T.S. Eliot and the
Myth of Adequation

Studies in Modern Literature, No. 29

A. Walton Litz, General Series Editor

Professor of English
Princeton University

Ronald Bush

Consulting Editor for Titles on T.S. Eliot
Associate Professor of Literature
California Institute of Technology

Other Titles in This Series

T.S. Eliot and the Myth of Adequation

by
Alan Weinblatt

UMI RESEARCH PRESS
Ann Arbor, Michigan

Copyright © 1984
Alan Weinblatt
All rights reserved

Produced and distributed by
UMI Research Press
an imprint of
University Microfilms International
Ann Arbor, Michigan 48106

Library of Congress Cataloging in Publication Data

Weinblatt, Alan.
T.S. Eliot and the myth of adequation.

(Studies in modern literature ; no. 29)
Revision of thesis (Ph.D.)–Harvard University, 1976.
Bibliography: p.
Includes index.
1. Eliot, T.S. (Thomas Stearns)–Aesthetics. 2. Creation (Literary, artistic, etc.) I. Title. II. Series.

PS3509.L43Z894 1984   821'.912   83-17863
ISBN 0-8357-1465-9

The profoundest obscurity enfolds the notion of *Adäquatheit* (adequateness), an ideal relation between the object of the idea and reality. . . . We are here in full cry after the familiar ignis fatuus of epistemology, the search for terms, which persist in dissolving into relations.

T. S. Eliot, *Knowledge and Experience*

Philosophy, precisely as "Being speaking within us," expression of the mute experience by itself, is creation. A creation that is at the same time a reintegration of Being: for it is not a creation in the sense of one of the commonplace *Gebilde* that history fabricates: it knows itself to be a *Gebilde* and wishes to surpass itself as *pure Gebilde*, to find again its origin. It is hence a creation in a radical sense: a creation that is at the same time an adequation, the only way to obtain an adequation.

Maurice Merleau-Ponty, *The Visible and the Invisible*

A fictional technique always relates back to the novelist's metaphysics. The critic's task is to define the latter before evaluating the former.

Jean-Paul Sartre, *Literary Essays*

The historical imagination may give us an awful awareness of the extent of time, or it may give us a dizzy sense of the nearness of the past. It may do both.

T. S. Eliot, *On Poetry and Poets*

To Didi

Contents

Acknowledgments

I wish to express my profound appreciation to those persons and institutions who have made this book possible: David Perkins and William Alfred, who directed my doctoral dissertation at Harvard University; Murray Krieger, for a summer fellowship to The School of Criticism and Theory, University of California, Irvine; Geoffrey Hartman and Haydon White, for their seminars at The School of Criticism; Ronald Berman, former Chairman, National Endowment for the Humanities, for an N.E.H. Fellowship; the Rev. Joseph Appleyard, S. J., and Anne Ferry, Boston College, former colleagues from whom I learned; James Olney, Louisiana State University, for his unsurpassed investigations into autobiography; Katy Brooks, for inestimable help in criticizing the final manuscript; and Ronald Bush, California Institute of Technology, for remembering the manuscript and recommending it to UMI Press.

To Roger and Ginny Rosenblatt I owe a debt of continuing friendship and encouragement that spans more than twenty years in Cambridge, Washington and New York. To Ernest May, John F. Kennedy School of Government, Harvard University, special gratitude for the questions he posed and the decisions he helped me make. For challenging me to think— and write—about how reality is perceived in a market society, I thank John Diebold, Chairman and Founder of The Diebold Group, Inc., and The Diebold Institute for Public Policy Studies, Inc. Finally, to my mother and father, and to my wife, Didi, to whom this book is dedicated, I owe more than I can say, including Nigel.

A portion of the original dissertation appeared as "T. S. Eliot and the Historical Sense," *The South Atlantic Quarterly*, 77, No. 3 (1978). Several of the ideas were touched upon in my review: "'Between the Idea and the Reality': *Eliot's Early Years* by Lyndall Gordon and *T. S. Eliot: The Longer Poems* by Derek Traversi," *The Sewanee Review*, 85, No. 3 (1977).

Preface

This book may be said to have been sparked into life one snowy afternoon in a Harvard seminar on Samuel Taylor Coleridge. David Perkins, offering the course together with Walter Jackson Bate and Richard Pipes, led us into a discussion dealing with symbols and sacraments. Our comments and questions moved us relentlessly into the essential area of the form, the structure shared by both: in the case of a symbol, the *necessary* connection between signifier and that signified; in the case of a sacrament, the *consubstantiality* of God and His creation, realized in a commitment to Christ, and sustained, as Coleridge's late Notebooks reveal, through rapt study of the Trinity. Heated discussion simmered on after class. The subject-object dichotomy. Kant. Dramatic illusion. Miracles. The agony of belief. As we made our way through the snow from Ash Street to the kiosk in Harvard Square, dusk turned to darkness. We lingered at the kiosk, arguing. Mantled in snow, we were as oblivious to the fury of a Nor'easter as we were to our own shivering.

The second impetus toward this study came in a quite different setting. One afternoon at the School of Criticism and Theory which Murray Krieger founded at UC Irvine, in seminars offered by Geoffrey Hartman and Haydon White, a similar passion seized us in argument. Focusing on Derrida and Deconstruction, our logic moved just as relentlessly toward the question of underlying structure, of form. In the case of De Saussure, linguistic disjunction had yielded an *arbitrary* and *conventional* bond between signifier and that signified. From this revolutionary axiom came Deconstruction's discovery of the "absence" lurking beneath literature's illusions of "presence"—those consoling fictions of voice and persona. Amidst heated discussion, we made our way from Irvine's campus to Laguna Beach. There, we sat on a hotel veranda overlooking the Pacific, copies of Freud in hand, arguing in detail about the infinite regress of representations of representations. What, we wondered, would be Deconstruction's ultimate legacy? Corrosive scepticism, claimed its foes. Humanizing indeterminacy, shot back its defenders. And still we argued as dusk turned to darkness, heedless of palm trees silhouetted against a postcard-perfect sunset, or gentle ocean breezes from the Orient or beyond.

These discussions have fructified in my life. When I sat down to write about Eliot, they generated a vigor and intensity never to be forgotten. Each discussion turned on a view of life that has yielded a succession of all-embracing theologies or ideologies. From each have arisen numerous canons of interpretation to help us make sense of the chaos of life. Each viewpoint inverts, subverts the other. But taken together, they comprehend and define two polar moments in the kinds of experience possible to the modern mind. Both are inevitable and necessary. The moot relation between signifier and that signified provides the scaffolding for much—if not most—of the intellectual debate of our age. But let there be no mistake. If we must choose a single poet who is heir to Coleridge and his successors through the nineteenth century, surely that choice must be T. S. Eliot.

Nowhere does T. S. Eliot speak with greater conviction or clarity than on the structure of symbols. "No symbol," he avers, "is ever a mere symbol, but is continuous with that which it symbolizes. Without words, no objects." And this last phrase—"without words, no objects"—raises the specter that would haunt Eliot's life, shaping every facet of his work, unifying his endeavors as poet, playwright, social critic, man of letters. For Eliot, art, language, literature, epistemology, theology, social theory, are all symbolic. Each instances what Eliot called "the incarnation of meaning in fact . . . ." Sunder the necesssary bond between signifier and that signified, and there remains only a world unredeemed by language, convention, form: a world of silence, emptiness, waste, and void. A world of dead fact.

Eliot's lifelong quest was in search of form adequate to his rich experience. My aim in writing this book has been to use the concept of adequation as a critical X-ray to disclose this quest as the underlying purpose that unifies and explains Eliot's diverse undertakings. Specifically, this study traces the evolution of adequation from its role in the earlier criticism, especially *Selected Essays*, where it functions as a *compensatory myth*, to its more far-reaching role in Eliot's later criticism, poetry, and drama, where it functions as a *three-stage method of interpretation*. In both cases, it is to the concept of adequation that Eliot turns in his attempt to formulate what I propose to call a poetics of process. By this I mean a poetics that could serve as a guide to those possible uses of language, convention, and form adequate to rendering on paper *and* exhibiting on stage the protean shapes of self.

In Eliot's earlier criticism, especially in his *Selected Essays*, and—with notable differences—in his social criticism, adequation—or the lack thereof—functions as a *compensatory myth* to rationalize, to artist and audience alike, the plight of the poet who fears that he dwells in a "late age of poetry," an epoch incapable of "produc[ing] great art," an era that dooms him to silence. Woven from an obsessive cluster of words and phrases that recur with musical regularity, *Selected Essays* is the counterpart in Eliot's literary historiography to the apocalyptic narratives so common to fundamentalist religion.

It boasts its own version of a "Second Fall of Man" ("dissociation of sensibility"); its own chronicle of religious, cultural, and literary decline from the Renaissance down to the late Victorian and early modern writers; its own portrait of language and literature in prelapsarian Europe (Dante's "allegorical" method); its own anatomy of how poetic creation takes place in a fallen world ("The Metaphysical Poets"); and its own dark vision of an Apocalypse (a future that is neither Christian nor even materialistic but only endless "chaos or torpor").

But as Eliot gradually came to a grudging acceptance of process, static myth gives way to (or comes to coexist with) a dynamic method of interpretation. Eliot came to believe that process was governed by a "law of nature" requiring that language—indeed *all* convention and form—must struggle to remain adequate to experience by dint of some deeper principle of "pure change" at the heart of things; to remain adequate to experience, form itself must be "always changing."

In consequence, there arose Eliot's later view of adequation, which holds that every moment of experience "tends" to struggle "towards intellectual formulation" and "pattern." This demands of the poet a reciprocal act of "exorcism"—creation—to transform the "demon" of experience—which in its first manifestation "has no face, no name, nothing"—into "the words, the poem he makes," the unique form of a particular experience. Philosopher Merleau-Ponty puts it this way: " . . . a creation that is at the same time an adequation, the only way to obtain an adequation." In a universe under the sway of process, every act of creation is at the same time an act of exorcism, a rediscovery and reaffirmation of the bond between signifier ("general words") and that signified ("particular feelings"), an adequation. Every act of creation is, therefore, a breakthrough into the dimension of the symbolic: at the moment of breakthrough the words, the poem made, to invoke Coleridge, "partakes of the Reality which it renders intelligible."

Serving both as an ethical imperative to the poet and as an anatomy of his creative act, Eliot's method of interpretation consists of three stages. First, there is "surrender" to—or "possession" by—the "bewildering minute" of experience. Second, there is the moment of "recovery" from that experience, the "process of de-possession." Finally, there is the quest of discovery for "meaning," the painful coming to consciousness of "pattern." Theology follows epistemology: " . . . sin," says Eliot, "may strain and struggle/ In its dark instinctive birth, to come to consciousness/ And so find expurgation." Indeed, in both form and theme, Eliot's most significant experiment in the drama, *The Family Reunion*, and his supreme poetic achievement, *Four Quartets*, are fully understandable only as symbolic dramas of "influence" or "possession" and "de-possession." All of Eliot's indefatigable experiments in portraying the shape of self clearly illustrate the three moments of this model. And Eliot's social criticism springs directly from the third moment of this interpretive scheme: the need for an adequate framework of theology and belief to anchor those bewildering minutes as they rush by on the currents of time both in one's own life and on the stage of history.

In drawing upon the word "adequation" to focus Eliot's abiding concern with form, my aim is heuristic, exploratory, speculative. Against charges that the term itself is alien, uncouth, Continental, I offer no defence. Says Eliot himself: ". . . there are words which are ugly because of rawness or because of antiquation; there are words which are ugly because of foreignness or ill-breeding. . . ." I ask only that the reader judge for himself. If this study succeeds in unifying the various facets of Eliot's quest and in rendering Eliot—the invisible poet—visible, I suspect that the term adequation may well be exorcised. Having served its purpose in a primary identification of the world around the poet, it moves the reader, the passionate arguers in Harvard Square or overlooking Laguna Beach closer to Eliot's essential pull, his drive, his obsession with social order and social issues as a counterpoise to exploring and mapping the geography of self.

On the other hand, adequation may yet prove useful as an instrument for reexamining those cultural artifacts created when the literary imagination engages in social criticism. Beginning with Ezra Pound's definition of an "image" as "that which presents an intellectual and emotional complex in an instant of time," the root formula of concord-turned-to-discord between form and experience repeats itself time and again on the pages of every period anthology. So, too, does the attendant sense of personal crisis, of existential anxiety, of historical inequity, of chaos come again, of radical disjunction and unjust disinheritance. These converge in shaping the root formula into myth, and in projecting it onto the face of history. These also produce the manifestoes, slogans, and emergency programs which promise to save the age for art.

In weaving a compensatory myth grounded in a metaphysical calamity or a violent shift of sensibility, Eliot was no more than representative of his age. In fact, such formulae (inadequate conceptual language compounded by discontinuity, crisis, imminent apocalypse) have even found their way into the writings of our own generation of social thinkers and policy analysts. For example, Zbigniew Brzezinski says that we are living *Between Two Ages*, entering a "technotronic era"; Peter Drucker contends that we are already immured in an "age of discontinuity," and Daniel Bell concludes that our postindustrial era is fraught with crisis and fractured by cultural contradiction.

At least in the case of our poets, the reason is clear. I propose as a law of cultural interpretation generally, and specifically in the case of literature and culture from the Romantic writers on down to T. S. Eliot, his contemporaries and successors, that the further a poet penetrates into the recesses of his self, the more desperately he finds himself in need of a sheet-anchor (be it a creed, a view of history, a dogma, a metaphysical calamity) to hold himself fast to an encompassing view of reality. The law I am proposing is a law of inverse proportionality between the portrayal of self and society.

For the man of action, the complex world of events exists at the forefront of his attention, relegating introspection or concern with the minutiae of felt experience to a position, at best, of secondary importance. But just the opposite holds true for the poet who would also write social criticism. The result is that language is tugged in two very different directions. Exploring the inner recesses of self demands a language that is infinitely nuanced, rich in figurative meaning, subtle and reflective beyond all reasonable expectations. Writing social criticism, on the other hand, requires language that can broadbrush a swath of history, resolve troubling complexity or ambivalence into sharp relief, and transform volumes of fine print or contradictory data into the simple message of a banner headline. In its need to be increasingly simple, outer reality as perceived by the poet is inversely proportional to the fragmentation and complexity of his inner self.

The upshot is what Eliot himself, in *After Strange Gods*, acknowledges to be "an apparent incoherence between my verse and my critical prose," adding that "in one's prose reflexions one may be legitimately occupied with ideals, whereas in the writing of verse one can only deal with actuality." The split between actuality and verse, on the one hand, and ideals and prose reflection, on the other, corresponds to the primacy of the "bewildering minute" of experience for the poet, and his concern with fixed "ideals" in his role as social critic. Each role demands a different use of language. Each represents the satisfaction of a different need for the poet. But the inverse relation of "actuality" and "ideals" illustrates in Eliot's case the law of inverse proportionality at work when the poet feels he must write about self *and* about society.

What role do Eliot's "ideals" play in making possible his vocation as poet? Broadly speaking, acceptance of the ideal or *compensatory vision* of a Christianity rooted in a monistic, hierarchic, telic, and closed society was the condition of stability that enabled Eliot to undertake and, more importantly, to continue his explorations into the geography of self. As sketched in Eliot's

Idea of a Christian Society, this ideal vision by definition finds itself at loggerheads with the actuality of the mundane world, attacking "a mechanised, commercialised urbanised way of life" with its "hypertrophy of the motive of Profit into a social ideal. . . ."

In some ways, perhaps, it is best not to interrogate a vision too closely. The answers are apt to be more mythic than mundane. But as students and admirers of T. S. Eliot who live, more likely than not, in a "commercialised urbanised way of life," we have three choices. In varying degrees we can assent to Eliot's vision, joining with him in his attacks on a liberal market society. But renunciation "of the motive of Profit" can also lead to a very different end: to the theology of liberation with its synthesis of Marx and the Gospel, which has sprung up in Latin America, especially in the writings of José Miranda (*Marx and the Bible: A Critique of the Philosophy of Oppression*) and Gustavo Gutierrez (*A Theology of Liberation: History, Politics and Salvation*). Lest we forget, other visions abound in Christendom. Recall John 14:2, "In my Father's house are many mansions."

At the opposite pole there is theologian and social thinker Michael Novak's vision of the relative *harmony* of Western economics, politics, and religious culture under democratic capitalism, deriving in part from Max Weber's view that democratic capitalism distinguishes itself from other commercial systems because it finds commerce imbued with religious and moral value. Unlike traditional societies, or the traditional cosmos (organic, hierarchic, telic) they sought to mirror, Novak portrays "democratic capitalism" as "differentiated into three social systems: a political system, an economic system, and a moral-cultural system."

A theology of economics is much-needed and long overdue, argues Novak in *Toward a Theology of the Corporation*. Not surprisingly, Novak charges that "most theologians of the last two hundred years have approached democratic capitalism in a premodern, precapitalist, predemocratic way; or else they have been socialists, usually romantic and utopian rather than empirical." Insists Novak: "The corporation is an expression of the social nature of humans. Moreover, it offers a metaphor for the ecclesial community that is in some ways more illuminating than metaphors based on the human body ('the mystical body') or on the family, the clan, the tribe, or the chosen people." Calling the modern corporation "a much despised incarnation of God's presence in this world," Novak draws upon theologian Bernard Lonergan's theory of "emergent probability" as one possible foundation for such a theology of economics. Understanding "world process," writes Lonergan in *Insight: A Study of Human Understanding*, makes necessary the use of our creative intelligence, especially in our willingness to accept "the complementarity of classical and statistical investigations" as complementary procedures in our quest for divine knowledge. Sparked by clues from "complementarity" about "the immanent intelligibility of the design or order in which things exist and events occur," there appears to "insight," which "pivots between the concrete and the abstract," the "inner design" of "emergent probability."

However much we may envy Eliot his *compensatory myth*, openness to our own rich and often bewildering "actuality" raises the real problem of religious affirmation in the contemporary world. "Modernity pluralizes," suggests Peter Berger, who goes on, in *The Heretical Imperative*, to define "modernity as the universalization of heresy." Discontinuity, competing frames of reference, endless alternatives, the marketplace which makes available to us both liberation theology and the theology of the corporation, often on the same bookshelf—such is our own "actuality," a market which offers a multiverse of views. "All markets trade in ideas," writes Lewis Lapham in *Fortune's Child*, "and the city's squalor is judged a fair price for its promise. The swarming exuberance of a city encourages the rise of such a thing as civilization precisely because the numbers of different people, so many of them unlike oneself and so many of them armed (either with weapons or dangerous thoughts), impose an appreciation of tolerance and restraint." Shall we call this chaos? How shall we deal with it? Shall we compensate for it? Do alternatives exist to the compensatory myth?

"Myths are the agents of stability, fictions the agents of change," observes Frank Kermode in *The Sense of an Ending*. "Myths call for absolute, fictions for conditional assent." Calling fictions "mental structures" which afford us "assistance" in a "contradictory" world, Hans Vaihinger, in his *Philosophy of 'As If,'* distinguishes among "paradigmatic fictions" (utopias, for example); "legal" or "juristic fictions"; the "fictions of the thing-in-itself" (as in causality); "mathematical fictions" (as in "probability" and "empty space"); and "abstractive (negative) fictions," which involve the "deliberate omission of certain elements of reality in complicated phenomena," the standard example being "Adam Smith's fiction in his political economy." Continues Vaihinger:

Adam Smith laid down as an axiom the fictional proposition that it appears *as if* all economic and commercial behaviour were dictated solely by egoism. . . . It is well known that Adam Smith . . . wrote in addition to his *Wealth of Nations*, another work, *The Theory of Moral Sentiments*. It has recently been shown that *The Wealth of Nations* does not strictly form an independent work or unit in itself, but is merely one portion of a complete moral philosophy. The one work examines mankind from the standpoint of egoism, the other from that of sympathy and altruism. He was unwilling to make an absolute distinction between ethics and economics any more than between economics and politics. . . . In order, therefore, to understand [Smith's philosophy] . . . both works must be considered together and regarded as one, for they are in fact two divisions of a single subject.

In our hunger to remain true to the bewildering complexities of our actual experience, Vaihinger's point that "economic" man and "moral" man are complementary "as if" constructions, meaningful only if understood together as instances of complementarity, may prove yet another avenue for exploration of the role of "the motive of Profit" in our culture, and the vexing question of its compatability with contemporary modes of religious affirmation.

For Eliot, modernism generated both a *compensatory myth* and a resounding attack on the "chaos" of modernization. Only by embracing the security of an ideal rooted in the myth of a premodern vision could Eliot continue to chronicle the shapes of self in a pluralistic, market society. Yet Eliot's dilemma was self-confessed and openly acknowledged. Many thinkers who venture forth to explore the complexities and nuances of our society do so only at the price of oversimplification committed twice over. On the one hand, they erect elaborate edifices of social theory on foundations that are little more than myopic interpretations of egoism or altruism. On the other hand, having missed the complexities and nuances of our society, they also fail to achieve a subtle and probing investigation of the true depths and hidden dimensions of the interior self. So mimesis is sacrificed to the law of inverse proportionality, or it is abandoned altogether. The question of the moment, which is also the besetting question for all who would construct a poetics adequate to our age, a poetics of process, is whether—and how—we can remain faithful to self and to society while portraying both.

I

The Quest

1

The Meaning of Adequation: The Central Quest

Ever an habitué of metaphysical gloom, Eliot is nowhere more so than in the stunning cry of despair in his play *The Family Reunion*: "I talk in *general* terms/ Because the *particular* has no language."[1] At once a confession, explanation and celebration of despair, it expresses Eliot's most characteristic fears. That the poet must be beggared by fruitless "talk," impoverished both in spirit and craft, and ultimately struck silent is an unbearable and unquestionable foreknowledge; this cry issues from the certainty that bequeathed to the poet there is only a puny heap of words—capacious "terms" which are irremediably "general"—while the "particular" for which he longs to find words, the "particular [that] has no language," consists of "feeling and emotion"—the heart and marrow of experience.

Incapable of summoning up language even remotely adequate to his own private experience, the poet, according to Kierkegaard, is reduced to "an emigrant from the sphere of the universal," debarred from that "relief of speech" which alone can "translate" his innermost feelings into "universal" expression.[2] Over time, as the "relief of speech" continues to elude his grasp, the poet finds himself, as Sartre brilliantly suggests in his dirgelike lament on "exorcism," deserted not only by the absent voice of "feeling and emotion" but also by commonplace meanings, the very names of things:

> I lean my hand on the seat but pull it back hurriedly: it exists. This thing I'm sitting on, leaning my hand on, is called a seat. . . . I murmur: "It's a seat," a little like an exorcism. But the word stays on my lips: it refuses to go and put itself on the thing. . . . Things are divorced from their names. They are there, grotesque, headstrong, gigantic and it seems ridiculous to call them seats or say anything at all about them: I am in the midst of things, nameless things. Alone without words, defenceless, they surround me, are beneath me, behind me, above me. They demand nothing, they don't impose themselves: they are there.[3]

Thus Eliot's edict that "feeling and emotion are particular, whereas thought is general"[4] imposes upon the poet's universe a frightening, perilous structure. It banishes his last haunting glimpse of a cosmos where "particular" and "general," feelings and words, raw experience and encircling form can marry and harmonize, where he can still partake of the "relief of speech," assume the existence of "an ideal unity in experience," and have "faith in an ultimate rationalization and harmonization of experience" and form.[5]

World of Process, Language of Form

In consequence, it poses the fundamental question that draws together every facet of Eliot's work. In a universe where general language, the sharable language of the community, is irreparably cleaved from the particular, unique language of feeling, how can any statement go to the heart? In a world where experience flows not in the mold of form, but where every moment of experience provides a triumphant annihilation of form, where "content of feeling is constantly bursting the receptacle" of language, where form is continually laid waste by an "anarchy of feeling," where "form" is no longer available "to arrest . . . the flow" of experience, how does the poet apprehend and judge such an agonizing universe? Words, language, grammar, conventions, hypothetical essences: how may form of any kind attain authenticity? And how, even if momentarily achieved, can such authenticity be sustained?

Eliot's work is shot through with this dilemma, where it assumes a multiplicity of guises, appearing as speculative philosophy, ruminative criticism, and poetic imagery. This central focus is already apparent, for example, in Eliot's powerful relish for the philosophy of F. H. Bradley, and in his successful assimilation of Bradley's major underlying theme: the insuperable dualism of thought and experience. Bradley argues this divide can never be transcended, because when thought ceases to be "relational and discursive," composed of artificial subjects and predicates bound together by a superstructure of grammar, of endless "whats" which denote qualities, contents and ideas pointing to the mysterious "that" of existence, when it attempts to approach the seamless unity of experience, "it commits suicide."[6] For Bradley it is a repulsive "notion that existence could [ever] be the same as understanding." With minor but significant variations, Eliot, in his doctoral thesis, *Knowledge and Experience in the Philosophy of F. H. Bradley*, paints a picture of a cosmos teetering perpetually between knowledge and experience, but with the latter in permanent ascendency. If knowledge and experience are the polar constituents of our paradoxical world, argues Eliot, their antithesis is irreconcilable, with thought always and everywhere inadequate to the ubiquitous, "vague, unprecise, swarming"[7] world of feeling. Thus the plight of the metaphysician redoubles the gloom of the poet.

On other occasions, this central dilemma so shapes Eliot's view of a particular historical period or era that its health or decadence becomes a partial explanation for Eliot's own situation. As early as 1916, before his far more notorious historical valuations in *The Sacred Wood* and, later still, *Selected Essays*, Eliot would trace the underlying "Emphasis upon *feeling* rather than *thought*"[8] as a narrow pathological Romanticism, with its accompanying tendency toward excess in every direction that afflicted nineteenth-century culture. "[V]ague emotionality"—unfocused, possibly unfocusable feeling and emotion—and "the apotheosis of science (realism)," with its unthinking, intellectually mordant "devotion to brute fact" instead of to cultivation of adequate language and form were, said Eliot with a flourish, the "two great currents of the nineteenth century,"[9] and the touchstone of its literary decadence.

But the dilemma declares itself most richly and starkly in crucial aspects of Eliot's imagery. In a tone of saddened pathos, Eliot often turns to reminiscence, the evocation of a haunting nostalgia, with the figure of Wordsworth uppermost in mind. Characteristically, Eliot will identify the relentless surge and flow of experience with the ceaseless ocean which continuously "throws up high and dry/ A crowd of twisted" forms "upon the beach," "skeleton[s]" of once meaningful speech, but now dead relics, detritus, "Stiff and white"[10] reminders of unrecapturable immediate experience. In vain do we seek to flee "the perpetual wash of tides," Eliot muses in despair, the pounding "intractable tide," stumbling pitifully to "lean on a rock" of permanent form, trying to catch, even for a moment's respite, "a firm foothold" of meaning.[11] Echoing the famous dream at the start of Book V of Wordsworth's *Prelude*, Eliot's metaphor recalls Wordsworth's figure of the poet, the Quixotic Arab, who hastens to bury the shell of poetry to preserve it from the onrushing deluge of experience, "the waters of the deep/ Gathering upon us." Wordsworth's dream may be thought to straddle both optimism and pessimism, to pivot between them, although coming to rest with the latter, since the frenzied effort to preserve the shell, which may still contain an echo of "the deep,"—or at least the intimation, the memory of one—is checked by the realization that, apart from these "waters of the deep," the shell is really inert and lifeless. It is at once an evasion and epitaph to the flow of experience, a "Poor earthly casket" unable to affirm a greater reality.[12]

Eliot is also capable of using this symbolism but reversing his conclusion. Or, as in the following passage from *Choruses from "The Rock,"* he will maintain a double vision, optimism arising from despair in a reciprocal dignity, both plainly visible, neither refuting the other, as the poet wrests his small victory from confronting two realities at once:

> Out of the sea of sound the life of music,
> Out of the slimy mud of words, out of the sleet
>   and hail of verbal imprecisions,
> Approximate thoughts and feelings, words that
>   have taken the place of thoughts and
>   feelings,
> There spring the perfect order of speech, and
>   the beauty of incantation.[13]

The moment of pure *experience* out of which, as if by an invisible grace, there springs the unexpected illumination of *meaning*, the hitherto opaque moment of feeling or passionate emotion from which there breaks suddenly an access to "the perfect order of speech," the moments of "meaningless practical shapes" and worse, the empty moments of "waste and void" which, penetrated by the beam of "the artist's eye," yield "new life, new *form*"[14]— yield a graspable and apprehensible *pattern*: these are the keystones of Eliot's poetic statement.

Moments, Patterns, and Revelation

Eliot's poetic terrain is a repeating history of moments and patterns, moments rendered in stark detail and moments barely visible beneath their twisting, surrealistic shape, patterns but dimly perceived in the early years, and patterns sharply etched and firmly embraced in the later work. One finds in Eliot recurringly a single, infinitely complex, infinitely rich moment of experience, hovering precariously on the edge of meaning, then slipping back toward the edge of chaos, momentarily accessible to the "relief of speech," then lost again through the nets of language. Such moments scrutinized first from this angle, then from that, remembered, suppressed, cogitated, investigated, meditated—this is the primary subject-matter of Eliot's poetic art.

The moments are those of cowardice and self-imposed deceit which we refuse, escapistly, "to force . . . to its crisis," the uncannily haunting moment of "sunlight in . . . [brown] hair" which "amaze[s]/ The troubled midnight and the noon's repose," the "moment" of secretly nurtured subterranean pride which "Revive[s] . . . a broken Coriolanus," the despairing moment of "Shape without form," the triumphant "predetermined moment" of Incarnation through which "time was made . . . for without the meaning there is no time, and that moment of time gave the meaning" to every moment of time. It is the inexplicable moment of natural arrest in which the "repose of noon" is transformed into an earthly reflection of the "still moment . . . set under the upper branches of noon's widest tree," the ecstatic moments in "the rose-garden," in "the arbour where the rain beat," and "in the draughty church at smokefall." It is the austerely, inhumanly "intense moment/ Isolated, with no before or after," the moment "unattended . . . in and out of time" in which dwells "The distraction fit, lost in a shaft of sunlight," the ordinary "moments of agony" and "moments of happiness," and the blighting moment in which, "at your touch, there is nothing but ruin. . . . "[15] The formal patterns remembered in which "we moved, and they" in a miraculous poise, a moment transfiguring the felt ecstasy of the rose garden into luminous meaning, or "the form, the pattern" by which "Words, after [ordinary] speech, reach [beyond the surface of experience]/ Into the silence" of the permanence of art. From these moments and patterns come discoveries: that "The detail of the pattern is movement," and hence the fluidities and fluxes of everyday experience may legitimately aspire to meaning; or the equally frightening recognition that the "pattern" to be deduced from "knowledge derived from experience" is in the end false, "For the pattern is new in every moment/ And every moment of [experience] is a new and shocking/ Valuation of all we have been." All work toward the final, achieved awareness, conferring both a quiet and despairing solace that "history is a pattern/ Of timeless moments. . . . " Like concentric circles widening outward from a scrutiny of our inner selves to the facts of personal chronicle to the events of national history, permanent meaning is circumscribed and won—this is the central subject matter for Eliot.[16] In every single poem Eliot was to write, in every single drama, we come again and again upon this solitary figure of the perplexed, perturbed consciousness confronting his isolated moments of experience, and we follow the sinuous twists and tortuous turns of his mind as he slowly attempts to uncover their hidden meaning. We witness as his mind both watches and enacts this progressive drama of revelation in which emotion and feeling struggle toward the "relief of language," moment attempts to become pattern, a drop of experience aspires toward adequate form. Played out in a recurring interior narrative or monologue, this drama of progressive revelation is what we propose to name the drama of *adequation*.

The Meaning of Adequation

Eliot never applied the noun "adequation" himself, nor does the word appear in any of his writings, except for the reference to "*Adäquatheit* (adequateness)" in *Knowledge and Experience*, which I have cited on the epigraph page. Seldom does the word appear in modern English except as an adjective to signal censure or reprobation—to level a charge of inadequacy.

Yet if Eliot nowhere refers to the drama of adequation, nowhere seeks to make use of the word's etymological suggestiveness to capture and focus an endless host of concerns, he everywhere invokes the adjectival form—the adjective adequate or inadequate—to praise or to blame. And in every instance, throughout Eliot's work, the adjective implies, stands for or points to the invisible noun of adequation—as to the missing X of an axiomatic equation. To prefer a charge of inadequacy against (or to confer the sobriquet of adequacy upon) an object is to point to the presence or absence of a condition of sufficiency or completeness, as well as to suggest the drama by which this condition of plenitude or vacancy arose. Adequation embraces both points. It is a "noun of action,"[17] composed of the particle *ad*, which indicates direction or movement toward, and the adjective *aequus*, level or equal. In the older, scholastic meaning of the term, now wholly inapplicable, it stood, as the "adequation of intellect and thing," for the traditional definition of truth in a static, hierarchical universe where intellect, supreme in its dominion over experience, could serenely intuit the names and informing essences of objects. But here, in Eliot's universe of process, where feeling and emotion reign supreme over displaced intellect, and where form and essence are feared to be subordinate and inauthentic, adequation now refers to the drama in which "thought," which is general, struggles toward equality with unique "feeling and emotion." Adequation, in other words, points to that drama in which experience seeks the true voice of form as "intelligence" operates to wrest from "sensation" the forms of "principle and definition."[18] Adequation implies that every emotion, no matter how vague, "tends" to struggle, whether successfully or otherwise, "towards intellectual formulation."[19] That is what the noted French philosopher, Merleau-Ponty, meant when he declared that "the only way ever to arrive at an adequation" is through the "creation" of form, for experience—feeling and emotion— "demands creation of us in order that we may have experience of it."[20] To grasp experience we must "quicken to creation"—"Out of the formless stone, when the artist united himself with stone,/ Spring always new forms of life, from the soul of man that is joined to the soul of stone"[21]—and that creation—that act of struggling to bring forth form adequate to experience—is an adequation.

Hence the theme of adequation runs like an obbligato through Eliot's imagination. Moreover, it may be seen, on closer inspection, to occupy a curious double or bipolar position in his thought. It bisects his speculation into bold historiography on one level and into the minutest pursuit of the complexities of creation on the other, while uniting these levels by means of logic and argumentation which are virtually identical. In his *Selected Essays*, Eliot apotheosizes the quest for adequation into a grand historical myth by projecting an underlying metaphysical dilemma onto the face of history and reading it back, tremblingly, as a prediction of the most dire consequence: as his besetting dualism of thought and experience assumes a menacing historiographic and political resonance, Eliot's own unease comes through in the poetry.

The Dualism of Thought and Sensibility

In the end, Eliot succeeds in bringing literary history to the support of his pressing metaphysical dilemma by fusing them into a united, overarching myth: his designation for this fused expression was the famous doctrine of dissociation of sensibility. Eliot first advanced the notion of a "dissociation of sensibility" in an essay, "The Metaphysical Poets" in 1921:

> The poets of the seventeenth century, the successors of the dramatists of the sixteenth, possessed a mechanism of sensibility which could devour any kind of experience. They were simple, artificial, difficult, or fantastic, as their predecessors were; no less nor more than Dante, Guido Cavalcanti, Guinizelli, or Cino. In the seventeenth century a dissociation of sensibility set in, from which we have never recovered; and this dissociation, as is natural, was aggravated by the influence of the two most powerful poets of the century, Milton and Dryden.[22]

His final pronouncement upon this theory came in his British Academy lecture on Milton, in 1947:

> I believe that the general affirmation represented by the phrase "dissociation of sensibility" . . . retains some validity; but . . . to lay the burden on the shoulders of Milton and Dryden was a mistake. If such a dissociation did take place, I suspect that the causes are too complex and too profound to justify our accounting for the change in terms of literary criticism. All we can say is, that something like this did happen; that it had something to do with the Civil War; that it would even be unwise to say it was caused by the Civil War, but that it is a consequence of the same causes which brought about the Civil War; that we must seek the causes in Europe, not in England alone; and for what these causes were, we may dig and dig until we get to a depth at which words and concepts fail us.[23]

If we ask what Eliot means by sensibility, why the sensibility of the artist has been dissociated, and in what array of elements or constituent parts this dissociation has resulted, a genuinely satisfactory answer cannot be supplied. Eliot himself backtracks rather lamely from the confident trumpeting of theory in the first passage cited above into the helpless silence which closes the second passage above. Neither recorded history nor literary historiography can supply a definition which will stand. The answer must be sought and found by a peremptory return to metaphysics.

Behind the notion of a "dissociation of sensibility" looms the specter, however ill-defined, of a *metaphysical* catastrophe. And in response to this hypothetical metaphysical catastrophe, during which thought and experience, formerly of equal metaphysical status and kindred ontology, were sundered at a stroke, so that "feeling and emotion [became] particular, whereas thought . . . [remained] general," the artist's sensibility, once a unified organ of thought and feeling, underwent a parallel—and related—catastrophe in which it too was sundered into separate faculties of feeling and thought, divided not only in internal function but in their skewed and diminished apprehension of reality. By themselves, neither faculty could "devour any kind of experience," whether "simple, artificial, difficult, or fantastic," because sensitivity to feeling and emotion, once so comprehensive and exquisite, had now been rendered crude and limited, while the vast resources of language so necessary to incarnate experience in form had likewise slipped away. Before this mythic catastrophe, adequation, both in literature and cognition generally, had held universal sway: adequation reflected and embodied the basic order of the cosmos. After this catastrophe adequation becomes not the rule but the exception—an infrequently wrested victory, a momentary achievement of art requiring always "a new beginning," an unending series of "raid[s] on the inarticulate/ With shabby equipment always deteriorating/ In the general mess of imprecision of feeling/ Undisciplined squads of emotion."[24]

Finding the Words

On the other hand, the plight of the artist is succinctly explained in precisely the same terms. Words cut adrift from sensibility, experience disjointed from intellect become the terms in which each and every one of Eliot's attempts to explain the creative act are drawn. In the act of creating a poem, he says, what we are really doing is to seek the "relief of speech" for that "inexhaustible and terrible nebula of emotion" which, buried deep beneath "The natural wakeful life of our Ego,"[25] fills our hidden souls, and in so doing we undertake the difficult burden of exploring, in Keats's words, "untrodden region[s] of . . . [the] mind"; or, to invoke Arnold's metaphor, we try to slip, however wrenching or draining the effort, "Below the surface-stream, shallow and light,/ Of what we *say* we feel—below the stream/ As light, of what we *think* we feel" in order to arrive at that "noiseless current strong, obscure and deep,/ The central stream of what we feel indeed."[26]

Of his numerous descriptions of the task of the poet, Eliot's most celebrated consideration occurs in his confession of "What Dante Means to Me." Above all else, Eliot finds in Dante a fulfillment of the poet's "obligation to explore, to find words for the inarticulate, to capture those feelings which people can hardly even feel, because they have no words for them"; as a result, the poet finds himself an "explorer beyond the frontiers of ordinary consciousness" who seeks to "comprehend the incomprehensible" by "enriching the meaning of words and showing how much words can do." By deliberately striving to increase the resources of language, the poet widens the range of his sensibility and increases the "*width of emotional range*" in his poetry, making "possible a much greater range of emotion and perception for other men, because he gives them the speech in which more can be expressed."[27] Hence the poet's twin obligations to language and sensibility are inseparable; both must cooperate—indeed become organically one—to complete the circuit of creativity. Attempting to illustrate this relationship, Eliot characteristically turns to three different metaphors: depth; center and circumference; and levels of consciousness. Often Eliot will picture the struggle for adequation as a quest—much as Matthew Arnold does—to raise "unknown, dark *psychic material*"[28] to the surface of consciousness. Seizing on a related metaphor from Gottfried Benn, the poet is viewed as having "something germinating . . . [deep inside] him for which he must find words; but he cannot know what words he wants until he has found the words; he cannot identify this embryo until it has been transformed into an arrangement of the right words in the right order. When you have the words for it, the "thing" for which the words had to be found has disappeared, replaced by a poem."[29] This "embryo," this "unknown, dark psychic material" of subterranean feeling which struggles for expression can be comprehended only as a powerful "demon" which "haunt[s]" the poet, "a demon against which he feels powerless, because in its first manifestation it has no face, no name, nothing; and the words, the poem he makes, are a kind of form of *exorcism* of this demon."[30]

Defining Emotion and Feeling

This description implies the distinction Eliot draws between surface emotions, which can either be intense or, more likely, tepid; and those vague, swarming, unnamed feelings which inhabit the depths. He distinguishes between "such emotions as observation can confirm, typical emotions,"[31] those "nameable, classifiable emotions and motives of our conscious life,"[32] and "something else that lies much deeper,/ Too obscure to rise to conscious emotion/ Or to have a name,"[33] the flux of "emotion[s] which cannot be expressed,"[34] that "fringe of indefinite extent, of feeling which we can only detect, so to speak, out of the corner of the eye and can never completely focus; of feeling of which we are only aware in a kind of temporary detachment from action."[35] Beneath and beyond our expressible emotions are those "deeper, unnamed feelings which form the substratum of our being, to which we rarely penetrate; for our lives are mostly a constant evasion of ourselves. . . ."[36] Apart from the poet's unremitting struggle, "The surface of existence coagulates into lumps which look like important simple feelings, which are identified by names as feelings," but which conceal from the poet the "simple, terrible and unknown" feelings which roil beneath.[37]

Frequently, as in the passage above ("fringe . . . of feeling which we can only detect . . . out of the corner of the eye"), the operative metaphor will change, as Eliot thinks of creation as involving a centripetal movement from the circumference of consciousness to its bright center where words and names may at least exist, a movement from the "frontiers of consciousness beyond which words fail"[38] to the more familiar territory of the ego, a movement which refines peripheral "feeling" into emotion that can be designated and fixed "by making it more conscious,"[39] thereby "refin[ing] our sensibility" by "enlarg[ing] our consciousness" through "the expression of something we have experienced but have [had] no words for."[40] Or, finally, as the fruit of this reciprocal growth of language and sensibility, we may unexpectedly achieve, as in a moment of sudden transport, a level of understanding and insight into ourselves and reality hitherto unimagined; such newly won insight, by giving habitation, name and meaning to feelings unfamiliar and fearful may render null those emotions which dominate mundane consciousness:

> It's only when they see nothing
> That people can always show the suitable emotions—
> And so far as they feel at all, their emotions are suitable.
> They don't understand what it is to be awake,
> To be living on several planes at once
> Though one cannot speak with several voices at once.
> . . . .
>   Only, that's not the language
> That I choose to be talking. I will not talk yours.[41]

In theory, then, if the poet cannot speak with several voices at once—voices which transfigure the hidden and affective dimensions of existence into familiar terms, voices which nudge us toward an apprehension of "some new experience, or some fresh understanding of the familiar,"[42]—he is free to be silent: "I will not talk yours." In practice, however, such silence is bravado, an embarrassed defense, a retreat from the task that awaits him. Sooner or later, the poet must again take up the burden of adequation, convinced in his heart that although "all language is inadequate . . . probably the language of poetry is the language most capable of communicating wisdom."[43] And, touched by wisdom, we are redeemed from our habitual dullness, we come alive on "several planes at once," we are "awake" to the engulfing, myriad richness of consciousness that spreads beyond the pinpoint ego, rich realms where dwell our reveries, our dreams, our memories, our nightmares—the multiple realities which, fitted together, constitute our true selves. Ordinary, practical "emotions," warns Eliot, "are only 'incidents,'" artificial, contrived, and fabricated, "In the effort to keep day and night together."[44] The stifling dullness of "The natural wakeful life of our Ego" staves off such knowledge of the night; poetry restores us, if momentarily, to such knowledge of ourselves. And that restoration is an affirmation, however temporary or tentative, of the cherished bonds between literature and the self.

2

Adequation as Myth in the Design of *Selected Essays*

High theory and the evocation of intensely immediate experience as embodied, respectively, in Eliot's "essays of generalization (such as *Tradition and the Individual Talent*) and [his] appreciations of individual authors":[1] the drama of Eliot's prose writings, especially of his *Selected Essays* is, at its most vital, to draw these poles together, to discover their mutuality, to declare them fully complementary facets of the same, common quest for adequation. At first this dramatic movement is not clearly evident. Dipping into *Selected Essays* at random, finding here the reassuringly familiar essay on "The Metaphysical Poets," there a relatively unknown, seemingly unrelated piece on the Church of England's Lambeth Conference of 1930 ("Thoughts after Lambeth"), the essays seem more independent, more self-contained—as befits their diverse publishing history as occasional essays, journalistic reviews or belletristic polemic. They do not at first reading appear implicated in the general meaning of each other. This deceptive impression of disconnection and autonomy is enhanced by Eliot's oft-rehearsed protest that he was no "systematic thinker," and that any search for system or architectonic in his work, erected on a structure of "sustained, exact, and closely knit argument and reasoning,"[2] must inevitably issue in failure or error.

What are we to think when at a certain moment, after sustained rereading, the argument of each essay, the conclusion, the summing up, the drawing forth of meaning from the subject at hand, begins to reveal a tell-tale similarity to each of the others? For, in almost every case, Eliot's method of procedure, his strategy of advance from premise to conclusion, is to invoke, to draw upon a highly limited repository of recurring words. These words echo and reecho themselves, catch up and pattern a multitude of disparate writers and situations into a common design, often amplifying each word's latent suggestivity in a variety of subject-matters (the compara-tive merit of specimens of poetry drawn from successive ages, or the contemporary dispute over humanism and religion, or disquisitions on education, sociology and the passing of the music hall era) until, almost without warning, each essay becomes but a particular, almost subordinate illustration of the more general, more critically important set of meanings, which it is Eliot's underlying aim to communicate.

The truth is, this technique of verbal refrain and reprise, this repertory of recurring words and phrases stems neither from genuine architectonic nor preconceived system but from an urgent, ongoing, underlying concern on Eliot's part to explore, to make sense out of and to illustrate the implications and consequences of his myth of failed adequation: the catastrophe of dissociated sensibility. Here "adequate objects" are repeatedly distinguished from "inadequate" ones, and "adequacy" unfailingly counterpoints "inadequacy." Here "intellect" struggles heroically to become adequate to "sensibility" and here "experience," "feeling," "emotion," "sensation," "enthusiasm," "passions," "emotional states," "emotional orgy," "emotional intensity and violence," and inexpressible "baffled emotion" surge over the bastion of "words," "language," "meaning," "receptacle," "gesture," "form," "expression," "clear purgation" and, of course, "objective correlative." Here the chiseled world of the "strong and simple outline," the "perfectly controlled" expression of emotion is set over against the unfocused world of that which is "inexpressible," the "incommunicable . . . vague and unformed," the world of "mistiness," "fluid haze," and shimmering "dream." Here swelling passion, unrelieved because undefined, is stymied from attaining to meaning in the form of "dogma," "revelation," "belief," and "religion."

Viewed from this perspective, the design of *Selected Essays* may be understood as a series of assays into the literary consequences of metaphysical pessimism, assays which depart from and return to this central myth. Taken in totality these assays chronicle the long, slow decline—in Eliot's eyes—of European literature from the time of Dante. Bearing directly on this point is a passage from Walter Jackson Bate's *The Burden of the Past and the English Poet*:

> A great deal of modern literature—and criticism—is haunted, as Stephen Spender says, by the thought of a "Second Fall of Man," and almost everything has been blamed: the Renaissance loss of the medieval unity of faith, Baconian science, British empiricism, Rousseau, the French Revolution, industrialism, nineteenth-century science, universities and academicism, the growing complexity of ordinary life, the spread of mass media.[3]

At one time or another, Eliot touches upon almost all of these issues, but quickly propels each one into orbit around his own metaphysical sun. As catalogued by Eliot in the great majority of his "appreciations of individual authors," the effects of this haunting Second Fall, this cosmic universal dissociation of form and feeling, group themselves into two categories.

Into the first category fall those essays which treat of the overall inadequacy of *doctrinal thought*—be it as dogma, theology, ideology, theory or a developed, articulated point of view—to the underlying affections in which a particular doctrine is rooted and from which it draws emotional sustenance. Under the second category are grouped those essays which illustrate the inadequacy of particular *works of art*—work of art being used in the broadest sense to include any poem, play, narrative, essay, image, word or even gesture—as vehicles to convey the emotions from which they spring. Both categories bear striking witness to the inexorable crumbling of form into the ruin of meaninglessness which is Eliot's starkest poetic fear.

Language, Feeling, and Emotion

Of the four "appreciations of individual authors" in which the central argument is the failure of equilibration between some structure of doctrinal thought and the feelings and emotions it once successfully conveyed, perhaps the most graphic—and famous—illustration is "Arnold and Pater." Matthew Arnold, in his extensive writings on the unraveling of ties between Christianity and Culture, was engaged in waging, according to Eliot, a "religious campaign," and the upshot of this succession of field operations was to "affirm that the *emotions* of Christianity can and must be preserved without the *belief*," an affirmation whose inevitable consequence was the "divorce" of that special sensibility possessed by "religion," with its heights and depths of feeling and emotion, from its superstructure of doctrinal "thought."[4] One outcome of this resulting imbalance—indeed severence—between emotions and belief where dogma no longer can function adequately to channel, shape and confer meaning on feeling, is "to leave Religion to be laid waste by the anarchy of feeling."[5] With religion thus split, fragmented, open to the eddying currents of individual feeling, it becomes possible to install, in the place of dogma, either "Morals" or "Art."[6] This substitution is accompanied by the need to translate everything either into morality—witness the "religious vapourings of Carlyle" or the "social fury of Ruskin"[7]—or into the dangerous cult of "emotion and . . . sensation" which marks Pater's own "peculiar appropriation of religion."[8] But for Eliot there exists also a third substitute for dogmatic religion, an outgrowth and later development of the foregoing, a substitute for which Arnold's campaign to elevate culture over dogma was incontrovertibly a "forerunner,"[9] and a substitute with which Eliot found himself, often to the exclusion of almost everything else, increasingly preoccupied and distressed: the substitute of Humanism. Dealt with at length over several years in a series of articles and heated rejoinders in the *Criterion* by such noteworthy controversialists as Herbert Read, G. K. Chesterton, and Allen Tate,[10] the topic surfaces, in *Selected Essays*, in "The Humanism of Irving Babbitt." The focal difficulty with Humanism, unlike dogma, is that, although it offered itself as an "*alternative* to religion,"[11] it could provide no clear definition of itself, no unchallengeable intellectual edifice, no anatomy of belief open to inspection and deliberative consideration. A loose amalgam of overlapping and often contradictory tenets, some drawn from religion, others from the classical tradition, and still others from the confluence of both, the generally accepted premises of Humanism—order, discipline, tradition, continuity, proportion, restraint, reason, authority, privilege, and aristocracy—might provide temporary solace for those "unable to take the religious view—that is to say . . . dogma or revelation" but would fail to provide "a view of life . . . durable beyond one or two generations."[12] The reasons for this failure are not far to seek. In terms of actual operation, the Humanism of Eliot's day split irreparably into morality in the form of what Babbitt, no doubt thinking of Matthew Arnold's "best self," called the "inner check,"[13] a doctrine of self-control by moral restraint, and simultaneously into an attempt, equally vital if futile, to provide, in Babbitt's words, "an enthusiasm"—an infusing or eliciting of feeling and emotion which "man" naturally "craves"—"that will lift him out of his merely rational self."[14] But between an influx of amorphous "enthusiasm" and an ideally defined "inner check" there is neither connection nor commerce: enthusiasm and inner check appear as mindless adversaries engaged in an endless tug of war, the former to inflate the ego with sporadic doses of a heady intoxicant, the latter to prick it back into place. Enthusiasm and inner check are shards of a broken whole, the fragmentary remains of Christian "theology in its last agonies."[15] Isolated "morality" must come to appear "hideous" because it loses all touch with the "personal and real emotions . . . this morality [once] supported and into which it introduced a kind of order."[16] Religion is always "in danger of petrifaction into mere ritual and habit," but lacking a central, articulated, and living framework of belief, it can never be "renewed and refreshed by" a mere "awakening of feeling" or by the unbiased scrutiny of "critical reason."[17] Humanism is a sham because it denies the supernatural, because its elevation of reason denies the dispossession of the intellect, because it denies the primacy of the emotive, and because it denies the quest for adequation.

This same decay of dogma is apparent, not surprisingly, in "Baudelaire," but the reaction of Baudelaire's self is strikingly different: it engages in a drama of positive, if agonizing, search to overcome this dogmatic vacuum. Although Baudelaire experiences a growing recognition of the "fact that no human relations are adequate to human desires," there is an accompanying battle to transcend this obstacle, to overcome, as Eliot sees it, the typical nineteenth-century "disbelief in any further [supernatural] object for human desires than that which, being human, fails to satisfy them."[18] With the swelling "content of [religious] feeling . . . constantly bursting the receptacle" of available dogma,[19] Baudelaire's answer was neither to suppress such feelings, deal with them in isolation, or limit their importance through a rejection of belief, but rather to accept them, to welcome them, to crave them in the form of "Satanism": for such rejoicing in the emotion of evil, stripped of its inevitable trappings of flamboyance and theatricalism, "amounts to a dim intuition of a part . . . of Christianity," an abandonment of "theological innocence" and religious ignorance by "discovering Christianity for himself."[20] And the part of Christianity which he investigated was the reality and meaning of "suffering," the reality of Original Sin that implies, even if always beyond the farthest hope of being reached, "the possibility of a positive state of beatitude." Recognizing, however imperfectly, the vast latitude of the religious sensibility, Baudelaire explored one small segment of that scale, but explored it with unmatched ferocity. Impressive for his thoroughgoing rejection of both the "naturalist" and "humanist" positions, Baudelaire is even more so for his positive recognition that his "business was not to practise Christianity"—that he could never bring himself to do—"but . . . what was much more important for his time . . . to assert its *necessity*."[21] Beginning with a self-intuited emotional reality, Baudelaire finds his way, if just barely, to the threshold of an intellectual reality, to the assertion of a supernatural, adequate reality.

Finding an Adequate Object

This same logic, writ large, informs the spiritual allegory that Eliot traces in "The *Pensées* of Pascal." Pascal begins in "despair," a pocket of despair so deep and dark, a clear-cut emotion that "corresponds [so] exactly to the facts" of an unillumined, spiritually sere world, that it "cannot be dismissed as mental disease."[22] Because Pascal was "a man of strong passions," his passions threatened, terrified, tyrannized so long as no "spiritual explanation"—no intellectual explanation adequate to his felt demon—"could be found." But then, by a process of logic that fills Eliot with awe, Pascal comes to recognize that "if certain emotional states . . . are inherently and by inspection known to be good, then the satisfactory explanation of the world"—the adequate explanation—"must be an explanation which will admit the 'reality' of these values."[23] It follows, therefore, that if the "emotional" state of "what in the highest sense can be called 'saintliness'. . . [is] inherently and by inspection known to be good, then the satisfactory"— the adequate—"explanation of the world" must accommodate and give lucid expression to the existence of this value.[24] The result of this spiritual conversion was the plan of the *Pensées*, a book which "was to have been a carefully constructed defence of Christianity, a true Apology and a kind of

Grammar of Assent, setting forth the *reasons* which will *convince* the
intellect."[25] To the right mind, Christianity is attractive precisely because of
the difficulty it poses "to the disorderly mind and to the unruly passions"[26]—
the mind turning over in an agony of doubt, the passions bottled up in
unending turbulence. In healthy religion we find, as Eliot would argue over
and again, not merely emotion and belief twined in ideal concord. We find,
in the first place, a means of attaining that *"intellectual* satisfaction" we
crave and without which we "do not want [religion] at all."[27] We find, in the
second, a means of "disciplin[ing] and training . . . emotion" by making it
significant, a means "only attainable through dogmatic religion."[28] We find,
finally, an object worthy of pursuit, even if unattainable, because of a
permanence—a permanence of adequation—that answers to the heart's
need:

> I should say that it was at any rate essential for Religion that we should have the
> conception of an immutable object or Reality the knowledge of which shall be the final
> object of that will; and there can be no permanent reality if there is no permanent truth. I
> am of course quite ready to admit that human apprehension of truth varies, changes and
> perhaps develops, but that is a property of human imperfection rather than of truth. You
> cannot conceive of truth at all, the word has no meaning, except by conceiving of it as
> something permanent. And that is really assumed even by those who deny it. For you
> cannot even say it changes except in reference to something which does not change; the
> idea of change is impossible without the idea of permanence.[29]

Composed roughly of thirteen essays, the second of the two broad
categories into which Eliot's "appreciations of individual authors" comes to
enclose themselves, focuses on individual works of art whose expressive
powers, either through authorial perplexity or linguistic debility, are flawed
by a practical, operative inability to transmute feeling into form. This
category is itself, of necessity, divisible into two groups, depending on
whether our momentary perspective or vantage point directs attention to
objects large or small: those essays which explore at length the failure of
language, of individual words—the smallest building block of literature—
either singly or collectively, to attach themselves to reality; and those essays,
dealing with complete works of art, which center on what Eliot came to call
the dilemma of "baffled emotion," works whose overall shortcoming Eliot
described using the notion of the "objective correlative." On the topic of
verbal insufficiency Eliot's most important commentary is to be located in
"Swinburne as Poet." Eliot begins by cataloguing Swinburne's highly
idiosyncratic style and peculiar verbal habits—the "adjectives [which] are
practically blanks," the "slightly veiled and resonant abstractions" which are
embedded in the large poem to no visible purpose, and become therefore
"destitute of meaning," the words chosen "merely for the tinkle," the general

absence of lines so singular and unique that they "can never be recaptured in other words,"[30] the penchant for "diffuseness" in place of "concentration," the sense of being seduced by "the most general word . . . because his [underlying] emotion . . . [is] never particular."[31] Finding here a distinct pathology of language, Eliot is driven to set forth the theoretical premise that "language in a healthy state," an ideal condition unlike that to be found in Swinburne, "presents the object, is so close to the object that the two are identified."[32] Ideally, words and their objects are inseparable; to exchange one word for another is, unwittingly, to transform reality, to alter it, to dismantle it. Swinburne scants objects, relishing the word in decadent isolation.

For Eliot, words never constitute a mere aperture onto an independent reality set over against them. Eliot assumes that "the name" of an object—be it physical, emotional, or a tangled complex of both—is never "merely a convenient means for denoting something which exists in complete independence of the name." For Eliot words cannot be merely *signs* for an independent, preexisting reality. On the contrary, words are *symbols* which cannot "be . . . arbitrarily amputated from the object . . . [they] symbolize," for "[n]o symbol . . . is ever a mere symbol, but is continuous with that which it symbolizes." Eliot goes further by stating that an "explicit recognition of an object as such" cannot actually occur "without the beginnings of speech," and as speech develops and evolves, growing in achieved nuance and complexity, an equal and corresponding evolution of reality takes place. In more drastic terms: "without words, no objects."[33] One might successfully argue, as both Eliot and Merleau-Ponty appear to, that language is a higher form of experience, continuous with it while nurturing it into adequate form.

Language and Reality

"Language," adds Eliot, is always "a development of reality as well," and whenever "language shows a richness of content and intricacy of connections," these "are as well an enrichment of the reality grasped.[34] For if a symbol were to be plucked from the soil of experience, it would become "a symbol that symbolize[s] nothing"—ceasing to "be a symbol at all" and becoming instead "another reality . . . [consisting of] certain [idle] marks on paper."[35]

Granting that "Swinburne was . . . a master of words," for Eliot this particular mastery consists not in a finelyhoned skill which renders the object more precise, more concrete, more palpable, but rather in a massive talent for obscurantism—for shrouding the object in an impenetrable verbal haze. The distinctive quality possessed by Swinburne's words is the ability to radiate "suggestions" which scatter endlessly in all directions while pinpointing nothing with "denotation." "If," as a result, "they suggest nothing, it is because they suggest too much;"[36] Swinburne fell prey to the illegitimate—because autonomous—blandishments of suggestive language, its associative richness leading to irresponsibility, its profusion of possible meanings which collectively mean nothing; it was "the word that [gave] him the thrill," laments Eliot, "not the object. When you take to pieces any verse of Swinburne, you find always that the object was not there—only the word."[37]

Eliot's judgment of Swinburne comes from his conviction that Swinburne has abandoned pursuit of experience for escape to an aerie from which the real world has been banished: "human feelings . . . in Swinburne's case do not exist." His "morbidity" is not of feeling—these are nowhere to be found—but of "language." For Swinburne the "object"—the felt object toward which adequation proceeds—"has ceased to exist," with the consequence that "meaning is merely the hallucination of meaning," and "language, uprooted, had adapted itself to an independent life of atmospheric nourishment." Only a "man of genius"—though the context transforms the term into a blatant misnomer— "could dwell so exclusively and consistently among words as Swinburne."[38] This genius manifests itself in that extraordinary ability of "so little material" to "release such an amazing number of words," all of which attempt to amplify and increase "the vague associations" they are capable of eliciting, without ever becoming anchored in a real "emotion" that is "particular," without ever being "focused."[39] Like the dream that fails to sustain its reality upon awakening, Swinburne's work possesses an air of dreamlike deception; like a dream, his work seems to hover tantalizingly on the brink of important meaning without ever attaining it, without ever trembling into adequate form. This is Eliot's meaning when he says that Swinburne's statements seem to counterfeit "tremendous statement[s], like statements made in our dreams." In Swinburne's work the quest for adequation becomes irrelevant, since his world "does not depend upon some other world which it simulates; it has the necessary completeness and self-sufficiency for justification and permanence."[40] Perfection for Swinburne is the perfection of irrelevance, for ultimately the kind of "language which is . . . important" is language which has embarked on the task of adequation, language that finds itself "struggling to digest and express new objects, new groups of objects, new feelings, new aspects" of the real.[41]

With some slight variation the same charge is made in such essays as "Philip Massinger," "Seneca in Elizabethan Translation," "Euripedes and Professor Murray," and, in more extreme form, in "Four Elizabethan Dramatists." Massinger, for example, is viewed as a poet whose "feeling for language," whose sheer lust for things verbal, has "outstripped his feeling for things; . . . his eye and his vocabulary were not in co-operation."[42] In Senecan drama, "the drama is all in the word, and the word has no further reality behind it," unlike the Greek drama or the drama of Shakespeare, where "[b]ehind the drama of words is the drama of action . . . and the particular emotion." In them, "[t]he phrase, beautiful as it may be, stands for a greater beauty still."[43] In his acid, frontal attack on John Gilbert Murray's translation of Euripides' *Medea* from the Greek, Eliot accuses Murray of a fundamental disregard for language which betrays him into the sloppiness of employing "two words where the Greek language requires one, and where the English language will provide him with one," and of "stretch[ing] . . . Greek brevity to fit the loose frame of William Morris, and . . . the fluid haze of Swinburne."[44] The problem also imbues "Four Elizabethan Dramatists," where the devaluation of words is compounded and exacerbated by a parallel loss of artistic conventions—convention defined as any "selection or structure or distortion in subject matter or technique" which results in "form or rhythm [being] imposed upon the world of action." The outcome is a loss of conventional "form[s]" capable of "arrest[ing] . . . the flow of spirit at any particular point before it expands and ends its course in the desert of exact likeness to . . . reality. . . ."[45] Here the desert of reality refers to the impoverished, circumscribed territory of the individual ego, cut off from the depths and heights of the emotional reality which lies outside its own narrow pale; since a lack of conventions or forms exists to describe this alien richness, this other existence becomes a reproach to the artist, taunting him with his own impotence. When conventions do exist, an impoverishment of language may render literature improbable; but when the conventions themselves are lost, literature becomes impossible, since conventions are the norms of reality which mediate our existence and make possible art in the first place.

In only two essays, "Marie Lloyd" and "Wilkie Collins and Dickens," does Eliot discern some slight grounds for optimism. Of Marie Lloyd, the renowned music hall artist, Eliot writes that there resided in "her smallest gesture"—her singular, theatrical vocabulary—a "perfect expressiveness" for what she felt; in consequence, "no other comedian succeeded so well in giving expression to the [emotive] life of . . . [her] audience . . . the soul of the people."[46] In the other case, that of Wilkie Collins and Dickens, Eliot seeks to draw a distinction between "pure melodrama," that form of art where we "accept an improbability"—a situation incapable of affording intellectual satisfaction— "for the sake of seeing the thrilling situation"—a climactic surge of raw emotion untethered to intellectual meaning—as opposed to a higher art where, instead of accepting melodramatic "coincidence, set without shame or pretence," we find "fate . . . which merges into character," and "the melodramatic—the accidental—becomes . . . the dramatic—the fatal."[47] After the momentary thrill of the melodramatic we demand a return to a higher art based on a harmonious intellectual scheme adequate not simply to the eliciting of emotions but to rendering them significant in an integrated, organic whole.

Eliot and the Objective Correlative

But Eliot's most compelling attention, as manifested in the turns, twists, and responses of his argument, is paid to that group of essays dealing with whole works of art in which the quest for adequation is mysteriously blocked, in which the endeavor to express "emotion" is "baffled." No "correlative" in the "objective" world of language and form can be found for the unarticulated feelings which underlie such works. In several of these essays, Eliot turns to a mode of argument that hinges on comparison and contrast, on mulling over the latent assets and hidden defects of two works set in juxtaposition or in weighing the comparative merits of two figures placed side by side, and watching as the scale balances, first this way, then that, on the point of an imaginary fulcrum.

Of those essays where a single figure alone is scrutinized, the case of Tennyson is both instructive and typical. Despite Tennyson's undisputed diversity of lyric form, Eliot delivers himself of a virtually formulaic summary of Tennyson's plight. His tragedy resides in the fact that his "real feelings . . . profound and tumultuous as they are, never arrive at expression,"[48] because of a paradoxical failure, despite their powerful intensity and Tennyson's own insistent poetic experimentation, to find a form adequate to their pent-up force, a form that would transform melancholia into meaning. Tennyson's long-harbored and long-submerged "emotional intensity and violence . . . emotion so deeply suppressed, even from himself, as to tend rather towards the blackest melancholia than towards dramatic action" could ultimately achieve "no . . . clear purgation." Tennyson committed errors which were grave to the degree that they thwarted adequation— "fundamental error[s in the choice] of form."[49] A closely parallel case is Cyril Tourneur. The emotions which rise to the surface in *The Revenger's Tragedy*—"cynicism," "loathing and disgust of humanity" are held by Eliot to be "immature in the respect that they exceed the [dramatic] object," they overwhelm the confines of the play because in the end the play proves a fundamentally inadequate vehicle for their full expression. Indeed, Eliot concludes that any "objective equivalents" for such emotions could be found only in "characters practising the grossest vices; characters which seem merely to be specters projected from the poet's inner world of nightmare, some horror beyond words."[50]

The four essays which pivot on comparison and contrast—"Francis Herbert Bradley" (to whom John Ruskin is unfavorably compared);

"Lancelot Andrewes" (who is applauded at the expense of John Donne); and "Hamlet and His Problems" which must be read in immediate conjunction with the essay on "Ben Jonson"—widen this circle of argument but scarcely alter the relentless flow of Eliot's thought. They comprise a brilliant triad whose purpose is to advance, augment, and amplify Eliot's argument. Bradley and Ruskin furnish a useful point of departure. The prose flights of Bradley, in which intellectual toil "is perfectly welded with the matter" to produce his "great gift of style," are the issue of a man whose "pleasure was the singular one of thinking." It is a poignant irony that Bradley's own underlying philosophic pessimism toward adequation is couched in a style which proves supremely adequate to its embodied matter. In the case of Ruskin, on the other hand, "[o]ne feels that the emotional . . . intensity . . . is partly a deflection of something that was *baffled* in life, whereas Bradley, like Newman, is directly and wholly that which he is."[51] And this terse analysis points back to the comparison of Donne with Andrewes in the previous year to which, though less volubly expansive, it is the logical successor. The "emotion" found in Andrewes's sermons "is purely contemplative" because it issues solely from a self-absorbing contemplation of an adequate object—the careful elucidation of the essential dogma of the Incarnation.

Having found an adequate object allows both for the harmonious absorption of feeling into object, and for the triumphant denotation of feeling by object, a reciprocal, self-enhancing process in which form renders feeling adequate and feeling renders form meaningful. The entirety of Andrewes's prose sermons is made "adequate"—and here Eliot is at pains to underscore his point—only by means of "his emotions [being] wholly contained in and explained by the object. But with Donne, there is always the something else, the 'baffling'" swarm of feelings which remains isolate, objectless. Donne is perpetually engaged in searching for "an object which shall be adequate to his feelings," whereas "Andrewes is wholly absorbed in the object and therefore responds with the adequate emotion."[52] In Donne there is discoverable a little of the nervous ascent and descent of "the religious spellbinder, the flesh-creeper, the sorcerer of emotional orgy," ready to play to a rapt audience, to whip up and indulge quivering and taut emotions. But this theatrical bent, this rhetorical ability is purchased at the price of "spiritual discipline," in that it prevents and is itself the offspring of some obstacle that hinders his "experience [from being] . . . perfectly controlled," perfectly ordered, made perfectly meaningful by the attainment of a satisfactory object. In consequence, there hovers about the edges of Donne's poetry and sermons some taint of the "incommunicable," feeling which is at once "the vague and unformed," and "experience" which, because imperfectly realized and therefore imperfectly understood, "is not perfectly controlled." No such taint darkens the pages of Andrewes, whose overspreading mastery is everywhere grounded in an achieved harmony of "[i]ntellect and sensibility,"[53] a harmonious perfection, unshadowed by tenuity or hesitation, of adequation. Indeed, the reader becomes the witness to this unfolding drama. He follows "the movement of . . . [Andrewes's] thought" as he "takes a word and derives the world from it; squeezing and squeezing the word until it yields a full juice of meaning," until this "examination of words" and meanings which can be wrung from them terminates "in the ecstasy of [intellectual and emotional] assent."[54]

By the time we reach Eliot's famous dyad of essays about "baffled emotion"—"Hamlet and His Problems" and "Ben Jonson"—we are fully habituated to his speculative and generalizing terms, to the origins and central concerns of his argument. Perhaps this allows us better to perceive the imperfections beneath this dyad's notoriety, its failure to formulate an all-embracing statement whose hard-surfaced, intellectual, abstract tone would suffice to stand alone, a formula whose a priori, scientific elegance and inescapable determinism would, once and for all, interpose itself between Eliot and the dilemma of adequation.

Eliot begins his discussion of *Hamlet* by noting that in a wholly successful work of art,

> The artistic "inevitability" lies in this complete adequacy of the external to the emotion; and this is precisely what is deficient in *Hamlet*. Hamlet (the man) is dominated by an emotion which is inexpressible, because it is in *excess* of the facts as they appear. . . . *Hamlet* . . . is full of some stuff that the writer could not drag to light, contemplate, or manipulate into art.[55]

To the extent that *Hamlet* remains a play about an unrecoverable, unfathomable emotion, unlike the lucidly defined emotional motivations animating Shakespeare's other tragedies—"the *suspicion* of Othello, the *infatuation* of Antony, or the *pride* of Coriolanus"[56]—our inspection of its shortcomings must commence with the "disgust . . . occasioned [in Hamlet] by his mother," while recognizing at the same time "that his mother is not an adequate equivalent for it; his disgust envelopes and exceeds her. It is thus a feeling which he cannot understand; he cannot objectify it, and it therefore remains to poison life and obstruct action." There is recognizable here an insidious overlapping of art and artist in which the dilemma of Hamlet and that of his creator are seen to join and become one: "Hamlet's bafflement at the absence of objective equivalent to his feelings is a prolongation of the bafflement of his creator in the face of his artistic problem."[57] Shakespeare himself had sounded the theme of the scourge of baffled emotion as early as *Titus Andronicus*, his first tragedy: "Sorrow concealed, like an oven stopp'd,/ Doth burn the heart to cinders where it is."[58] Thus far Eliot's analysis is beyond reproach; but then, in the face of this dilemma of baffled emotion, Eliot, with a striking lack of elaboration in an essay of barely six pages, proceeds to erect a massive theory.

"The only way of expressing emotion in the form of art," says Eliot, "is by finding an 'objective correlative'; in other words, a set of objects, a situation, a chain of events which shall be the formula of that *particular* emotion; such that when the external facts, which must terminate in sensory experience, are given, the emotion is immediately evoked."[59] The first clause of this ill-begotten formulation merely repeats that emotion must attain to the nobility of form to find expression and achieve meaning. Eliot then engrafts a second formula, bedecked with scientific ostentation, that is both contradictory to the sense of his initial premise and erroneous in its own right. He posits nothing less than the existence of a fixed hierarchy of emotions whose existence would be reflected and confirmed by a corresponding hierarchy of "formula[s] . . . for [each] . . . *particular* emotion," such that when a particular formula—a word, a phrase, a situation, a chain of events, an adequate vehicle of whatever description—is supplied, the emotion is automatically elicited. This latter formulation rings with automatism, and is steeped in the logic of stimulus and response. It comes across as wholly invalid in a universe of process, and untrue to the underlying drift of Eliot's thought as we have followed it thus far.

Pessimism Inherent in the Quest for Adequation

For if such a project of fitting together hierarchies of emotion and adequate vehicles of form could be undertaken and achieved once and for all, adequation would cease to be a dilemma and the very task and endeavor of art—"the fight to recover what has been lost/ And found and lost again and again"[60] would at a stroke be subverted, indeed disappear forever. In the midst of a cosmos in process, as Eliot sadly concludes elsewhere, the attainment of such final certitude, either in life or art, is impossible.

This expansive general theory, however, does not affect Eliot's sure central insight into the underlying structural conundrum which flaws *Hamlet* where he is unerringly correct and incisive. *Hamlet* is composed of a diversity of sources and earlier plays, each imperfectly melded and fused with those that preceded; it is a "stratification" in which each layer "represents the efforts of a series of men, each making what he could out of the work of his predecessors." Although an early version of the play fitted neatly into the "revenge-motive" mold, in which "the action or delay is caused, as in *The Spanish Tragedy*, solely by the difficulty of assassinating a monarch surrounded by guards," in the final play, the handiwork of Shakespeare, "there is a motive which is more important than that of revenge, and which explicitly 'blunts' the latter; the delay in revenge is unexplained on grounds of necessity or expediency; and the effect of the 'madness' is not to lull but to arouse the king's suspicion."[61] As Reuben Brower puts it, "[Hamlet] has moved *toward* action, toward the simplification of the agile avenging hero. This aim, a 'purpose mistook,' might if realized have satisfied a Fortinbras, but not Hamlet, the man of many selves, of which the soldier"—the heroic figure at the focus of revenge tragedy— "was only one."[62] Shakespeare superimposes another drama onto the "revenge-motive" scheme, a second drama where adequation is, with perverse horror, blocked.

Because the role of avenging angel, in its defined simplicity, is closed to him, and because Hamlet is unable to bring to light and articulate a consistent, fully developed attitude toward "the effect of a mother's guilt upon her son,"[63] Hamlet is unable to choose, as Brower aptly notes, "any single one of these well-defined roles." In consequence, "Hamlet's tragic complexity and pathos arise from this terrible openness to so many possible modes of thought, feeling, and action. In the gestures and words of the final scene, his various selves, concerns, and loyalties come to expression in flashes of poetic and theatrical power,"[64] without resolving or reconciling themselves into a single, integrated human identity which could successfully bring to the surface of consciousness and reckon with a nameable, articulable emotion. On the contrary, baffled emotion blocks "the relief of speech," and only in speech, in the choice and selection of words to body forth his true self—for "an implicit program of action" is contained in the "attitude" which every word displays and "[t]he ideal word is in itself an act, its value contained in its use at the moment of utterance"[65]—could a program for action be found. Blighted by sincerity, Hamlet stands helpless before his swarming, contradictory feelings. His failure to arrive at words to propel him into cathartic action and help him to reestablish a single, rounded identity defines the tragedy of Hamlet.

If the problem of Hamlet is the "intense feeling, ecstatic or terrible, without an object or exceeding its object" which the ordinary person "puts . . . to sleep, or trims down . . . to fit the business world,"[66] the polished achievement of Ben Jonson, although unacknowledged by reason of Eliot's own desperate attempts to whittle down the imposing burden of Shakespeare's greatness to a more manageable size, is an achievement of retrenchment, a victory won in default of battle by circumventing the enemy—the dilemma of adequation. For if, as Eliot speculates, Shakespeare's characters were "perhaps the *satisfaction* of more and of more complicated feelings . . . the offspring of deeper, less apprehensible feelings," Ben Jonson eschewed altogether—perhaps deliberately, perhaps as the natural tropism of his own native bent—such "emotion deeper and more obscure" in favor of emotion plainly at the center of consciousness, nameable, identifiable emotion, emotion as "intense" perhaps, as "strong" as Shakespeare's, but never as deep, as peripheral, as inapprehensible.[67] "Shakespeare, and also Donne and Webster and Tourneur . . . have a depth, a third dimension . . . which Jonson's work has not," remarks Eliot without foreseeing that the future context of *Selected Essays* would transpose this note of involuted praise into the minor key of derogation. "Their words have often a network of tentacular roots reaching down to the deepest terrors and desires. Jonson's most certainly have not."[68] Jonson was content to rest with the conquerable task, to repose with an art not of exploration but of completion, to devote himself to the "precise filling in," with known, unambiguous emotion, "of a strong and simple [artistic] outline," and "at no point" to feel compelled, at no point to feel driven by some inner necessity, to "overflow the outline."[69] In the dual portraits of Shakespeare and Ben Jonson, the one tormented by adequation, the other oblivious to its cruel demands, we have Eliot's most graphic and most revealing studies in pessimism.

The Fall from Allegory

To suggest that all of Eliot's "appreciations of individual authors" explore only the reaches and depths of pessimism, would be to misstate the case. Beyond these studies of failure and inadequacy, (which dominate *Selected Essays*), looms still another triad of essays, these moving towards a limited optimism. The first and most crucial of these essays, "Dante," is the center point around which the assays into pessimism circle. The reason is plain. If Dante is reverenced by Eliot as the distant master in a foreign tongue who poses no threat to the aspiring poet, he is, at the same time, like Virgil before him, the ideal poet who dwells in a cosmos still whole, still free of the fragmentation that ensued in the wake of the cataclysmic "dissociation of sensibility." Dante is, in other words, the figure of the poet still situated in a static universe, precariously yet indubitably free of the ravages of process, a universe in which language is still miraculously adequate to the full "spectrum" or "gamut" of emotion of which man's sensibility is potentially capable. He is the poet who can still fashion a work of art in which an image of that cosmos may be caught up and reflected in an all-embracing structure of allegory that most fully unites language and experience in an immense, closely knit, and comprehensive tableau of meaning.

Allegory is Eliot's name for the highest achievement of art possible in an unfallen universe. As a fitting capstone to his explorations into the dilemmas of adequation, and as a powerful counterweight to his extensive chronicling of the precipitous decline of art after the fall, Eliot's discussion of allegory is central to his thought. Indeed, nothing so obsessed or refreshed the springs of his thought as speculating about the nature of such a work of art, supreme in its achieved perfection; and to a leisurely examination of its salient characteristics, as embodied chiefly in *The Divine Comedy*, Eliot gave himself up wholeheartedly in "Dante." To begin with, as already noted, allegory is capable of displaying not simply a single emotion carefully nurtured from inchoate feeling into mature form, but rather, all together, in a vast and harmonious orchestration, "a complete scale of the *depths* and *heights* of human emotion," leaving far off for the distant future the fallen, "ordinarily very limited human range" of emotion now typical of the wakeful ego.[70] In the second place, the language of allegory is so close to its object, so close—because so adequate—to the texture and intensity of the original experience depicted, as to be characterized by a singular, unique "*poetic* . . . lucidity"[71] which enables it to manifest that drop of experience in "*clear visual images*," lucid "visions" which highlight the already inherent clarity and meaningfulness of the original experience. Moreover, such "visions" or "clear . . . images" may be thought of, in an ideal way, as reconciling and harmonizing the very disconnection and diversity of fallen experience—the discontinuous realms of "dreaming,"[72] reverie, fantasy, memory and the like. And, because such "clear images"[73] possess a network-like coherence among themselves, they may likewise be viewed as achieving what, in the fallen world, could be achieved only through a massive and powerful fusion of "actual experience . . . , intellectual and imaginative experience (the experience of thought and the experience of dream),"[74] a chain of radiant nodes of experience far more whole, more real, more palpable, and more terrible than any single, half-formed experience that occasionally strays within the perimeter of the limited ego. In allegory as Eliot envisions it, abstract "ideas" and general words are no longer shucked or lopped off from the experiences which they endeavor to express, but rather, as functioning symbols, remain continuous with their underlying experiences, every "idea" successfully "express[ed] . . . in images,"[75] and every "image" informed by an idea ultimately apprehensible and alive. Third, no matter how far allegory seems to intrude into realms of phantasmagoric experience now alien to our own dull world, we can still enjoy (Eliot is at pains to assure us) full confidence that the experiences recounted in allegory are, by definition, anchored to stable "meaning;" and although we may initially fail to grasp in its entirety this "meaning"—indeed, allowing for our present ignorance, at first "we do not [even] need to know what that meaning is"—eventually, in due course, allegory will bestow that meaning upon us, will render us "aware that the meaning," as well as the experience, "is there too."[76] Hence allegory may be said to restore us, momentarily, to a prelapsarian cosmos where every shred of experience is invested with meaning. Finally, because every single experience and its coordinate, corresponding meaning is inseparably twined, and because every such fused whole is ordered, articulated, and related to every other such whole along the parallel scales of sensibility and intellect, "the whole poem" becomes "one vast metaphor," with the consequence that "there is hardly any place for metaphor in the detail of it."[77] Eliot would urge that language, prior to the "dissociation of sensibility," functions in a radically different fashion from its later counterpart in the fallen world. In consequence, Dante found it necessary to employ only "very simple language, and very few metaphors, for allegory and metaphor do not get on well together." Settled comfortably into a circumambient metaphysical framework of stable meaning and exorcised emotion, Dante was needful only of simple "comparisons," and for this the "simile," drawing two known, magnetically attracting quantities together, was adequate. The aim of this sort of simile is wholly "intensive," its goal "solely to make us see *more definitely*"—more starkly, more concretely, more immediately, more meaningfully—"the scene which Dante has put before us." This simile draws out, highlights and intensifies, as it were, an interpretation which is both before the mind and preexistent in the grand scheme of the cosmos, latently, from the start. A settled, mapped-out cosmos requires only simple comparisons, simple links to forge together its basic elements, instead of the complex, tortured, involuted, perpetually unfolding metaphors which must begin their work by first attempting to bring these basic elements—defined emotion and stable meaning—into existence. Similes employed for such an "explanatory" function served Dante well;[78] there was no need to struggle after the difficult language of exorcism and adequation.

The Language of Adequation

The language of adequation, on the contrary, is prodigal of difficulty; in its struggle to overcome a profound metaphysical debility, it must proceed by an "expansion" of the unknown, the half-formed, the embryonic, the intrinsically unclear instead of by a simple process of intensifying known meaning. In other words, it must expand by exploring, by explaining (in the sense of the Latin *explico*, to unfold), by unfurling meaning after meaning to jog the mind from lower to ever higher steps of understanding, by analyzing everything, theoretically, to its farthest, most infinite reach. Because the comprehensive and self-contained "whole from idea to image"[79] which once comprised allegory has now been fragmented and dissociated, the "purpose" of the language of adequation becomes analytical and exorcist. Its intent is always "to *add* to what you see . . . either on the stage or in your imagination," always to etch ever more clearly and firmly, always to prevent newly won clarity from softening and slipping away in a blur or meaningless haze. Such language must always be "more elusive,"[80] more difficult, more treacherous for both poet and reader. The existence of such language forms the bond, the bridge, and the link between the historical practice of the metaphysical poets, as essayed in "The Metaphysical Poets" and "Andrew

Marvell," and Eliot's private view of his own poetic needs and his own struggle with language.

This personal bond is established as Eliot casts his eye back from his own desperate plight to a particular period of the past, and is renewed as his eye travels forward from a familiar past to a kindred present: for as Eliot later confessed in speaking about this dual perspective, "both in my general affirmations about poetry and in writing about [those] authors [of the metaphysical school] who had influenced me, I was implicitly"—and simultaneously—"defending the sort of poetry that I and my friends wrote."[81] In writing about them, the metaphysical poets became surrogates, virtually alter-egos, and in confronting their problems, Eliot could achieve a measure of perspective on his own. The metaphysical poets "were at best, engaged in the task [of adequation,] of trying to find the verbal equivalent for states of mind and feeling."[82] In so doing, in so setting off down the twisting and turning path of "expansion," they were compelled to "become more and more comprehensive, more allusive, more indirect, in order to force, to dislocate if necessary, language into . . . meaning.[83] We note this in the lush, almost tropical "variety and order of the images," and again in "the high speed," accelerating pace at which this "succession of concentrated images" rushes past, "each magnifying the original fancy,"[84] each expanding and compounding the initial set of meanings, each heaping up this accumulating suggestivity to new heights of meaning—and all following the general law of adequation which dictates the necessity of forcing "the elaboration . . . of a figure of speech to the farthest stage to which ingenuity can carry it."[85]

This difficulty, this complexity, this involution and convolution of thought extends from the small space of the individual image or metaphor in which meaning is drawn out or unraveled to the larger contours of overall sentence structure as well. For if "the *structure* of the sentences . . . is sometimes far from simple," this is out of a necessary "fidelity to [actual] thought and feeling"[86] as the poet struggles to set down an accurate transcription of the lunging, darting, abruptly zig zagging drama unfolding before his own mind. Indeed, in the "skill of these . . . sudden . . . transitions" from one meaning to the next, from one metaphor to the next, from an entire thought to its unexpected successor—transitions which arc across the unprepared mind—lie the true mark of an exhalted "sincerity" of style. Here the poet's method consists in "faithfully and easily [following] the movement of his own mind,"[87] that quality of sincerity which is yet another attribute of the drama of adequation. But if these qualities are to be located among the metaphysical poets, almost exactly the same qualities are discoverable in modern poetry, as Eliot observes on another occasion, a fond remembrance of Charles Whibley, and for exactly the same reasons.

Critics sometimes comment upon the sudden transitions and juxtapositions of modern poetry: that is, when right and successful, an application of somewhat the same method without method. Whether the transition is cogent or not, is merely a question of whether the mind is *serré* [tight, closely-knit, closely-woven] or *délié* [loose, untied, disconnected], whether the whole personality is involved; and certainly, the whole personality of Whibley is present in whatever he wrote, and it is the unity of a personality which gives an indissoluble unity to his variety of subject.[88]

What Eliot has done is to yoke epistemology and poetic style, for the attainment of "a *living* style, whether in prose or in verse"[89] depends directly on whether the mind is "*serré*," on whether the "whole personality" has been kindled into a state of activity, sweeping away habitual dullness and disconnection before a rush of insights. Only in this way can the mind continue to leap from illumination to illumination in its quest for adequation. Unlike the Dantesque universe of circumscribed fixity, where the simile functions as little more than an equals signs between known entities, in a fallen universe, a universe of process, a universe where adequation is both starting point and terminus for the artist, the poet's mind—and the metaphors it spins out— when "perfectly equipped for its work,

. . . is constantly amalgamating disparate experience; the ordinary man's experience is chaotic, irregular, fragmentary, [because his mind is *délié*]. The latter falls in love, or reads Spinoza, and these two experiences have nothing to do with each other, or with the noise of the typewriter or the smell of cooking; in the mind of the poet these experiences are always forming new wholes.[90]

In a universe which consists of no single whole, it is inevitable that, unless we fall prey to habituation, "new wholes" will always be forming in "the mind of the poet," as the cosmos ceaselessly defines, redefines, and transforms itself, assuming new and often terrifying shapes. And, indeed, a countercurrent of fear of such new wholes—of confronting a universe of process—manifests itself in Eliot's simultaneous quest for precision, for fixities, for definitions, for limits, for boundaries, for termini. But the very existence of this tendency merely lends poignance and courage to the quest of the poet by underscoring the risks he must perpetually encounter, and serves in the end to enhance his calling.

By yoking epistemology and poetic style, mental activity, and the birth of metaphor, Eliot, moreover, places himself squarely at the end of a broad tradition of theoretical speculation in English poetry that runs from at least the early eighteenth century to the present. Thus Eliot finds himself overturning and inverting Dr. Johnson's impeachment of the metaphysical poets—that cluster of premises, assertions, and stylistic shortcomings which Dr. Johnson alleges in his famous brief—into terms of necessary praise. As a pointed rejoinder to Dr. Johnson's disparaging claim that in the meta-physical poets "the most heterogeneous ideas are yoked by violence together," Eliot pleads that "a degree of heterogeneity of material compelled into unity by the operation of the poet's mind is omnipresent"—and necessary—"in poetry."[91] Nor is Eliot's description of the poet's mind very far, either in spirit or underlying conception, from Wordsworth's claim that when the mind, in its most active, exhalted mood, gives birth to a metaphor, the "two objects unite and coalesce," so that "a sense of the truth of the likeness" of the objects, "from the moment that it is perceived, grows—and continues to grow—upon the mind,"[92] producing new wholes of experience and thereby transforming the world. Even more profound and telling, in his attempt to describe the reciprocal movement between mental activity and poetic style as adequation struggles to occur, is Eliot's invocation, with considerable fanfare, of Coleridge's famous elucidation of Imagination:

> This power . . . reveals itself in the balance or reconcilement of opposite or discordant qualities: of sameness, with difference; of the general, with the concrete; the idea with the image; the individual with the representative; the sense of novelty and freshness with old and familiar objects; a more than usual state of emotion with more than usual order; judgment ever awake and steady self-possession with enthusiasm and feeling profound or vehement . . . ."[93]

Coleridge's categories of the "general," "idea," "representative," "order," and "judgment" are all subsumed under Eliot's declaration that "thought is general." Coleridge's rubrics of the "concrete," "image," "individual," "emotion," and "feeling profound or vehement" all fall under Eliot's claim that "feeling and emotion are particular." When a balance or reconcilement of these opposites takes place, Coleridge would claim that a symbol is educed, a symbol which for Eliot marks a fleeting moment of adequation. Indeed, to set Eliot's definition of the mind of the poet beside Coleridge's elucidation of imagination is to be struck by their nearly identical reasoning. Both the mind of the poet exercising its characteristic activity and the completed work of art display, in operation and accomplishment, similar powers, and attributes.

Wit as Artistic Instinct

In casting about for a term adequate to describe this process, Eliot sought to avoid both the commonplace Romantic designation of imagination and "the equally unsatisfactory nomenclature of our own time," turning instead to an attempt to resurrect "the dim and antiquated term wit."[94] Yet despite Eliot's attempt to rewrite literary history in terms of a "fluid" phrase whose own slippery "meaning [always] alters with the age,"[95] Eliot is only partly successful. On the one hand, it was vital to keep repeating to himself and others alike, over and again, that for him "wit" meant "something more serious than we usually mean [by that term] today."[96] On the other hand, he sought diligently to sidestep the intricate complexities indigenous to the knotty Romantic dispute over the "difference between imagination and fancy," emphasizing that in both the clear primacy of mental activity, whatever the particular differences in degree of intensity or area of application, rendered the distinction "a very narrow one."[97] And so Eliot inches backward, not unreluctantly, from the temptation to undertake any comprehensive historical survey or chronological account of the problem, contenting himself with the improvisory—yet pivotal—declaration that "wit forms the crescendo and diminuendo of a scale of great imaginative power"[98] which culminates in the achievement of adequation. In other words, wit never consists principally in verbal festooning, in ornamentation, in illustration or sportive decoration of preexisting ideas or conceptions. Rather, it always signals the discovery of a new reality, a breakthrough to a more adequate conception of the real. The metaphor framed by wit does not merely combine or fuse "into a single phrase, two or more diverse impressions"—much more importantly, it "identifies itself with what suggests it" to produce "that perpetual slight alteration of language, words perpetually juxtaposed in new and sudden combinations, meanings perpetually *eingeschachtelt* into meanings" which is at once a new version of reality.[99] As a functional term, wit comprehends and blends a progression of meanings which range from mental brilliance and the cutting power of the insightful mind to seize new reality to the use of language which demonstrates, embodies, and incarnates this power. It manifests itself often, but never exclusively, as "a tough reasonableness beneath the slight lyric grace,"[100] reasonableness by necessity tough and agile because intellect, from the very outset inferior and inadequate to dominant experience, is always in peril (even at those rare moments when it appears close to victory) of falling back into its more natural condition, of "los[ing] some [further] contact with reality," of further withdrawing from "a constant inspection and criticism of experience" which "involves," ultimately, "a recognition, implicit in the expression of every experience, of other kinds of experience which are possible"[101] to the broadest range of human sensibility and intellect. At its best, the poetry of wit is the poetry of adequation, allowing us to break through the habitual "mistiness of . . . [our] feeling[s]" and "the vagueness of its object,"[102] restoring both to a communion of equality, and restoring us to a momentary communion with the real.

3

Adequation and Personality in "Tradition and the Individual Talent"

Most recently we esteem Eliot's "Tradition and the Individual Talent" as among the most enduring of his theoretical essays; yet this was not always the case. F. R. Leavis's dudgeon, which flogs the essay for "its ambiguities, its logical inconsequences, its pseudoprecisions, its fallaciousness, and the aplomb of its specious cogency,"[1] is a case in point. But though Leavis's appraisal may seem to us wrong, the process by which it is arrived at is understandable. Undeniably, "Tradition and the Individual Talent" consists of a tissue of fragments, richly suggestive passages, and boldly resonating phrases whose overall unity is nowhere to be found within the confines of its nine pages. Moreover, the underlying themes which ultimately animate these fragments—themes which run the length and breadth of Eliot's work in all literary forms—here remain embryonic, unamplified, unexplored, unconnected, unreticulated. The essay is characterized by a striking failure to weld together parts which, looked at carefully, have an excellent reason for being together.

To sound the full depth of meaning and reconstruct the overall panoramic import of Eliot's essay it is best to begin at the invisible point where his two main themes—the nature of impersonality in works of art and the mysterious nature of selfhood—intersect to produce the essay's most tantalizing question: What is meant by "personality"? Throughout the course of his prose writings the term personality crops up repeatedly, being invoked, without prior hint or proper warning, in at least two dramatically different and often distinctly opposite ways. Most often Eliot thinks of personality in negative terms: an encrustation of habits, postures, attitudes, and social roles which provide us with an effective means of staving off confrontation with the incessant flux of experience, with those "deeper, unnamed feelings which form the substratum of our being, to which we rarely penetrate."[2] Personality is an everthickening encrustation of the inauthentic which sits atop and blocks salutary interchange with our deeper, truer, emotive selves. Personality is an "invented self" which interposes itself "between myself and [my true, subterranean] me,"[3] an artificial "self that is largely a deliberate fabrication" crafted lovingly by "thorough-going . . . actor[s]" who long only "to play . . . [their] role" in the outside world without hindrence or painful interference from true feeling or genuine knowledge, actors who are "so occupied with . . . [themselves] and with the figure . . . [they are] cutting [that] nothing could be altogether real."[4] To be certain, society itself helps to conspire in this outcome since "the ordinary processes of society . . . consist largely in the acquisition of impersonal ideals which *obscure* what we really *are* and *feel*."[5] And on an early leaf from *The Waste Land* manuscript we find Eliot crying out against a London which withers the sensibility and intellect of its inhabitants, a mass "Huddled between the concrete and the sky,/ Responsive [only] to the momentary need,/ . . . [but no longer] Knowing . . . how to think, nor how to feel."[6] This depersonalization at the hands of society, as Hazlitt put it, causes "our sharp angular points [to] wear off" as we "are [first] drilled into a sort of stupid decorum, . . . [then] forced to wear the same dull uniform of outward [and inward] appearance . . . [and finally] neutralized by intercourse with the world."[7] Abetted by our own deep-seated, entropic hunger for ignorance and blissful anesthesia, it becomes easy to busy ourselves solely with a "self" that is our "own invention," a "self" that we "under[stand] perfectly" because we have "invented" it.[8] Habits, postures, attitudes, roles, performances, inventions, actors, acting—the theatrical metaphor is both obsessive and apt, and has its taproot in Matthew Arnold's "The Buried Life," where "the mass of men" are pictured as beings condemned to live and move "Tricked in disguises, alien [both] to the rest/ Of men, and alien to themselves. . . ." So effective are these entrenched "disguises" that we can almost never return to "ourselves" nor "utter one of all/ The nameless feelings" that, at rare moments when we become aware of them, "course through our breast . . . for ever unexpressed."

> Yet still, from time to time, vague and forlorn,
> From the soul's subterranean depth upborne
> As from an infinitely distant land,
> Come airs, and floating echoes . . .

as "A bolt is shot back somewhere in our breast,/ And a lost pulse of feeling stirs again."[9] But except in the special case of the receptive and willing artist, for whom such moments may herald the onset of the quest for adequation, Eliot is more pessimistic about the human condition than is Arnold, transforming the latter's bittersweet pathos into a rich vein of comic, mordant wit as he explores the moment of panic that can accompany this sudden "loss of personality."

It is an unimpeachable article of faith for Eliot that we struggle to hold fast to our personalities as to a barrier reef before the onrushing, thundering tide of experience. "You are nothing but a set/ Of obsolete responses," the protagonist of *The Cocktail Party* is told as he finds himself stripped of his "invented self," shorn of his social role, naked before a sudden welter of unaccustomed, inexplicable feelings and the frightening tug of unexpected events. "[Y]ou've lost touch with the person," he is further informed,

> You thought you were. You no longer feel quite human.
> You're suddenly reduced to the status of an object—
> A living object, but no longer a person.
> It's always happening, because one is an object
> As well as a person. But we forget about it
> As quickly as we can.

The workings of this process are more precisely described in two analogies that follow without pause.

> When you've dressed for a party
> And are going downstairs, with everything about you
> Arranged to support you in the *role you have chosen*,
> Then sometimes, when you come to the bottom step
> There is one step more than your feet expected
> And you come down with a jolt. Just for a moment
> You have the experience of being an object
> At the mercy of a malevolent staircase.

In the second metaphor, loss of personality is likened to the loss of consciousness experienced during "a surgical operation."

> In consultation with the doctor and the surgeon,
> In going to bed in the nursing home,
> In talking to the matron, you are still the *subject*,
> The *center of reality*. But, stretched on the table,
> You are a piece of furniture in a repair shop
> For those who surround you, the masked actors;
> All there is of you is your body
> And the "*you*" is withdrawn.[10]

Both metaphors turn on a single irony: neither the "role" chosen to be played before an audience of assembled guests nor the feeling of being a "subject" in control, a commanding "center of reality," an active "you" is valid, since such conceptions are euphemisms for that *mauvais-foi* personality which must be painfully relinquished if the true self is to be uncovered through that downward descent leading to true knowledge of "What you really *are*. What you really *feel*."[11] Partly out of pride and ignorance, partly out of habit, and partly out of a more haunting, compelling concern that flows from the elusive metaphysical ramifications of personality, we mistakenly seek to think of ourselves as "something *positive*, Always the subject of the sentence;/ As having arranged, having been responsible/ For the part we play in every scene." In truth, our encrusted, fixed personalities are nothing more than sad, exhausted, reviled objects "Among others, like a broken cup/ Or a stalled engine."[12]

Personality as Artifact in a World of Process

Why, then, pay lifelong obeisance to a broken object, a tedium-filled scenario whose threadbare actor repeats his pitiful, unchanging lines in performance after performance? Why accept these walls of limitation that reduce us to shadows of our true selves? That answer, like most others after which Eliot quested, was to be found in an amalgam of metaphysics, poetry, and drama. As Eliot looked harder and harder at the dilemma of personality, seeking not only an explanation for the bleak specter of human existence, but a key that would explain its enduring metaphysical allure, he came to realize, early on, that personality is the weapon we employ not simply to defeat feeling, but to vanquish process itself, to overcome the ravages of time and history. Through the invention of a fixed, immobile, unchanging personality we seek an illicit apotheosis of that "something *positive*" into an artifact that dwells serenely in a timeless realm of eternal stasis, a transformation of the life-infected quotidian into a permanent conditon of unchanging, immutable being. We seek, above all, simply to "*be*: for how can I act," asks one of Eliot's characters in perplexity, how can I enter into the rough and tumble of human existence, how can I make decisions and commitments, how can I enter into the world of the ethical, "unless I [already] *am*,"[13] unless I already possess a fixed being, an eternal selfhood beyond the hungry encroachments of time? How else can we hope to escape the remorseless cycle of change, development, and decline, the painful search after meaning and the more painful certainty of loss of meaning, unless, by clinging to personality, we can stumble upon the secret to permanent being in the midst of time?

Is it possible, asks Eliot, that a fixed, stable self presupposes a fixed, stable cosmos—self and surrounding reality sharing the same permanence—in which meaning and being are both achieved and complete? Hence the quest for a stable personality, a fixed self, is really another version of the quest for adequation, the eternal hunger for adequate *meaning* and its attendant corollary, fluxless *being*. "It is . . . possible that *being* is only possessed completely by the dead," said Yeats,[14] and the sense of his epigram here augments and reenforces Eliot's thought. Only the dead can truly "be." Or, as Ortega y Gasset puts it, "Only when the Man, the you, *has died does he have a fixed being*—what he has been, which he can now no longer alter, contradict, or add to. This is the meaning of the famous line in which Mallarmé sees the dead Edgar Allan Poe: *Tel qu'en lui-même enfin l'Éternité le change.*" And, continues Ortega, "Life is change; at every new moment it is becoming definitely itself. *Only death, by preventing any new change, changes man into a definitive and immutable himself, makes him a forever motionless figure—that is, frees him from change and renders him eternal.*"[15] Plucked into the land of the changeless dead, both meaning and being can exist in unperturbed reciprocity, liberated from the nausea that clings to the moments of daily existence, the currents of time that lap jealously at the permanence of death.

The human equivalent of death must be objecthood: the firm, chiseled, shapely, marmoreal solidity of personality to which we cling in the face of process. Even Prufrock, who with half his tormented soul lashes out against the glance of the Other that condemns him to objecthood, lashes out with mingled self-pity and withering self-scorn against "The eyes that fix you in a formulated phrase," craves, simultaneously, with the other half of his damned soul, the security of that "formulated phrase," the security of objecthood which reduces him to a balding actor in a "morning coat, my collar mounting firmly to the chin,/ My necktie rich and modest, but asserted by a simple pin," a dull participant in an endless ritual of measuring "out . . . life with coffee spoons."[16] If personality is a form of death, death is what, in the end, we really seek.

This search for the fixity of selfhood beyond life is what Eliot refers to, in another form, when he speaks of the embalming, hypostatizing power of the *reflexive glance* to confer instant objecthood on a living person by gathering up past, present, and future in a remembered continuity beyond the exigencies of time; the power of this reflexive glance to circumscribe and fuse together the totality of one's life in a retrospective *sub specie aeternitatis*, is instanced especially, Eliot thinks, in "situations" in Shakespeare "where a character . . . *sees himself in a dramatic light*:

OTHELLO. And *say*, besides,—that in Aleppo once . . .
CORIOLANUS. *If you have writ your annals true*, 'tis
                            there,
                    That like an eagle in a dovecote, I
                    Fluttered your Volscians in Corioli.
                    Alone I did it. Boy!

TIMON. Come not to me again; but *say to Athens,*
 Timon hath made his everlasting mansion
 Upon the beachèd verge of the salt flood . . .

"It occurs also once," adds Eliot, "in *Antony and Cleopatra*, when Enobarbus is inspired to see Cleopatra in this dramatic light: 'The barge she sat in . . . ' "[17]

Unlike *Romeo and Juliet*, where "the profounder dramatist shows his lovers melting into unconsciousness of their isolated selves, shows the human soul in the process of forgetting itself,"[18] the characters above are "contemplating their own dramatic importance"[19] by viewing themselves from an imaginary vantage point beyond death, by fixing their legends, so to speak, while they still enjoy a few moments of life to relish the spectacle. Othello, Coriolanus, Timon, and Hamlet all are engaged in authoring a view of themselves to cling to in their moment of greatest need. But this "attitude of self-dramatization assumed . . . at moments of tragic intensity"[20] is in fact a method of escaping from dire reality, of shunning the agony of the present for an aesthetic contemplation of the self safely ensconced, as it were, beyond the power of time. Summarizing the crux of this argument, Eliot notes with considerable acumen that Othello, to take but a single case,

is endeavouring to escape reality, . . . has ceased to think about Desdemona, and is thinking about himself. Humility is the most difficult of all virtues to achieve; nothing dies harder than the desire to think well of oneself. Othello succeeds in turning himself into a pathetic figure, by adopting an *aesthetic* rather than a moral attitude, dramatising himself against his environment.[21]

The Surrender of Personality

Personality conceived of in this way—(be it as the disguises of social role, the self-dramatizing reflexive-glance of the mind's inner eye, or the metaphysician's attempt to locate the self once and for all as a continuous philosophic monad)—calls forth a resounding imperative from Eliot to cast away personality altogether, to relinquish its tyrannical sway. Eliot's favorite word to describe this process is the verb "to surrender." He cries out repeatedly for a ready "surrender" to our hidden feelings, for a willing "surrender" to the invincible tides of process, for a continuing "surrender" to the ceaseless flow of reality.

To understand personality as a rigid denial of process is to be compelled, willingly or otherwise, to subscribe to the negative declaration on which "Tradition and the Individual Talent" turns: a declaration which attacks, refutes, and rebuts the metaphysical dimension of personality, a declaration which soundly denies the existence of any "metaphysical theory of the substantial unity of the soul."[22] In truth, the self, the soul, the "I" possess no "substantial unity," no monadic sameness that can weather the ebb and flow of time. Man can never attain to a "substantial unity of the soul," for Eliot would agree with Ortega y Gasset's formulation that man

> ... has no nature. Man is not his body, which is a thing, nor his soul, psyche, conscience, or spirit, which is also a thing. Man is no thing, but a drama—his life, a pure and universal happening which happens to each one of us and in which each one in his turn is nothing but happening. ... Existence itself is not presented to him ready-made, as it is to the stone; rather, shall we say, ... on coming up against the fact of his existence, on existence happening to him, all he comes up against, all that happens to him is the realization that he has no choice but to do something in order not to cease existing. This shows that the mode of being of life, even as simple existing, is not a *being already*, since the only thing that is given us and that *is* when there is human life is the having to make it, each one for himself. Life is a gerundive, not a participle: a *faciendum*, not a *factum*.

The upshot of all this is that

> I am free *by compulsion*, whether I wish to be or not. Freedom is not an activity pursued by an entity that, apart from and previous to such pursuit, is already possessed of a fixed being. To be free means to be lacking in constitutive identity, not to have subscribed to a determined being, to be able to be other than what one was, to be unable to install oneself once and for all in any given being. The only attribute of the fixed, stable being in the free being is this constitutive instability.
>
> Human life is thus not an entity that changes accidentally, rather the reverse: in it the "substance" is precisely change, which means that it cannot be thought of ... as substance. Life being a "drama" that happens, and the "subject" to whom it happens being, not a thing apart from and previous to his drama, but a function of it, it follows that the "substance" of the drama would be its argument. And if this varies, it means that the variation is "substantial."

As a result,

> To comprehend anything human, be it personal or collective, one must tell its *history*. This man, this nation does such a thing and is in such a manner, *because* formerly he or it did that other thing and was in such another manner. Life only takes on a measure of transparency in the light of *historical reason*. ... *Man, in a word, has no nature*; *what he has is ... history*. Expressed differently: what nature is to things, history, *res gestae*, is to man.[23]

Almost exactly these sentiments can be found in tones of ringing conviction in a passage drawn from the writings of the philosopher Josiah Royce, under whose partial influence Eliot fell during the period of his graduate studies, and whom he was later to endow with the sobriquet "That extraordinary philosopher":[24]

The rule that *time* is needed for the formation of a conscious community is a rule which finds its extremely familiar analogy *within the life of every individual human self*. Each one of us knows that he just now, at this instant, cannot find more than a mere fragment of himself present. *The self comes down to us from its own past. It needs and is a history.* Each of us can see that his own idea of himself as this person is inseparably bound up with his view of his own former life, of the plans that he formed, of the fortunes that fashioned him, and of the accomplishments which in turn he has fashioned for himself. *A self is, by its very essence, a being with a past.* One must look lengthwise backwards in the stream of time in order to see the self, or its shadow, now moving with the stream, now eddying in the currents from bank to bank of its channel, and now strenuously straining onwards in the pursuit of its own chosen good.

At this present moment I am indeed here, as this creature of the moment,—sundered from the other selves [of my past and future]. But nevertheless, if considered simply in this passing moment of my life, I am hardly a self at all. *I am just a flash of consciousness,— not a coherent personality.* Yet, memory links me with my own past,—and not, in the same way, with the past of any one else. This joining of the present to the past reveals a more or less steady tendency,—a sense about the whole process of my remembered life.[25]

This striking metaphysical law denying the existence of a fixed, static personality accounts for the numerous points these passages have in common, points which "Tradition and the Individual Talent" makes by means of epigram, indirection, and suggestive hint.

The Dialectic of Surrender and Decision

One might enumerate these key points, the building blocks of Eliot's notion of selfhood, and the groundwork for his subsequent views concerning that quality of impersonality which should properly characterize works of art. First, no "substantial unity of the soul" exists, no timeless monad serenely above the currents of process can be conceived, no matter what the level on which such a notion is advanced or under whatever guise it is proposed or upheld. As a result, we can never "be" prior to feeling or action, prior to becoming engaged with the world; indeed, the reverse holds true, since our volitions, our feelings, and our plans, once discovered through liberation from the prison of personality, are paramount. Second, the true self, the self which has for the moment brushed away the remaining encroachments of false personality, must constantly be engaged in the unending task of keeping itself free of ever new encrustations of personality. In addition, it must continually try to recover from the depths our feelings, raise them to the surface of consciousness where they acquire meaning and direction and, then, act so as to confront life, engage existence, and transform our "irresponsible and undeveloped nature" into an ethical being capable of "that frightful discovery of morality."[26] The true self is dynamic, oscillating between two characteristic and overwhelmingly important moments: the moment of "surrender," when we plunge into the depths to recover our emotive selves; and the double moment of "decision" which launches us toward the act of surrender and, guided by the newly revealed meaning of our conscious emotions, binds together past, present and future in a decision which commits us to a task. In other words, it leads toward engagement with the world, toward shaping a revisionary self in and through the toils of action. Selfhood is, in its inner mechanism, a process of dialectic between "surrender" and "decision," a process that becomes possible only after our liberation from the strictures of personality.

Whenever the self cannot feel authentically, it is effectively blocked from action. Whenever the self fails to act authentically or to define itself through its commitments, it loses its authentic actuality and fades like an ember into darkness. We recognize the true self only by surrendering it to the plenitude of a particular time and place, a concrete moment of actuality, a particular program of action. A lifetime of such moments is required to establish—not a brittle mask of personality—but an authentic identity, a continuum from the distant past into the beckoning future. And third, insofar as the self *is* forged anew in each fresh moment of existence, the self must be conceived in positive terms that are temporal, historical and dramatic. Since history and drama are temporal, telic, directional, they are grounded in an "organic," "holistic" or "existential" view of time, in which past, present and future—or the beginning, middle and end of a task or action—constantly infiltrate each other, interpenetrate and co-mingle in a continuing immanence to produce a succession of whole selves, each right and proper for a particular period of our existence. Only such an "organic" view of time can explain the paradoxical workings of memory; for, despite the fact that our lives are bound together by a continuity of memory, memory itself always

> Goes on changing. Everything you do,
> Everything you discover about yourself—
> That is to say, everything you discover
> About your past self, for the present,
> Like the future, you cannot [fully] know—
> Everything you think and feel, accept, deny,
> Is altering the past . . . [27]

And the altered past, in turn, refashions the present and transforms the still hidden future while shaping and bodying forth, amidst this change and transformation, our authentic identities.

This view of "organic" time is expressed, most succinctly, in the first half of "Tradition and the Individual Talent," in Eliot's memorable phrase that "the historical sense involves a perception, not only of the pastness of the past, but of its presence."[28] The past is not an atomistic instant that passes away into an empty void but a force that continues to live, inform, and direct the present. It remains for the diligent reader to couple this epigram with the denial, in the second half of the essay, of any existence of "the substantial unity of the soul: for my meaning," continues Eliot, "is, that the poet has, not a 'personality' to express, but a particular medium, which is only a medium and not a personality."[29] In the first half of the essay, history radiates the design of organic time, whereas in the second half, the shape of self radiates, on a smaller scale, the identical design. The self becomes a microcosm of history, and history is seen as autobiography writ large.

The writer's task, his goal, his program of action is, at every moment, not the expression of personality, which has at this point already been relinquished and surrendered, but rather to wrestle with the medium of language, to transform the public dimension of received language into the subtle interiorities of his own private meaning, to find language adequate to his deepest, most elusive feelings. Then, through a second decision—or, perhaps, a reaffirmation of the first—the writer struggles to craft the material raised from his depths into a viable work of art. In short, only through an initial decision to surrender, followed by and reaffirmed in a second decision to labor at his craft, does the writer fulfill his particular destiny to write, and in this succession of reciprocating acts he discovers and rediscovers, over and again, his slowly emerging, developing, authentic identity.

History and Art, Self and Language

And what holds true in the particular case of the artist retains equal validity for selfhood in general in Eliot's view. The growing recognition "not only of the pastness of the past, but of its presence" is perhaps the central theme in all of Eliot's poetry and drama, culminating especially in the *Four Quartets,* which move from a quizzical, tentative exploration of the possibility that "Time present and time past/ Are both perhaps present in time future,"[30] to the more comprehensive, more positive dual conclusions embodied in the joint epigrams about selfhood which postulate that "In my beginning is my end" and "In my end is my beginning,"[31] to the final, climactic assertion in *Little Gidding* of a tempered bond between self and history, a heartfelt cry that "history is now and England."[32] Here the immediacy of the present and the span of history are fused: a declaration that personal history, cultural history, and religious history unfold on parallel but identical tracks, that past, present, and future must be caught up and transfigured in the moral calling of a poet dedicated to his own past, which is also the past of his people. The devastating failure to connect past, present, and future becomes the archetypal pattern of the remainder of Eliot's poetry, whose respective *personae* dwell "immured," as Matthew Arnold wistfully remarked, "In the hot prison of the present,"[33] isolated in an empty, solitary now with no before or after, men who "have no ghosts"[34] to stir them to nostalgia, desire or regret, women who "can connect/ Nothing with nothing."[35]

For Eliot, the same formula which expresses the immanence of the past in the present and the present in the future applies equally whether to the vast sweep of history or the narrow field of the self. The principle of immanence resembles a series of concentric circles, each circumscribing an area of human experience, each overlapping and mirroring the other two. The innermost circle represents the fluidity of experience, its incessant eddying from past to future. The second circle characterizes the temporal character of all our experience, its structuring into a continuum of past, present, and future. The third circle carries these experiences onto the field of history, which gives meaning to society as a collection of individuals. In an organic view of time, the past always exists as a distanced present, a present that has already been, but the fact of "having been" does not blunt its bearing on the experienced present. The past "has been," but it is not over, finished with, as one might speak of discarded instants which have been shuttled across the stage of the present and are of little further use. The past continues to bite into the present, to affect its direction and meaning, to play a vital role in man's decisions. The past provides us with a storehouse of materials for shaping the present, for the past alone can provide us with its precious legacy of language, ritual, and belief.

Still, "Only by acceptance/ Of the past . . . [can] its meaning" be altered, can its legacy be rendered understandable and meaningful.[36] The present is an imminent past, a past ready to hasten from its momentary station in the present backwards to its final destination. The present is always on the verge of slipping into the past. Yet the present holds within it the fullness of the past. The present passes away incessantly, flicks by in the blink of an eye, and its breathless quality of transiency, of fleetingness is displayed in the urgency of choice, in the experience of the present as the "right time" or "opportune moment"[37] for *decision*, for the actualization of our inescapable tasks. The present lies before us to be chosen, to have its profusion of latencies and potentialities transmogrified into actualities which expand to give content to the here and now. This notion of the present in organic time as the moment in which we experience the upswelling pressure of choice—the upswelling pressure to render an immediate decision—distinguishes it from the present conceived by chronological or atomistic time, which is represented as a discrete instant in an undifferentiated, colorless, uniform series. In this view of the present as the critical "moment of choice,"[38] the commingling of the past and present is readily visible: The present passes on its way, and the possibilities which it enfolds can be seized and affirmed or neglected and escaped from.

With this mutual interpenetration of past and present goes hand and glove a symmetrical interpenetration of present and future. From this angle of vision, we grasp the present as it flows towards us from its hidden source in the future. The present comes from the future. Hence the present displays a dual character: it is constantly slipping away to become the past, and constantly refreshing us, giving us hope, with its sudden arrival from the future. The present, in other words, is never a mere instant: it displays thickness, breadth, span; it straddles past and future.

The future is an impending present, a present just about to be, and a removed past, a past which eventually will come to be. Although the future cannot be viewed from the vantage point of the present, its power can be apprehended as an "anticipatory presence."[39] In organic time the future is never a column of successive nows marching towards the present, ready to break into reality at a later date—it is an anticipated region, craved or shunned, hoped-for or feared, which informs and gives meaning to the present. The future in chronological time is a cruel fountainhead of empty instants

> Older than the time of chronometers, older
> Than time counted by anxious worried women
> Lying awake, calculating the future,
> Trying to unweave, unwind, unravel
> And piece together the past and the future,
> Between midnight and dawn, when the past is all deception,
> The future futureless, before the morning watch
> When time stops and time is never ending.[40]

In organic time, we do not simply await the future, we anticipate it, we allow it to fructify or lay waste the present, to invade the immediate now of experience with its anticipatory meanings. For without the future the present would collapse, its fluidity would grow sluggish, harden, and solidify; without the future the vital human quest for renewed hope and possible redemption would become a mockery; without the future spread before us, the hope of the artist for one more desperate attempt at adequation, one more attempt to create a work of art of equal stature to those monuments of the past, would be foreclosed; without the future beckoning toward us in perpetual hope, history itself would be beyond redemption, doomed to an unending linear design of random and meaningless succession or a cyclical design of perpetual recurrence and reenactment.

The future seems to foretell the past for Eliot. It displays the figures of possible choice which can either be plucked at their moment of ripeness and endowed with the actuality of chosen possibilities or neglected and relegated to the sad junkheap of "what might have been." When the future is blocked or rendered inaccessible, despair or death result. When it is believed to be beyond present reach, depression or boredom are born. With the loss of the future, either actual or believed, the present and past become equally impoverished because the self no longer can look upon the future as a way of redeeming or retrieving the past and fructifying the present. Past and future clash to produce the inescapable, ineluctable now, the moment of choice and decision, the crucial instant which we must seize to shape our life into a positive drama. The starkness of *now*, the hereness of the present which poses for us its multiple, dizzying decisions, is the moment which alone can affirm and unite past, present, and future into a coherent whole, which can mitigate and defeat the anxiety, boredom, loneliness, guilt, despair, and death which shadow all human time and stand ready always to exact their cruel penalties on the victims of impoverished time. In other words, the present can exist either as an empty *now*, impoverished of meaning, hollow of content, prey to the anxieties of disconnection and isolation, or as a creative moment of decision, uniting past and future in a drama which focuses on and exalts the resoluteness of commitment and engagement.

4

The Quest for Adequation in the Poems, Plays, and Essays

"Decision," then, both as a key word and an overarching concept, is central to Eliot's thought and to his continuing attempt to defeat the seductive power of false personality. Perhaps the most moving case is embodied in the drama of *Prufrock*. Because J. Alfred Prufrock cannot bring himself to relinquish his personality, to be reborn as an authentic identity, because he craves and savors the illicit security of an "etherized," fantasy-ridden, dreamlike world, hermetic and insular, from which the clash and tumult, the pressure and anxiety of real time have been banished, he lulls himself into the perilous delusion that the pressing *now* of human time may be disregarded with impunity, that he may absent himself from and return to the exigencies of the present at his own whim, that there will always be "time yet for a hundred indecisions,/ And for a hundred ... revisions," for "decisions and revisions which a minute will reverse." Prufrock cannot conceive a decision so conclusive that revision becomes impossible, a commitment so steadfast, agonizing, and wrenching that flight becomes impossible.

The reason for Prufrock's blindness to the true meaning of decision is his self-imposed, jealously guarded blindness to the real nature of human time. The overwhelming failure of Prufrock's existence, echoed and embodied in his comic, rhetorical drone, is his failure "to force the moment to its crisis" (*crisis* being the Greek word for decision), to force a turning point in his own spiritual malaise, to escape once and for all from the theatrical world of "cups, ... marmalade, ... tea,/ ... [and idle] talk of you and me" by an irreversible decision to face the dangerous truth that time is running out, that he is "grow[ing] old," that little time remains to discover an authentic identity beneath his vaporous inner dialogue of sterile subjunctives and coiling interrogatives. This cloud of subjunctives and interrogatives that encircles Prufrock's personality is simply another strategem for evading reality, for keeping time at bay. In his failure to confront the insidious moment of the present, in his perpetual flight from the necessity of making a final decision, Prufrock seals and reseals his own living death.[1]

Self and the Surrender of Self

Other instances of Prufrock's dilemma abound in Eliot's work. The failure of DIVISION to resolve itself into new VISION, and the failure to make a DECISION that turns love to DERISION, is a paradigm of great significance to Eliot. In the minor lyric "Eyes that last I saw in tears" the speaker, not unlike Prufrock, is riveted by "Eyes of decision," eyes which once shed "tears" but now hold him in "derision" for his culpable failure to escape his own inner "division" and make an affirming "decision." There is the further suggestion that what has caused eyes formerly capable of shedding "tears" of human affection to turn to stony "derision" is the speaker's own failure, as Eliot says elsewhere, to shed his personality, to melt "into unconsciousness of ... [his own] isolated ... [self]," to become capable of "forgetting" himself, a failure which transports him to "death's dream kingdom," unable, in his self-paralyzing indecision, to move backward into human time or forward through "the door of death's other kingdom" to the true peace of death.[2]

Murder in the Cathedral moves this theme from lyric to fullblown drama. In *Murder in the Cathedral*, the fourth temptation is the crucial one because this final tempter, unexpected by Thomas, tempts him with an aesthetic vision of himself as Saint in Heaven after a glorious death, a vision, tainted by pride, which Thomas himself, in the secret recesses of his soul, has carefully nurtured. Thomas has committed the sin of the reflexive glance, meditating on a vision of himself that simply extends the earthly glory he will reap from a martyr's death into the celestial glory of Heaven beyond time. This final temptation brings to Thomas the temptation of "[his] own desires," his own earthly longing for a fixed, eternal self, his sinful intimations of attainable immortality, a transfiguring vision of himself

> Dwelling forever in presence of God ...
> What earthly glory, of king or emperor,
> What earthly pride, that is not poverty
> Compared with richness of heavenly grandeur?
> Seek the way of martyrdom, make yourself the lowest
> On earth, to be high in heaven.
> And see far off below you, where the gulf is fixed,
> Your persecutors, in timeless torment,
> Parched passion, beyond expiation.

This transcendent vision of the consecrated Martyr in Heaven is simply an extension and final fruition of Thomas's own view of himself on earth—his fixed self, his prideful personality—that nourishes itself by

> . . . think[ing] of glory after death.
> When king is dead, there's another king,
> And one more king is another reign.
> King is forgotten, when another shall come:
> Saint and Martyr rule from the tomb.
> Think, Thomas, think of enemies dismayed,
> Creeping in penance, frightened of a shade;
> Think of pilgrims, standing in line
> Before the glittering jewelled shrine,
> From generation to generation
> Bending the knee in supplication,
> Think of the miracles, by God's grace,
> And think of your enemies, in another place.

"I have thought of these things," admits Thomas belatedly, recognizing that such fantasies of pride disguised as holiness are really "Dreams to damnation," the "soul's sickness" of mortal, brittle "pride."[3] This sudden self-realization is a turning point back to spiritual health. This crisis marks the onset of the play's denouement, as Thomas begins the painful ingathering of faith and spiritual energies that will finally allow him to overcome self-division by a surrender of personality and an acceptance of physical death. The gathering and focusing of his faith reaches its climax in Thomas's moment of decision— "If you call that decision/ To which my whole being"—unriven by doubt or division— "gives entire consent."[4]

In *The Family Reunion*, the minor characters, who characterize themselves as solitary "watchers and waiters"—characters intended only "To swell a progress, [or] start a scene or two," as Prufrock would put it[5]—find themselves incapable of the surrender which is so integral a part of decision making: "there is no decision to be made [by us];/ The decision will be made by powers beyond us/ Which now and then emerge."[6] It is for Harry alone, the protagonist and eldest son, after a long agony of struggle in which he exorcises his feelings, discerns their true meaning and pieces together the events which have befallen him, to recognize, ultimately, his true destiny—to recognize the meaning of his unhappy past and intuit the dim shape of the future and then affirm them as inseparable in one lucid moment of decision, uniting past and future in a meaningful destiny. So long as Harry tries to flee his past, personified in the play by those omnipresent Furies, its meaning will continue to elude him, leaving the present a sickly void from which escape is impossible and the future a terror-filled promise of continuing torture. But once he confronts his past, following in the direction it points, the Furies are transformed into "bright angels," and this transformation of dreaded pursuers into guiding angels becomes an icon of time's continuity and fruitfulness forged through an affirming decision.

> I know that I have made a decision
> In a moment of clarity, and now I feel dull again.
> I only know that I made a decision
> Which your words echo. I am still befouled,
> But I know there is only one way out of defilement—
> Which leads in the end to reconciliation.
> And I know that I must go.[7]

In *The Cocktail Party* dual dramas unfold along parallel tracks. Having been left unexpectedly by his wife Lavinia, an event which has precipitated a shattering loss of personality, Edward assumes that her return will serve to restore his sense of his own identity as well. He therefore agrees to her return under the proviso that she return as a stranger, a person shorn of her accustomed personality just as Edward is bereft of his, certain that her return will restore to them both their accustomed, habitual identities. "What we know of other people," Edward is duly warned,

> Is only our memory of the moments
> During which we knew them. And they have changed
>   since then.
> To pretend that they and we are the same
> Is a useful and convenient social convention
> Which must sometimes be broken. We must also remember
> That at every meeting we are meeting a stranger.

But though Edward listens to this admonition, he fails to grasp its meaning. So, he makes his "decision" to accept the return of his wife, wrongly convinced that their reunion will prove successful in restoring his lost identity, and equally convinced that he will not desire to "change . . . [his] mind," even though at that point, after the reunion, "It will be too late."[8] Predictably, the reunion fails; it confirms Edward in his isolation while increasing his terrified solitude.

> What is hell? Hell is oneself,
> Hell is alone, the other figures in it
> Merely projections. There is nothing to escape from
> And nothing to escape to. One is always alone.[9]

There is nothing to escape from because Edward can look back on no real past; there is nothing to escape to because the future has been withdrawn. The present alone exists, empty and meaningless, with no companion other than an invented self whose brittle unreality cannot be escaped. Hell is oneself only because Edward is incapable of surrendering to his hidden feelings, terrified of discovering his true self, and unable to experience that creative solitude from which the seeds of a genuine decision might come forth. The persons who surround him remain "[m]erely projections" because Edward is incapable of forgetting himself, of reaching out beyond his invented self, of feeling the restorative human presence of another. So Edward remains "divided" and paralyzed, "much too divided to know what ... [he] want[s]," or to reassume his old personality or to move forward in quest of a new, authentic identity.[10] "O God, O God,/ if I could return to yesterday," he wails,

> Before I thought that I had made a decision.
> What devil left the door on the latch
> For these doubts to enter? And then you came back, you
> The angel of destruction—just as I felt sure.
> In a moment, at your touch, there is nothing but ruin.
> O God, what have I done? The python. The octopus.
> Must I become after all what you would make me?[11]

In his desperation, he seeks renewed flight from the exigencies of *now*, and can bring himself only to announce a cessation of responsibility for his actions, a total abandonment of the world of the ethical: "I can no longer act for myself. . . . I cannot take any further responsibility" either for my own life or the lives of those around me.[12]

But interestingly this too passes as Eliot shows one more version of the compromised life. As the play progresses, both Edward and Lavinia are shown the way back to a partial restoration of their old identities—less selfish, less proud, less brittle—but still incapable of true surrender or true decision; we are shown a vision of life where they will

> Maintain themselves by the common routine,
> Learn to avoid excessive expectation,
> Become tolerant of themselves and others,
> Giving and taking, in the usual actions
> What there is to give and take. They do not repine;
> Are contented with the morning that separates
> And with the evening that brings together
> For casual talk before the fire
> Two people who know they do not understand each other,
> Breeding children whom they do not understand
> And who will never understand them.[13]

Meanwhile, another drama has been unfolding, less visible but of greater consequence, as Celia, Edward's erstwhile paramour, prepares "To make a decision"[14] that will, unlike Edward's or Lavinia's, be genuine and authentic. Instead of evading responsibility, she confesses eagerly, at her own moment of crisis, that "I know it is I who have made the decision"[15] to cast off her invented self and accept the "terrors of the journey"[16] into the recesses of her soul. This will be a journey of total surrender to her deepest feelings in order to discover an adequate reason for existence. "To speak about . . . [such voyages into the interior]/ We talk of darkness, labyrinths, Minotaur terrors"[17] beyond the pale of the ordinary ego, beyond the dull understanding of the ordinary person. Hence Celia follows, as it were, in the footsteps of Harry, allowing her emergent feelings to carry her across the threshold of authenticity into the realm of religion, where she alone will find a way of life adequate to and consonant with her own, overwhelmingly intense experience of reality.

Finally, in *The Confidential Clerk*, Eliot paints a portrait of two selves, both known, competing for domination of Colby, the confidential clerk: a former, truly authentic self as an aspiring musician battles to displace a newly invented self as a confidential clerk in the successful world of business. Colby struggles to hang onto this invented self, but at times, without warning, his former self steals back to take momentary possession, rekindling his buried delight in music and reawakening his early dreams of pursuing art. Colby finds his newly invented self "exhilarating," and feels it exhilarating

> To find there is something that I can do
> So remote from my previous interests.
> It gives me, in a way, a kind of self-confidence
> I've never had before. Yet at the same time
> It's rather disturbing. I don't mean the work:
> I mean, about myself. As if I was becoming
> A different person.

For that is exactly what is happening to Colby as he hovers between two selves, drawn to one in the hope of pleasing his father and benefactor, drawn to the other by an inextinguishable, unquenchable love. "Just as, I suppose," continues Colby, searching for analogies,

> If you learn to speak a foreign language fluently,
> So that you can think in it—you feel yourself to be
> Rather a different person when you're talking it.
> I'm not at all sure that I like the other person
> That I feel myself becoming—though he fascinates me.
> And yet from time to time, when I least expect it,

When my mind is cleared and empty, walking in the
 street
Or waking in the night, then the former person,
The person I used to be, returns to take possession:
And I am again the disappointed organist,
And for a moment the thing I cannot do,
The art that I could never excel in,
Seems the one thing worth doing, the one thing
That I want to do. I have to fight that person.[18]

In the end, "that person," that authentic identity does come to prevail, and we are led to believe that Colby will return not simply to his music, but that his art will point the way to something beyond—a religious vocation—that will unify his divided existence.

Thus in every poem that Eliot was to write, in every drama, we return again and again to the solitary figure of a perplexed, roiled consciousness confronting its isolated moments of experience. We follow the sinuous twists and torturous turns of this mind as it slowly attempts to uncover the hidden meaning of these moments. Alternately we watch with rapt fascination as these dense, swarming moments of feeling struggle to emerge out of the darkness toward the luminous "relief of language."

The Decision To Surrender

But there is a second dimension or level to this drama, a necessary, omnipresent dimension which also is characteristic of every poem or play written by Eliot, and which arises organically from and completes his original quest. This is the drama of surrender and decision. As often as not, Eliot's *personae* hover indecisively—dividedly—on the brink of a revelation, unwilling, on the one hand, to surrender their fixed personalities to the hidden feelings which comprise their subterranean experience; but equally unwilling to make the crucial decision to abandon this known self for one more painful, more engaged with the agony of real experience, and ever in the process, as every authentic identity is, of always being forged anew. During the span in which a typical poem or play unfolds, a drop of experience aspires toward adequate form, and we are also spectators to an individual's terrified reactions to this process; we watch him procrastinate, make excuses, practice evasion to avoid confronting that elusive drop of experience, to avoid searching out its meaning and deciding to recover authentic identity by engaging the world. All of Eliot's *personae* nurture, deep in their breasts, the Wordsworthian desire that their "days . . . be/ Bound each to each" by the memory of an experience, affirmed and reaffirmed each day in the inexhaustible fullness of its meaning, and reaffirmed each day through a conscious, deliberate, courageous decision. Almost all of Eliot's *personae* are incapable of this, cringing before the necessary imperative of such a choice, shrinking back into the shell of their habitual selves. All of them hunger to cry, with Wordsworth, in a triumphant celebration of temporal continuity,

> So was it when my life began;
> So is it now I am a man;
> So be it when I shall grow old,[19]

as the authentic self rejoices and pleasures itself in its synchronicity forged from understanding wrested from an erstwhile hidden moment of experience; but few of them reach this heroic plateau, and fewer understand why they do. The typical poem or play of Eliot proceeds through at least two moments, in which at first the author's own quest for poetic adequation is mirrored in a similar quest on the part of the dramatic *persona*. The author's quest for an authentic identity is achieved through surrender and decision, furnishing the prototype for the action that is embodied and dramatized in the work of art.

Eliot deals in many passages with those who "are terrified and cannot surrender."[20] This includes the typist who clings to her anesthetized "indifference" and "automatic" routine,[21] the speaker from *Ash Wednesday* who doggedly refuses to relinquish the memory of "The infirm glory of the positive hour,"[22] the hollow men whose "Lips," at "the hour when we are/ Trembling with tenderness . . . *would*"—but are unable to—"kiss," instead "Form[ing] prayers to broken stone,"[23] the narrator of *La Figlia che Piange* who, still struggling against the haunting recollection of the maiden with "Her hair over her arms and her arms full of flowers," finds that "these cogitations still amaze/ The troubled midnight and the noon's repose,"[24] and Marie, the archduke's cousin, who helplessly allows her mind to wander back to her childhood trips to "the mountains . . . [where] you feel free," but is now imprisoned in a cycle of insomnia and social travel, "read[ing], . . . much of the night, and go[ing] south in the winter."[25] None is more powerful than the penultimate passage from *The Waste Land*, the moment of successful surrender:

> *Datta*: what have we given?
> My friend, blood shaking my heart
> The awful daring of a moment's surrender
> Which an age of prudence can never retract
> By this [act], and this only, we have existed
> Which is not to be found in our obituaries

Or in memories draped by the beneficent spider
Or under seals broken by the lean solicitor
In our empty rooms[26]

Standing at the center of Eliot's poetic exploration of surrender, this passage ties together a dense network of verbal repetition, refrain, and echo. The question "what have we given?" recalls Thomas's forthright affirmation:

It is not in time that my death shall be known;
It is out of time that my decision is taken
If you call that decision
To which my whole being *gives* entire consent[27]

as well as, in *Portrait of a Lady*, the anticipatory parody, in stilted social accents, of this act of self-surrender, of a total, selfless giving of oneself:

You are invulnerable, you have no Achilles' heel.
You will go on, and when you have prevailed
You can say: at this point many a one has failed.
But what have I, but what have I, my friend,
To *give* you, what can you *receive* from me?
Only the friendship and the sympathy
Of one about to reach her journey's end.
I shall sit here, serving tea to friends. . . .[28]

And this, in turn, is rehearsed in *The Cocktail Party*, with the bleak, dispirited vision of those who do not give, are incapable of giving, are incapable of surrender:

They may remember
The vision they have had, but they cease to regret it,
Maintain themselves by the common routine,
Learn to avoid excessive expectation,
Become tolerant of themselves and others,
Giving and *taking*, in the usual actions
What there is to *give* and *take*. They do not repine.[29]

The phrase "awful daring" is reminiscent of Prufrock's failure *to dare* ("Do I dare/ Disturb the universe?"[30]) and also of the "Eyes" that the hollow men "dare not meet in dreams,"[31] eyes of judicial terror which reflect their inner division and hold them in derision. The "blood shaking my heart" is "The dance along the artery/ The circulation of the lymph"[32] which, all too often, can be ignored, or totally denied: thus the simple soul, *Animula*, paralyzed by indecision, wrought asunder by self-division

> Unable to fare forward or retreat
> Fearing the warm reality, the offered good,
> Denying the *importunity of the blood,*

becomes a "Shadow of its own shadow, specter in its own gloom,/ Leaving disordered papers in a dusty room,"[33] immobilized by its own blind, willful denial of reality's importuning. It is consigned, at the end, to the pitiful isolation of a dusty room, papers everywhere disordered waiting for the lean solicitor, the same rooms inhabited by the "lonely men in shirtsleeves, leaning out of windows"[34] who so affright Prufrock with a warranted premonition of his own fate, the same room in the same "rented house" where Gerontion, unredeemed and isolated from past and future, will "Stiffen"[35] in death. To surrender is to "open one's heart" even "When one is sure of the wrong response," it is to "make a confession" even "with no hope of absolution,"[36] it is to risk all in the face of certain failure, else one remains a craven disciple of "prudence," risking nothing, losing everything.

This extraordinary importance of surrender bulks equally large in the mass of Eliot's critical writings, especially his numerous attempts to describe the way in which the act of creation, practiced and nurtured across the span of a lifetime, results in the formation and reformation of an authentic self. Surrender itself provides us with a clue to what Eliot would call the paradoxical and simultaneous presence of authentic or positive personality in great authors, and the attendant impersonality which is a quality of the art they create. A passage embedded in "Tradition and the Individual Talent," although allowed to remain dormant and unelaborated in that essay, figures prominently in Eliot's train of thought. This passage, which is situated directly after Eliot's attack on the metaphysical unity of the soul, and follows his proposal that the writer has a medium—his language—to develop through a lifetime's struggle of devoted workmanship rather than a personality to express, is a striking quotation from *The Revenger's Tragedy*, lines which seized and held fast Eliot's imagination, for he invoked them again in the essay on Tourneur of 1931—

> Are lordships sold to maintain ladyships
> For the poor benefit of a *bewildering minute?*
> Why does yon fellow falsify highways,
> And put his life between the judge's lips,
> To refine such a thing—keeps horse and men
> To beat their valours for her? . . .[37]

—and once again, sixteen years after "Tradition and the Individual Talent," in an important letter to Stephen Spender. That occasion was to offer a comment on Spender's critical book, *The Destructive Element,* but as in so many of Eliot's other occasional utterances, the true theme was a sounding of his own experience.

Surrender Through Art

"[Y]ou don't," said Eliot, "really criticize any author to whom you have never *surrendered yourself*. . . . Even just *the bewildering minute* counts; you have [first] *to give yourself up*, and then *recover yourself*, and the *third moment* is having something to say, before you have wholly forgotten both *surrender* and *recovery*. *Of course the self recovered is never the same as the self before it was given.*"[38] Surrender, recovery, the wresting of meaning: the sudden possession of the self by an overwhelming, irresistible feeling, the slow process of recovery or dispossession, and the final quarrying of meaning from the depths of that bewildering intensity—this is the process of adequation. And the self surrendered—be it to the experience of coming under the influence of a new author for the first time or the experience of the raw, impinging world—is never the same as the self before it was given. Experience, then, is formative, and this dialectic of surrender and recovery, this sudden lurching or reeling backward under the shocking impact of a new experience followed by the slow drawing forth of meaning from the overwhelming encounter, shapes us, forms us, and reforms us throughout a lifetime. The experience of the bewildering minute in poetry, as Eliot had written two years earlier, in 1929, in the essay on "Dante," is

> the experience both of a moment and of a lifetime. It is very much like our intenser experiences of other human beings. There is a first, or an early moment which is unique, of shock and surprise, even of terror (*Ego dominus tuus*); a moment which can never be forgotten, but which is never repeated integrally; and yet which would become destitute of significance if it did not survive in a large whole of experience; which survives inside a deeper and calmer feeling.[39]

Eliot had expressed almost the identical sentiment in 1919, the same year as "Tradition and the Individual Talent," in some remarks which appeared in *The Egoist*. These remarks provide a brilliant gloss, moreover, on the relation between tradition and the artistic formation of the individual talent. "[I]t is possible," suggested Eliot in *The Egoist*, "that there is a close analogy between the sort of experience which develops a man and the sort of experience which develops a writer." When we come under the influence of another writer, when we fall under his spell, when he takes possession of our innermost self, his influence "overcome[s] us suddenly," producing a "crisis"; and especially "when a young writer is seized with his first passion of this sort he may be changed, metamorphosed almost, within a few weeks even, from a bundle of second-hand sentiments into a *person*." Possession of "this secret knowledge," combined with being possessed by the "dead man . . . is a cause of development, like personal relations in life. Like personal intimacies in life, it may and probably will pass, but it will be ineffaceable," leaving the writer permanently changed, ineradicably transformed. "[W]e are changed; and our work is the work of the changed man; we have not borrowed, we have been quickened, and we become bearers of a *tradition*."[40]

The mysterious dialectic of surrender and recovery stands at the point of intersection between the individual talent and tradition. For tradition can neither be imbibed, as in a magical draught, nor can it be imitated, as in a conscious, sterile act of obeisance. Tradition is the view that "the whole of the literature of Europe from Homer and within it the whole of the literature of [the artist's] own country [which] has a simultaneous existence and composes a simultaneous order"[41] must be surrendered to, never as a whole, but author by author, in a slow process of assimilation and digestion spanning a lifetime.

The "historical sense," which Eliot calls "indispensable to any one who would continue to be a poet beyond his twenty-fifth year," is simply another name for the formative impact produced by this succession of surrenders and recoveries, another name for the transformative powers of art, and the artist who is, as a result, dramatically transformed.[42] Moreover, the same process transpires, in both the developing writer and sophisticated reader, in the gradual formation of *taste*. "I happened to pick up a copy of Fitzgerald's *Omar* which was lying about," says Eliot in one of the lectures that comprise *The Use of Poetry*, "and the almost overwhelming introduction to a new world of *feeling* which this poem was the occasion of giving me . . . was like a sudden conversion; the world appeared anew, painted with bright, delicious and painful colours."[43] Transfigured into bright, delicious and painful shapes, we are really engaged in viewing the world through the dazzling, miraculous prism of a new self. For

> At this period [of adolescence], the poem, or the poetry of a single poet, *invades the youthful consciousness and assumes complete possession for a time*. We do not really see it as something with an existence outside ourselves; much as in our youthful experiences of love, we do not so much see the person as infer the existence of some outside object which sets in motion these new and delightful feelings in which we are absorbed. The frequent result is an outburst of scribbling which we may call imitation, so long as we are aware of the meaning of the word "imitation" which we employ. It is not a deliberate choice of a poet to mimic, but writing under a *kind of daemonic possession by one poet*.

By contrast, the third or "mature stage of enjoyment of poetry" comes when we recover, although ourselves now transformed, from this state of intoxicating possession, when we cease to identify ourselves with the poet we happen to be reading; when our *critical faculties* remain awake; when we are aware of what one poet can be expected to give and what he cannot. The poem has its own existence, apart from us; it was there before us and will endure after us."[44]

A similar model of self-development through surrender and recovery is sketched in another passage, this one drawn from the essay "Religion and Literature":

> Everyone ... who is at all sensible to the seductions of poetry, can remember some moment in youth when he or she was completely carried away by the work of one poet .... The reason for this passing infatuation is not merely that our sensibility to poetry is keener in adolescence than in maturity. What happens is a kind of *inundation, of invasion of the undeveloped personality by the stronger personality of the poet* .... One author takes complete *possession* of us for a time; then another; and finally they begin to affect each other in our mind. We weigh one against another; we see that each has qualities absent from others, and qualities incompatible with the qualities of others: we begin to be, in fact, critical; and it is our growing critical power which protects us from *excessive possession* by any one literary personality .... The very different views of life, cohabiting in our minds, affect each other, and our own [authentic] personality asserts itself and gives each a place in some arrangement peculiar to ourself."[45]

This growth in our critical powers, this emerging arrangement within our psyche that reflects a true development of one facet of authentic personality, is therefore a "development of genuine *taste*, founded on genuine *feeling*" and "is inextricable from the development of . . . [authentic] personality and character."[46] Even among persons who acquire a taste for the same poetry, "this poetry will be arranged in their minds in slightly different *patterns*; our individual *taste* in poetry bears the indelible traces of our individual lives with all their experience pleasurable and painful."[47] Taste, in other words, always "springs from a deeper source,"[48] a source which forms and crystalizes that unique pattern which comprises the individual self at any given moment, a pattern which, in turn, is the expression of a confluence of forces exerted by self and world, consciousness and the unconscious, massive feeling and arbitrating taste; and this pattern or arrangement peculiar to oneself, kindled into incandescence by an act of surrender, appears to us as an ever more sharply etched point of view, the beginnings of an authentic personality, the lineaments and contours of an emerging self.

Depicting the successive stages of the act of creation, Eliot invokes, in "Tradition and the Individual Talent," yet another metaphor to explain the unconscious and assimilative aspects of the act of surrender. This is the famous analogy, intended to throw light on the "relation of the poem to its author," which suggests that two of the three facets of the act of creation—

the initial surrender and the subsequent recovery—bear a powerful re-
semblance to "the action which takes place when a bit of finely filiated
platinum is introduced into a chamber containing oxygen and sulphur
dioxide."

> When the two gases . . . are mixed in the presence of a filament of platinum, they form
> sulphurous acid. This combination takes place only if the platinum is present; nevertheless
> the newly formed acid contains no trace of platinum, and the platinum itself is apparently
> unaffected; has remained inert, neutral, and unchanged. The mind of the poet is the shred
> of platinum. It may partly or exclusively operate upon the experience of the man himself;
> but, the more perfect the artist, the more completely separate in him will be the man who
> suffers and the mind which creates; the more perfectly will the mind digest and transmute
> the passions which are its material.

The materials which "enter the presence of the transforming catalyst, are of
two kinds: emotions and feelings . . . . [The ultimate work of art] may be
formed out of one emotion, or may be a combination of several; and various
feelings, inhering for the writer in particular words or phrases or images,
may be added to compose the final result. Or great poetry may be made
without the direct use of any emotion whatever: composed out of feelings
solely."[49]

The analogy is not however wholly successful. It appears to have been
pressed into service for two reasons: first, to bolster Eliot's attack on the
metaphysical unity of the soul and to offer a partial explanation, albeit by
tenuous analogy, of how the various elements of the writer's medium—his
language—enter into combinations beyond his conscious control in the
depths of his emotive being, enacting a process of adequation at the
preconscious level; and second, to stress the passivity of the act of surrender
considered apart from the other two stages of the act of creation, the way in
which unexpected combinations of language rise from the depths in the act
of recovery to produce those arrangements of language which display a
preliminary adequation to our hidden feelings, and which are characterized
by that difficulty or quality of wit that becomes, for Eliot, the hallmark of
adequation. As an analogy, however, its shortcomings are considerable. In
the first place, it scants entirely the third facet of the act of creation, the
conscious wresting of meaning, the conscious wrestle with language, the
dedication to craft and workmanship, the daily combat with a recalcitrant
medium. More serious, however, is its failure to suggest, as Eliot stresses
elsewhere, that the artist *does* change and evolve through the act of creation.

This evolving and renewing of the artist's self in no way, however,
contradicts the assertion that "the man who suffers and the mind which
creates" are separate. The statement of this separation within man simply
upholds Eliot's later assertion that feelings and emotions are particular,

whereas language is general. Experience is always alien to its embodiment in language, and language itself presents a formidable obstacle to be overcome.

The very process of "transmut[ing his] . . . passions" into language, of bringing his particular feelings up to the light of day, alters the artist's self, and alters all future attempts to transmute passion, to perform the act of creation, the act of adequation. For each act of surrender and recovery produces a new design of self, a new pattern of magnetic attraction, which unconsciously transforms the materials of art into new patterns. "[M]agnetised in its own way . . . the mind of any poet," muses Eliot, "select[s] automatically, in his reading (from picture papers and cheap novels, indeed, as well as serious books . . .) the material—an image, a phrase, a word—which may be of use to him later." To help provide this unending cornucopia of materials is the broad function of tradition.

> And this selection probably runs through the whole of his sensitive life. There might be the experience of a child of ten, a small boy peering through seawater in a rock-pool, and finding a sea-anemone for the first time: the simple experience (not so simple, for an exceptional child, as it looks) might lie dormant in his mind for twenty years, and reappear transformed in some verse-context charged with great imaginative pressure.[50]

And "Why, for all of us," wonders Eliot out loud as his speculations conclude,

> out of all that we have heard, seen, felt, in a lifetime, do certain images recur, charged with emotion, rather than others? The song of one bird, the leap of one fish, at a particular place and time, the scent of one flower, an old woman on a German mountain path, six ruffians seen through an open window playing cards at night at a small French railway junction where there was a watermill: such memories may have symbolic value, but of what we cannot tell, for they come to represent the *depths of feeling into which we cannot peer*. We might just as well ask why, when we try to recall visually some period in the past, we find in our memory just the few meagre arbitrarily chosen set of snapshots that we do find there, the faded poor souvenirs of passionate moments.[51]

This metaphor of the bewildering minute, with its felicitous, tripartite division of the act of creation and its accompanying stress on the continued development and growth of the artist's authentic identity, can be seen to have come to dominate Eliot's imagination as the chemical catalyst analogy could not, and therefore to have superseded it in all his later speculation. Only four years after "Tradition and the Individual Talent," in "The Function of Criticism," (1923), Eliot himself appears to have recognized the inadequacy of the catalyst metaphor with its undue emphasis on the passivity and unconscious locus of the act of creation. For in "The Function of Criticism" Eliot refers to "the capital importance of criticism"—the third stage of creation after surrender and recovery—"in the work of creation itself," and suggests that "the larger part of the labor of an author in composing his work is critical labor; the labor of sifting, combining, construction, expunging, correcting, testing." He calls such labor "this frightful toil," and distinguishes it from obedience to the Inner Voice, a manifestation of unwarranted emphasis on the passive aspect of creation. "There is a tendency," adds Eliot, "to decry this critical toil of the artist; to propound the thesis that the great artist is an unconscious artist," whereas, in truth, "The *critical* activity finds its highest, its true fulfillment in a kind of union with *creation* in the labor of the artist."[52] The point that Eliot wishes to drive home is that "you never rest at the pure feeling,"[53] for that is at best a moment of bewilderment; the moment "you try to put the impressions"— the feelings and emotions: the *particulars*—"into words"—*universals* or *forms*—"you either . . . begin to create . . ." a true work of art if you are an artist or you "begin to analyse and construct, to 'eriger en lois'" your impressions[54] "to the point of principle and definition"[55] if you are a critic or reader.

Impersonality and Adequation

Thus we circle back to the crucial question that informs Eliot's criticism: how does forging an authentic personality in the artist through surrender, recovery and the struggle for meaning—the quest for adequation—give rise to works of art which are characterized by an unmistakable quality of impersonality. The answer lies in the multiple and often antagonistic meanings which Eliot, from decade to decade, assigns in his criticism to the concept of personality. False, inauthentic or object-like personality, that personality which the artist must perpetually flee, is an encrustation, an accumulated debris of personal, social, and literary habits which, like protective armament, serves to stave off all revivifying contact with our emotive selves. In its fundamental denial of the primacy of our massed feelings and the supremacy of all particular experience, false personality thwarts the true artist's quest to overcome the inadequacy of all form and language. Of course false personality can contrive works of art, but such art is likely to be insincere, mannered, *mauvais-foi*, imitative, and derivative. It will prove not a triumph of adequation—the attempt to find a unique form adequate to a particular experience—but an excrescence of habit, a mirror which reflects back to artist and audience alike the dehumanization of self into the nullity of objecthood. But, adds Eliot quickly, in a phrase distilled from his attack on the metaphysical unity of the soul, "No artist produces great art by a deliberate attempt to express his personality," for how, if he is honest and sincere, can he give expression to that which he does not have? He can, at best, express only false personality, an essence of objecthood, dooming him from the outset to failure. The true or authentic artist "expresses his [authentic] personality *indirectly* through concentrating upon a task"—adequation—"which is a task in the same sense as the making of an efficient engine or the turning of a jug or a tableleg."[56] The continual struggle to transmute into adequate form the feelings which have surfaced— these are the undeniable essentials of his task.

The struggle of the artist involves, first, a decision to obliterate, at least temporarily, his false personality, or at least set it aside, while he embarks on the upcoming quest. The true artist's struggle involves, next, a succession of acts—surrender, recovery, and criticism or the wresting of final, adequate meaning from cloudy feeling—which, in the creation of new works of art, produces also a succession of changed, transformed selves. Finally, it involves the recognition that, insofar as "feeling and emotion are particular, whereas thought is general," every instance of form will be impersonal, metaphysically speaking, impersonal and inadequate to the elusive experience it sought to capture and fix. To term a work of art impersonal is, in this sense, to pass judgment upon its sincerity. To the degree that all form is *mauvais-foi*, and all language is seen as constraining us into insincerity, all works of art are, to greater or lesser extents, impersonal. And yet the lash of impersonality, no matter how slight, the inevitable failure of adequation spurs us on to renew our quest: so that each work of art, however impersonal from the metaphysical perspective, displays the shape of a unique self, an authentic self. Thus, while the individual work of art is characterized by impersonality, it displays, simultaneously and paradoxically, the hallmark of a particular artist's quest to achieve authentic selfhood. Authentic personality refers not to an objectlike ego, secure in its detachment from life, but to an incessant struggle to achieve adequation, the never-ending struggle toward the sacred condition of sincerity.

And this is how Eliot can declare a work of art to be impersonal while maintaining, at the same time, that it bears the indelible imprint of a unique, human personality. As form, it is ipso facto impersonal, but as the product of a struggle for adequation, a struggle to escape the torment of baffled emotion, it reflects the emerging stamp of a unique self. And for Eliot there are other, lesser kinds of impersonality. The "religious poetry of public worship," for example, often displays "the impersonal eloquence of the Latin language."[57] And a similar, impersonal eloquence "is natural to the mere skillful craftsman" who fashions the typical "anthology piece"—the poem which slips effortlessly and gracefully out of a predetermined mold—to a cusp of perfection.[58]

By contrast, in those rare cases where we come upon a great artist, an authentic poet, there is always "that sense of a unique personality"—a buried self yearning for the precise, momentary definition of form—"which makes one sit up in excitement and eagerness to learn more about the author's mind and feelings," about how he will confront and engage this overwhelming "intensity of experience," and whether or not this quest for exorcism will succeed. If success comes, in a moment filled with exhaustion, relief, and triumph, there emerges art characterized by an "impersonality" peculiar to the authentic artist "who, out of intense and personal experience," through total submission to the ordeal and trial of adequation, "is able to express a general truth; retaining all the particularity of his experience, to make of it a general symbol."[59]

Only the artist who has once tasted the victory of breaking through to a general symbol, of achieving an adequation of particular and universal, truly "know[s] what it means to want to escape from ... personality and emotions," can truly appreciate the pressing urgency to "escape from personality."[60] The work of art which has achieved the status of a general symbol is never "exclusively for the author, [for then] it would be a poem in a private and unknown language; and a poem which was a poem only for the author would not be a poem at all." On the contrary, the general symbol twists, bends, and warps public language—the language of tradition and usage—into "the eventual form [which] will be to a greater or less degree the form for that one poem and no other," at the same time developing and bringing to light, as from an invisible image deposited on a photographic plate, the form for that self and no other.[61]

This dichotomy helps to explain why an impersonal theory of poetry such as that espoused by Eliot can never be grounded in a theory of language as communication. Provisionally, of course, in a loose and rather imprecise way, we may hold that "in poetry there is communication from writer to reader, but [we] should not proceed from this to think of the poetry as being primarily the vehicle of communication." Such a theory of communication however errs grievously in "putting the emphasis upon the poet's feelings," the rudimentary stuff from which his poetry will be wrought, "instead of upon the poetry" itself.[62] For "what is ... [this] experience that the poet is so bursting to communiate? By the time it has settled down into a poem it may be so different from the *original experience* as to be hardly recognizable."[63] When the poet remains true to himself, when he remains open to the torment of pain and pleasure, when he refuses escape to an ego locked in a void beyond experience, he

finds himself in a different world in every decade of his life; as he sees it with different eyes, the material of his art is continually renewed. ... Most men either cling to the experiences of youth, so that their writing becomes an insincere mimicry of their earlier work, or they leave their passion behind, and write only from the head, with a hollow and wasted virtuosity.[64]

But the poet who undergoes willingly the baptism of experience, becomes a "true experimenter," an artist "impelled [always] . . . by compulsion to find, in every new poem as in his earliest, the *right form for feelings* over the development of which he has, as a poet, no control."[65] If we peer closely enough at the life of a genuine experimenter, there is always to be discerned, no matter how lightly etched, that "continuity of . . . a positive personality," focused by "such a single purpose," that "the later work cannot be understood, or properly enjoyed, without a study and appreciation of the earlier; and the later work again reflects light upon the earlier, and shows us beauty and significance not before perceived."[66]

Wholeness and Adequation

For the authentic poet, the true experimenter, two inescapable corollaries follow. First, his life remains committed to artistic development. From this central belief Eliot never wavered. It remains a fixed point of reference, an integral part of the formula employed by Eliot to celebrate the greatness and scope of achievement of contemporaries and predecessors alike. As early as 1917, referring to Pound's stylistic alterations from volume to volume in a warm defence of the latter's early career, Eliot would assert that

> When a poet *alters* or *develops*, many of his admirers are sure to drop off. Any poet, if he is to survive as a writer beyond his twenty-fifth year, must alter; he must seek new literary influences; he will have different emotions to express. This is disconcerting to that public which likes a poet to spin his whole work out of the feelings of his youth; which likes to be able to open a new volume of his poems with the assurance that they will be able to approach it exactly as they approached the preceding.[67]

A year later, in 1918, Eliot would claim that Henry James's "greatness" lay "both in his capacity for development as an artist and his capacity for keeping his mind alive to the changes in the world. . . ."[68] And twenty-two years later, in his magnanimous salute to Yeats, Eliot would voice the sentiment that "to have accomplished what Yeats did in the middle and later years is a great and permanent example—which poets-to-come should study with reverence—of what I have called Character of the Artist: a kind of moral, as well as intellectual, excellence." Despite the many difficulties which attend upon generalizing "about ways of composition," proceeds Eliot,

> so many men, so many ways . . . it is my experience that towards middle age a man has three choices: to stop writing altogether, to repeat himself with perhaps an increasing skill of virtuosity, or by taking thought to adapt himself to middle age and find a different way of working. . . .

Except for figures of Yeats's towering stature, very few poets, concludes Eliot, "have shown this capacity of adaptation to the years. It requires, indeed, an exceptional honesty and courage to face the change."[69]

The second corollary here is an outgrowth of the first. It holds that to grasp this ongoing personality from beginning to end, and to trace the many intricacies and small movements of its trajectory we must read an author's work whole, regarding every word that flows from his pen or typewriter as part of a single, unfolding oeuvre. "The important difference" between a major and minor poet, claims Eliot, "is whether a knowledge of the *whole*, or at least of a very large part, of a poet's work, makes one enjoy more, because it makes one understood better, any one of his poems. That implies a *significant unity* in his whole work."[70] This expanding web of cross-relations is, of course, reciprocal; as we come to sense the "unifying personality" behind the diversity of an author's work, "we get to know this personality better by reading all of his poems, and for having read all of his poems we enjoy still better the ones we like best."[71] Eliot repeatedly enjoins us to read the works of any important author whole. "No part of Kipling's work," he writes on one occasion, while trying to puzzle out the reasons for Kipling's literary eclipse, "and no period of his work, is wholly appreciable without taking into account the others: and in the end, this work, which studied piecemeal apears to have no unity beyond the haphazard of external circumstances, comes to show a unity of a very complicated kind."[72]

Much more than Kipling, more than the metaphysical poets, more than any other author—and Eliot's own contradictory utterances notwithstanding—Eliot marveled and stood in awe before the spectacle of "Shakespeare's work as a whole."[73] True, in nearly all of Shakespeare's lesser contemporaries there is discernible "some inchoate pattern" which may be called an incipient "personality";[74] in one or two figures of still lesser rank, there is apparent no coherence, no unity, no personality, no "point of view," merely a "name which associates six or seven great plays."[75] But "[t]he standard set by Shakespeare," on the other hand,

> is that of a continuous development from first to last. . . . What is "the whole man" is not simply his greatest or maturest achievement, but the *whole pattern* formed by the *sequence of plays*; so that we may say confidently that the full meaning of any one of his plays is not in itself alone, but in that play in the order in which it was written, in its relation to all of Shakespeare's other plays, earlier and later: we must know all of Shakespeare's work in order to know any of it. No other dramatist of the time approaches anywhere near to this perfection of pattern, of pattern superficial and profound; but the measure in which dramatists and poets approximate to this unity in a life-time's work is one of the measures of major poetry and drama.[76]

In other words,

The whole of Shakespeare's work is *one* poem; and it is the poetry of it in this sense, not the poetry of isolated lines and passages or the poetry of the single figures which he created that matters most. A man might, hypothetically, compose any number of fine passages or even of whole poems which would each give satisfaction, and yet not be a great poet, unless we felt them to be united by one *significant, consistent, and developing personality.*[77]

If we choose to believe that a "person is a unity," a developing, emerging unity, "however inconsistent his conduct" upon any number of single occasions, and if we hold, further, "that acquaintance with him over a span of time makes him more intelligible," then to grow in intimacy with another man's work, to participate, at a remove, in the growth of his own authenticity, to bear witness to his struggle for sincerity through his quest for adequation, to take into our hearts another man's authenticity is to augment our own.[78] Or, as Eliot puts it by drawing upon Keats's great phrase, "Men of Genius are great as certain ethereal chemicals operating on the Mass of neutral intellect—but they have not any individuality, any determined character—I would call the top and head of those who have a proper self Men of Power."[79] In the act of witnessing adequation become formative in the lives of Men of Genius, we create the opportunity for it to become richly formative in our own.

II

The Historical Paradigm

5

Adequation and the Historical Sense

From Static to Dynamic Adequation

Eliot's preoccupation with weaving in his *Selected Essays*, the outline of a Second Fall of Man—the compensatory myth which Stephen Spender, among many others, perceived to haunt his generation, is striking. It is an extraordinary demonstration of how the poet can spin his own tribulations into full-blown historical myth, the counterpart in literary historiography of the apocalyptic narratives so common to fundamentalist religion. But it also serves to illustrate a gradual shift in Eliot's views—a shift away from a Second Fall of Man, a myth of failed adequation, toward acceptance of process and adequation as inevitable and necessary in every age—and this is a shift which has been mostly overlooked. This mature view I call dynamic adequation. It marks Eliot's acceptance of what he called the historical sense, a reconciliation that was to have major consequences for his art.

Eliot's most concise statement of dynamic adequation occurs in his brilliant essay on "American Literature and the American Language" in *To Criticize the Critic*:

> From time to time there occurs some revolution, or sudden mutation of form and content in literature. Then, some way of writing which has been practised for a generation or more, is found by a few people to be out of date, and no longer to respond to contemporary modes of thought, feeling and speech. A new kind of writing appears, to be greeted at first with disdain and derision; we hear that the tradition has been flouted, and that chaos has come. After a time it appears that the new way of writing is not destructive but re-creative. It is not that we have repudiated the past, as the obstinate enemies—and also the stupidest supporters—of any new movement like to believe; but that we have enlarged our conception of the past; and that in the light of what is new we see the past in a new pattern.[1]

As Eliot gradually came to an acceptance of process, static myth gives way to (or comes to coexist with) acknowledgment of a "law of nature,"[2] which requires that language, struggling to remain responsive to some deeper, unfathomable principle of "pure change"[3] at the heart of things, "some deeper cause incapable of formulation,"[4] must itself be "always changing,"[5] always in a state of transformation such "that something is always being lost, as well as something being gained."[6] If language may from one point of view be regarded as fundamentally an attempt to grasp and fix the shifting contours of process, then "living literature [must itself be] . . . always in process of change"[7] as it tries desperately to maintain lifegiving contact with "ordinary everyday language," the "changing language of common intercourse"[8] whose inexplicable "changes" and sudden mutations from day to day and year to year stem from even more profound and more fundamental "changes" occurring at the bedrock level of "thought and sensibility."[9] Hence language, and by extension all "forms of art," must be viewed as a continuing attempt to apprehend in every successive moment of time the "different and necessarily different combinations of the eternal and the changing," a tacit admisssion that "we cannot banish *becoming*" from the realm of art "any more than we can banish *being*." Of the fact "that there can be no art *greater* than the art which has already been created," Eliot is certain; there remains only the struggle of each age to affirm the possibility of greatness in its own time, to recognize that if "our individual problems and duties are the same as they have been for others at any time—[so] . . . equally [are] our opportunities."[10]

The Structure of Artistic Revolutions

But in the actual attempt to mirror faithfully "a particular relation in time of the permanent and the transient,"[11] neither art nor language is in fact characterized by a smooth and keenly responsive evolution whereby "the good New [is found to grow] . . . naturally out of the good Old";[12] instead "forms have to be broken and remade" in a roughly "cyclical movement," and language appears to swing precipitously between moments of accelerating change and respites of consolidation, development, and decay, a movement that on occasion resembles a lurching between "perpetual revolution" and sloughs of inertia where an "obstinate adherence to the idiom" is ascendent. Between such polar extremes may flourish a healthier cycle of artistic "exploration" and "development" as art moves first from revolutionary "artificiality to simplicity, from stiffness to suppleness," in which form approaches asymptotically the axis of the real. Inevitably, in trying to "find out how far [it] . . . can go," art "oversteps the mark." Then, having reversed its direction from hardwon "simplicity towards elaboration," art "tends to become fixed to the idiom of the moment of its perfection. It quickly loses contact with the changing colloquial speech, being possessed by the outlook of a past generation; it becomes discredited when employed solely by those writers who, having no impulse to form within them, have recourse to pouring their liquid sentiment into a ready made mold in which they vainly hope that it will set." By its very nature, then, art must be always engaged in "revolt against dead form, . . . [or] a preparation for new form or for the renewal of the old."[13]

By its very nature, process looms both as threat and liberation to the great writer. On the one hand, it raises the specter of eventual extinction of his own culture and his language, consigning him to a future oblivion penetrated only by a handful of "scholars who will dispute the meaning of [his] many passages and will be completely in the dark as to how [his] . . . beautiful lines should be pronounced." On the other hand, Eliot looks upon "constant change" as, paradoxically, "a necessary condition for the *continuance* of a literature." A static universe, from which all significant "change" was absent, would mean that "new writers [could] have no escape from imitating classics of their literature without hope of producing anything so good."[14] Thus, for the poet fully conscious the historical sense, the awareness of process becomes a double symbol of continuing servitude and of partial freedom. But beyond art which retrospectively ushers a new era into existence, there is a lesser art of consolidation and elaboration, devoted not to bold exploration but to a "development of the territory acquired," an art of "developers"[15] whose less daunting appearance belies its vital role in the necessary elaboration of mature possibility and the equally necessary exhausting of all potential. But what of the third kind of art, the work of the pedestrian craftsman who is utterly without the "impulse to form within" him and seeks only for the "ready-made mold" near at hand? Though railed at by posterity, and scoffingly dismissed by their contemporaries, these legions of undistinguished practitioners nevertheless carry on a vital task: they "provide collectively . . . an important part of the environment of the great writer" and, even more important, they provide an historical "continuity" by producing "a body of writings which is not necessarily read by posterity" but which forms "the link between those writers who continue to be read."[16] It falls to their lot to delineate and articulate the accepted norms of reality which characterize a particular moment of time. In short, reality is normative and conventional, a vast network of customs, usages, and accepted perceptions which bind us together and organize us into viable communities of men; it is the task of pedestrian art through its repertory of genres, literary practices, and accepted types, to uphold and faithfully reinforce at every level these conventions and norms no less than it is the destined task of great art to labor at the opposite function, to work to overturn the habitual and customary in an effort, even if only fleetingly successful, to "see the world afresh, or some new part of it."

Thus, when Eliot says that the appearance of "a new kind of writing" leads to an "enlarged . . . conception of the past"—a suggestion first broached some thirty years earlier, stating that "the new (the really new) work of art" requires that "the past . . . be altered by the present as much as the present is directed by the past"[17]—he is really giving voice to a twofold insight. First, he is suggesting that in almost every realm of knowledge, but especially, as Ortega notes, "in artistic creation and scientific theory,"[18] the sudden revision or unexpected transformation of accepted truths comes about neither by a progressive "accumulation" or "chronicl[ing]"[19] of fact nor by an "incremental process" of predictable evolution, but rather through a thoroughly "revolutionary" upheaval in which, in Eliot's phrase, "the conventional modes of perception and valuation," both those of the individual and, in time, those of the surrounding community, undergo a "revolutionary transformation of vision."[20] Second, he is suggesting that such new "modes of perception" or novel perspectives on reality (perspectives which are "prerequisite to perception itself"[21] and often signal a "fundamental revision of man's attitude towards life" brought about in part by "changes of collective sensibility,"[22]) explain the ability of truly innovative art to accomplish a "reevaluation of prior fact" or a "reconstruction of prior"[23] reality. Across its mysterious epochal divides art works both to entrench and shake loose its hold on man.

The parameters of knowledge are always shifting, contextual, subject to the vagaries of point of view and social outlook. Hence, too, the extraordinary ability of art to reflect the eternal conflict between the need for the finality of metaphysical closure and the need for continuing openness, between a desire to repose in the certainty of completed pattern—*harmonia*—and a troubled awareness of the need to acknowledge fresh influxes of concrete experience—*mimesis*. The haunting dream of impersonal and explicit knowledge, of certain and objective experience, whether in art, science, or theology, is an offshoot of the quest for a stable reality, a static cosmos. "The human mind," Eliot notes "is perpetually driven between two desires, between two dreams each of which may be either a vision or a nightmare: the vision and nightmare of the material world, and the vision and nightmare of the immaterial."[24] In a universe of process where art must undergo a "periodic divagation from reality,"[25] where the individual perspective is subject to wracking uncertainty, and where commonplace reality, if not hopelessly fragmented, stands in the almost certain knowledge of its own future transformation, art, like reality, evades easy definition. The greatest danger is when art itself attempts to evade reality. "Has human feeling altered much from Aeschylus to ourselves?" asks Eliot, "I maintain the contrary."[26] And if, from age to age, the central occupation of art has been to reflect "the permanent as well as the changing," that "hint of something behind, something impersonal, something in relation to which the author has been no more than the passive (if not always pure) medium,"[27] then its modern preoccupation, certainly for the contemporary author, has been with what Eliot styled the "historical sense": the inescapable fact of process, the backdrop of history, and the whispered call to a life of exploration to discover adequate meaning.

Development of the Historical Sense

In the development of Eliot's "historical sense" there exist two preliminary stages or models. Perhaps the most famous of all is found in "Tradition and the Individual Talent." At the same time, however, it is flawed and, as I have suggested, fragmentary. His title notwithstanding, Eliot evades the substance of its meaning: the conflicts which the "individual talent" must surmount in his anguished attraction and recoil before "tradition" are nowhere explored. To be sure, there is the notably famous injunction to acquire "the historical sense" directed at any poet who would continue beyond his "twenty-fifth year," but this does not confront the questions either of how a writer is to acquire his own poetic voice amid the treacheries of the overpowering influence of deepening self-consciousness, or whether "tradition" itself is really a monument to permanence or rather a testament to insuperable process.

Indeed the essay seems to strain toward both interpretations simultaneously. On the one hand, "tradition" is that to which "men . . . [give] allegiance . . . outside themselves," the objective "spheres of fact" which exist only "outside of ourselves," and therefore "may provisionally be called truth."[28] On the other hand, at the core of the essay's most famous passage, an assertion that the existing configuration of the past, however stable it may appear, is always dislodged and reshaped by the advent of a really new work of literature—"the *whole* existing order must be, if ever so slightly, altered; and so the relations, proportions, values of each work of art toward the whole are readjusted; and this is conformity between the old and the new"[29]—is the view, less memorably put, that "every period of history is seen differently by every other period" because the "past is in perpetual flux, although only the past can be known."[30] If the past is to be viewed as an effective ballast or counterweight to the present, in this context it is at best relative and uncertain, a "kind of cog regulating the rate of change"[31] rather than a bedrock principle of permanence. Moreover, this awareness of change as perpetually ongoing, of revision and transformation as abiding laws of nature, inspires both an extreme wariness of the finality of even the most secure knowledge—in a moment a pattern may alter, a truth crumble—and an almost heroic, indeed desperate attempt to compass within the mind everything that has been known: to circumnavigate the bounds of the past in order to seal it within definite limits. Of course the latter strategy is futile—at best a gesture of renunciation toward life, an attempt to shut off awareness of change at the very instant it is admitted. Forced to admit that no experience may be regarded as "an isolable event, having its value solely in itself and not in relation to anything else,"[32] Eliot is equally unwilling to concede as a general premise that all knowledge is wholly relative because passed "through the sieve of our own interpretation."[33] The result is that Eliot tries to mitigate the relativity inherent in his doctrine of perspective by setting it against a principle that might loosely be termed the social nature or periodicity of knowledge. Although only present in embryo at this point, it is a principle that assumes great importance in Eliot's later writings. If to some extent knowledge is always unique, it is also to some degree shared, socially determined, shaped by the prevailing circumstances of a particular time and place. Hence "each generation," suggests Eliot, is destined to view the past from a "different perspective"—but one to some extent uniform or homogeneous *within* its purview—whose unique character derives from being molded and stamped by a "greater number of influences than those which bore upon the generation previous."[34] From this point issues Eliot's deliberate use of the assertion that "dead writers are remote from us because we *know* so much more than they did," and his equally noteworthy rejoinder: "precisely, and they are that which we know."[35]

In the unfolding of Eliot's paradigm an intermediary stage is marked in *The Use of Poetry and the Use of Criticism*, where earlier insights, suggestive but rudimentary, are further sharpened into tenets, and the notion of reality as socially determined—what has been described elsewhere as "the social construction of reality"[36]—is brought into greater focus.

> From time to time, every hundred years or so, it is desirable that some critic shall appear to review the past of our literature, and set the poets and the poems in a new order. This task is not one of revolution but of readjustment. What we observe is partly the same scene, but in a different and more distant perspective; there are new and strange objects in the foreground, to be drawn accurately in proportion to the more familiar ones which now approach the horizon, where all but the most eminent become invisible to the naked eye. The exhaustive critic, armed with a powerful glass, will be able to sweep the distance and gain an acquaintance with minute objects in the landscape with which to compare minute objects close at hand; he will be able to gauge nicely the position and proportion of the objects surrounding us, in the whole of the vast panorama.[37]

When, in "Tradition and the Individual Talent," Eliot observed that the "introduction of the new (the really new) work of art" modifies the "existing order"[38] or pattern, he left unspecified by whom such tasks of "readjustment" are to be undertaken, and how often they may be expected. On the personal level, both for the developing poet and the sensitive and informed reader, there is always a continuing process of scrutiny and revision of the past: for the poet this assumes the form of a personal quest to acquire his own voice through exploration of the past, and for the reader there is a kindred quest for a fully ripened and mature sense of *taste*; and while perhaps "only the exceptional reader" will come "in the course of time . . . to classify and compare his experiences, to see one in the light of others; and . . . as his poetic experiences multiply . . . to understand each more accurately," the ideal remains valid nevertheless. Hence the process is envisioned as a threefold development. At the outset,

> The element of enjoyment is enlarged into appreciation which brings a more intellectual addition to the original intensity of feeling. It is a second stage in our understanding of poetry, when we no longer merely select and reject, but organize. We may even speak of a third stage, one of reorganization; a stage at which a person already educated in poetry meets with something new in his own time, and finds a new pattern of poetry arranging itself in consequence.

But this involves a personal "pattern," one "which we form in our own minds out of our own reading of poetry that we have enjoyed"[39] and assimilated.

Thus, in *The Use of Poetry*, the question is again taken up on a more general plane, and instead of limiting his inquiry to the question of how the artist, young or old, may best pursue his personal quest for self-development, Eliot widens the scope of his investigation to include an exploration of that inexplicable social phenomenon by which an entrenched public perception of the past may pass swiftly from a stable valuation to a shattering revaluation. As a social phenomenon, such "readjustment" becomes linked to the idea of a necessary periodic occurrence; and while Eliot's metaphor confines itself to a description of literary upheavals and revolutions, clearly he is looking beyond literature to confront that larger mystery of how reality itself seems now and again to give way before a major overturning of accepted truths in an upheaval that is discontinuous, periodic, and revolutionary.

6

Adequation and Self-Consciousness: From Johnson to Valéry

Dr. Johnson and the Age of Confidence

After *Selected Essays*, Eliot's appreciations of individual authors tend to focus on the corrosive effects of time on increasing their self-consciousness, instead of on the myth of adequation per se as causal explanation. To begin with, there is Eliot's telling description of his ideal or classic age as one encapsulated in a moment of suspended time, "a moment of order and stability, of equilibrium and harmony," a precarious moment of balanced forces and checked energies which inevitably disintegrate. It is of course a compensatory vision, one that conceives and renders a moment of stasis in the only terms available to a fallen, temporal mind: those of dynamic forces momentarily arrested before resuming their chaotic motion. It is a rendering of poised stillness, a metaphor of existence outside the limits of time, an evocation of an ideal age imbued with natural confidence toward the temporal because it is essentially innocent of the temporal, a mythic world poised on the brink of a radical awareness of time and terror of history. In short a single metaphor becomes the vehicle for describing both an attitude toward time ("the moment when men have a critical sense of the past, a confidence in the present, and no conscious doubt of the future") and an attitude toward art (only at such a "moment" do we find "a common style"[1]); in the end, the two are virtually indistinguishable as the moment of stasis and the moment of cultural unity are fused into a dream of impossible art.

The first stage from the ideal to the real is marked in Eliot's imagination by the figure of Johnson. Of course there are glancing references to Renaissance figures—the dramatists of that age are "blessed" because of their absence of any "sense of a 'changing world,'" an innocence that fosters a *belief* in their own age "in a way in which no nineteenth- or twentieth-

century writer of the greatest seriousness has been able to believe in his age.
... We recognize the same assumption of permanence in [Shakespeare's]
minor fellows"[2]—but these references are mostly scattered and fragmentary.
On the other hand, Johnson's is an age of "innocence"[3] because one into
which the "historical sense"[4] had made as yet but few and insignificant
inroads. The direct result, Eliot thinks, is that Johnson, taking stock of the
"body of English poetry" in his monumental *Lives of the Poets*, could take
"for granted a progress, a refinement of language . . . along definite lines," an
attitude impossible without a concomitant and far-reaching "confidence in
the rightness and permanence" of the styles and genres wrought to near
perfection in his own time; confidence of an intensity and depth, Eliot adds,
"much stronger than any we can place in the style, or styles, of our own age.
. . ."[5] And whether envied or spurned by future judgment, a confidence
which involves a frame of mind able to flourish unblighted only when
innocent of "the historical and comparative methods"[6] so integral to Eliot's
own view of things.

From this quixotic portrait of Johnson, three conclusions emerge. First,
the virtual perfection of a neoclassic common style arose, Eliot insists
repeatedly, out of a fundamental agreement—often acknowledged but more
often healthily unconscious[7]—on "the nature of the world . . . on the place
of man in it and on his destiny."[8] Thus a common style may be said to
reflect—indeed assert—a broad consensus of opinion and belief about the
ultimate nature of reality. Given this basic premise, it follows that unity of
culture which gives rise to a common style will likely also produce a powerful
belief that art has achieved, potentially at least, an access of knowledge into
the mystery of reality: "style" to Eliot here subsumes the neoclassic concept
of *decorum* which holds that art may attain to a "cousinship . . . (in its best
moments something approaching the fraternal) to the process of nature
itself. . . ."[9] But Eliot holds the neoclassic achievement of art to have fallen
short, to have rendered a view of reality that was incomplete because the
sensibility of that age, "especially in the scale of religious feeling," was
seriously restricted, despite its relative freedom from self-consciousness.[10] In
exhibiting this flaw—a too narrowly circumscribed and continously shrinking scale of religious feeling—the neoclassic age is portrayed as the
harbinger, though certainly not the proximate cause, of our own besetting
"disintegration of . . . common belief and a common culture."[11] Thus the
nub of Eliot's perplexity centers on whether the neoclassic conception of
decorum carries within itself, both as goal and guiding premise at hand, a
profound metaphysical flaw—one inherent in its canons and conceptions of
art as noetic—a hypothesis which, if affirmatively answered, must lead to
Eliot's other allegorical figure, the figure of Valéry.

Valéry and Self-Consciousness

For Eliot, Valéry becomes a cautionary figure in an allegorical tale, a striking exemplar in whom the characteristics of the historical sense—the decay of language, the decline of belief, the near disappearance of a cohesive logic of sensibility, the atrophy of the affective life, the growing obsession with method in both life and art—culminate in the blight of morbid self-consciousness.

Although Eliot employs the phrase self-consciousness loosely, referring to habits of mind, characteristics of art, or general traits of society—often with reciprocity between all three—his overall meaning seems clear, particularly with regard to the dilemma of the artist.

Clearly, the most striking characteristic of self-consciousness is the need to distance experience, the inability to "accept" it in all of its possible forms, from the commonplace emotions of the daylight world to the darker "forms of imagination, phantasmagoria, and sensibility."[12] Typically we distance experience by embracing reductive "explanation," or some particular "method which . . . gropes toward wider and deeper connexions,"[13] carrying us relentlessly "further and further away from . . . [reality itself] without arriving at any other destination."[14] The upshot is modern culture's intense self-consciousness which nullifies and defeats what Keats called "Negative Capability, that is when man is capable of being in uncertainties, Mysteries, doubts, without any irritable reaching after fact & reason."

This affliction betrays itself in several ways. If the recoil from experience is both massive and acknowledged, it may give rise to "moral and spiritual qualities, of a stoic kind,"[15] in which uncertainty and doubt elicit a protective philosophy of detachment that can look, as in the case of Charles Eliot Norton, "upon the passing order without regret, and towards the coming order without hope."[16] It is manifest time and again in what Eliot views as the doomed attempt "to preserve emotions without the beliefs with which their history has been involved," a desperate "rear-guard religious action"[17] typified as much by the centrifugal diffusion of culture across the last two centuries as by the personal quests of such figures as Matthew Arnold or I. A. Richards. Certainly it presents specific dangers for the poet, corrosive pressures, "both direct and indirect, to make him overconscious of his beliefs as *held*";[18] these may foster attempts to overcome doubt or perplexity, as Eliot observes archly of Yeats, by single-handedly taking "heaven by magic," searching defiantly if hopelessly for those concepts, rituals or other formal doctrines of belief—as with Yeats's imposing arsenal of "self-induced trance states, calculated symbolism, mediums, theosophy, crystal-gazing, folklore and hobgoblins" to say nothing of "Golden apples, archers, black pigs and [other] such paraphernalia"[19]—no longer at hand in society at large to render experience transparent.

But in the enumeration of these qualities, as they come together to thwart the aspirations of the poet, Eliot turns inevitably to the figure of Valéry. Above all in Valéry the "process of increasing self-consciousness" bends art back upon itself, turns it away from the mystery and suffering of experience towards refuge in the private fascination of reflexive scrutiny, bringing about a profound "change of attitude toward the subject matter" of art in which reality recedes to the subordinate role of attendent *"means"* while "the poem" itself is proclaimed the new *"end"* of art. But this apparent triumph of aestheticism is in fact only temporary. In due course the "doctrine of 'art for art's sake'" is also relinquished, for Valéry was in truth "much too sceptical to believe even in art."[20] With Valéry, then, the self-created flight from life leads first to abandonment of the traditional ends of art, then to a desertion of art itself.

Forsaking art, Valéry is left only with a self-consuming "method and . . . occupation—that of observing himself write."[21] Eliot notes "the number of times that [Valéry] describes something he has written as *ébauche*—a rough draft."[22] Perhaps in the end Valéry "continued to write poetry," Eliot speculates,

> simply because he was interested in the introspective observation of himself engaged in writing it: one has only to read the several essays—sometimes indeed more exciting than his verse, because one suspects that he was more excited in writing them—in which he records his observations. There is a revealing remark in *Variété V*, the last of his books of collected papers: "As for myself, who am, I confess, much more concerned with the formation or the fabrication of works [of art] than with the works themselves," and, a little later in the same volume: "In my opinion the most authentic philosophy is not in the objects of reflection, so much as in the very act of thought and its manipulation."[23]

The danger, courted by Valéry and finally welcomed with the abandon of deliberate self-destruction, is that "penetration of the poetic by the introspective critical activity" will be carried to the "limit at which the latter begins to destroy the former."[24] In both life and art Valéry "had ceased to believe in *ends*, and was only interested in *processes*."[25] Of course the "result of offering an *activity* . . . to replace an *end* may terminate merely [in] a restless search for more sensation . . . of the same kind,"[26] but for Valéry the case is quite otherwise. The upshot is not simply a withdrawal from practical endeavor, struggle or pursuit, but a radical program to banish process: for without *ends*, time must cease to exist. Whether spiritual or artistic, the sweeping away of ends is a manoeuvre to demolish that necessary prop of human thought: teleology. Hence desertion of *ends* produces Valéry's "extreme scepticism,"[27] transforming him into a model of the type of "adult mind playing with ideas because . . . too sceptical to hold convictions."[28] And as Valéry contrived to fashion a "language [that] remains fixed," cutting it off from "spoken language, the vulgar speech" which embodies and reflects reality on both the natural and supernatural planes in a particular culture,[29] his goal—shunning alike all reference to life or common nature—is simply to induce a sense of time's denial, a deathlike facsimile of a static universe.

Language and Method

Several of Eliot's cardinal beliefs, as they emerge into critical premises hinge upon this view. To begin with, Eliot seems to have believed that the language of his own age was doomed to a long twilight of disintegration and decay. If so, this would mean the very capacity of his own civilization to experience broadly and deeply and actively—"to feel any but the crudest emotions"[30] would, in time, be seriously impaired. The ruinous upshot would be, predictably, that

> people everywhere would cease to be able to express, and consequently be able to feel, the emotions of civilized beings. This of course might happen. Much has been said everywhere about the decline of religious belief; not so much notice has been taken of the decline of religious sensibility. The trouble of the modern age is not merely the inability to believe certain things about God and man which our forefathers believed, but the inability to *feel* towards God and man as they did. A belief in which you no longer believe is something which to some extent you can still understand; but when religious feeling disappears, the words in which men have struggled to express it become meaningless.[31]

The heart of Eliot's concern lies with the plight of the poet, since it is "equally possible that the feeling for poetry, and the feelings which are the material of poetry, may disappear everywhere."[32] Often believing himself caught in this slope of decline, Eliot's personal nightmare involves the artist who discovers that the culture in which he lives cannot provide him with adequate resources of language (and all the word implies) to express what he feels. If a poet dwells in an age when the language around him "is deteriorating, he must make the best of it," ever mindful that the "quality of . . . poetry is dependent upon the way in which the poeple use their language."[33] In one sense poetry may be thought of as "the vehicle of feeling,"[34] and the "great poet," unlike the "eccentric or mad," who "may have feelings which are unique but which cannot be shared," is he who discovers "new variations of sensibility which can be appropriated by others. And in expressing them he is developing and enriching the language which he speaks."[35] Thus Eliot's chain of logic terminates in the careful elaboration of what he came to call "the social function of poetry,"[36] the "duty of the poet" directly "to his *language*, first to preserve, and second to extend and improve,"[37] and in so doing to reclaim, unheralded by his own age since largely unbeknownst to it, and in the face of implacable history, a spark of his former glory. Sounding a rather unconvincing note of Shelleyan exhuberance, for the moment Eliot proclaims himself ready to acquiesce in personal failure and future inconsequence—though not without a hint of rhetorical legerdemain—in order to stand ready to accept the larger mission thrust upon his shoulders, the task of assuring the perpetuation of civilization itself.

This is reflected in a second theme that reappears with striking regularity: Eliot's overriding concern with questions of method,[38] especially as they turn on his important distinction between "explanation" and "understanding."[39] Although Eliot nowhere undertakes a sustained treatment of the problem—wary of the logical paradoxes and linguistic pitfalls that beset his earlier venture into epistemology—the remarks scattered throughout his criticism are both cumulative and suggestive. Given the assumption that reality does in fact possess, to an extent unknown and perhaps ever changing, "an organization coincident with the organization of the human intellect,"[40] method is the result of our attempts to put forth hypotheses of organization, axioms of consonance between mind and reality, rules which—however tentative at first—gradually and inexorably aspire to universal import. By method Eliot aims to indicate habits of mind or implicit rules of procedure mandated by culture or education; but although such habits or rules, however necessary, may lead us closer to the truth, they may also come to hold tyrannical sway over the delicate processes of human cognition, either shutting out reality completely or filtering and distorting its fluid shape into predetermined and artificially rigid patterns.

Typically, Eliot will distinguish between two generic types of method: explanation and understanding. On the one hand, to approach reality by attempting to "explain" it is, for Eliot, to invoke a procedure characterized at worst by the evils of psychologism, reductionism, atomism, or mechanism: reality is successfully evaded by chopping it up blindly into a multitude of static and discrete parts under the guise of "investigating what it is made of and the causes that brought it about."[41] On the other hand, to approach reality ever cognizant of its fluid nature, ever mindful that in every successive moment of reality fully observed "something new has happened, something that cannot be wholly explained by *anything that went before*," is to exemplify a true hunger for genuine "understanding." Correctly grasped, reality is always in flux, in the process of "creation."[42] True understanding aims, so far as possible, to grasp the dynamic character of experience, to capture not only its past design, or its static shape during the present moment, but what it "is aiming to be"—its end, purpose or goal—"its entelechy."[43] When understanding occurs, when we suddenly discern in place of the habitual past the existence of "a new whole,"[44] we proceed "not by explanations" or by "trying to dissect" reality "but in a kind of *vision/* For which there are no words,"[45] in which pure concept and concrete image are fused to produce a nonverbal and intuitively satisfying ground of meaning. In speaking of human understanding, Eliot concludes that, at the height of its concentrating and focusing powers, it is "*active* rather than accumulative";[46] beneath the most disorganized or random scattering of facts, entities, objects or data, the mind, in a moment of activity that yields sudden insight or understanding, may penetrate to "a unity of underlying pattern"[47]—pattern, in its broadest sense, being roughly synonymous with shape, design, or meaning—an intuitively grasped "whole" of experience that exceeds and transforms the "sum of its parts."[48]

By thus remaining open to the future through constant "comparison and analysis"[49] of our experience, we allow reality to jog the mind into a moment of intuition, insight, or understanding in whose sudden illumination a new pattern may be revealed: mind and reality interact so that mere "facts" are enabled to "generalize themselves."[50] Accordingly, it is not isolable events as such (or their philosophic counterpart, discrete facts), but the proliferating network of relations and points of contact which subsist among them in designs of infinite range and meaning, that are of true significance. Often such networks of pattern or meaning are thought of, metaphorically speaking, as maps, and in Eliot's view they bear much the same relation to experience as their topographical counterparts do to unfamiliar or alien terrain. Of course Eliot rarely expects that any attempt to map the flow of reality will actually achieve conclusive finality, or indeed even begin to approach the true depth and complexity of reality itself, but rather that it will attain, at least momentarily, a degree of detail and precision sufficient to offer us a minimal degree of orientation. In a passage that echoes, among others, John Henry Cardinal Newman, Eliot is able to speak of the aim of education as kindling the power of understanding to "such an apprehension of the contours of the map of . . . the past, as to see instinctively where everything belongs, and approximately where anything new is likely to belong."[51]

Method forms a bridge between explanation and understanding, a point of transition between the fixity of "known pattern" and "new variation," between the impulse to recoil into a static universe of immutable regularity and the continuing struggle to bend our will to an acceptance of process: between the polarities, as George Kubler suggests, of "Time and history [which] are related as rule and variation: time is the regular setting for the vagaries of history."[52] But the preoccupation with method also threatens dangers to the artist. As it comes to assume a position of dominance both to society and the artist, the craving for method represents, for Eliot, a dangerous denial of process. Indeed, a fear of process may give rise to just such an obsessive interest in method. "The *true enemy was the accidental*," wrote Valéry in this vein in "A Conquest by Method," adding that by means of it alone "Surprises can be forseen" by diminishing if not altogether eliminating "the role of chance."[53]

7

Adequation and Revolution:
The Function of Art

Periodic Revolution and Art

Art and religion are inseparably twined, whatever shifts in importance or redresses of imbalance between them may occur from age to age. "Literature can be no substitute for religion," Eliot warns repeatedly, "not merely because we need religion, but because we need literature as well as religion."[1] On one occasion Eliot puts forward the suggestion that their relative weight at any moment in time may vary according to a law of inverse proportions. "Can we not take it," he asks, "that the form of art must vary from age to age in accordance with the religious assumptions of the age?" If so, then art would represent "a relation of the human needs and satisfactions to the religious needs and satisfactions which the age provides."

In eras marked by "set religious practice and belief," eras decidedly unlike Eliot's own, it becomes a duty of art to "tend towards realism." And despite a noticeable reluctance to pursue this observation at length, a reluctance evident especially in his wary caveat— "I say *towards*, I do not say arrive at" —Eliot lets fall the pregnant suggestion: "The more definite the religious and ethical principles" of an age, the more adequate its conception of reality, "the more freely . . . [its art] can move towards what is now called photography." But when the "religious and ethical beliefs" of an age threaten to become "more fluid . . . more chaotic" then, Eliot beseeches us, the art it produces would do well to "tend in the direction of liturgy. Thus there would be some constant relation between . . . [art] and the religion of the time." With the passing of time art veers to and fro, in some epochs tending toward a more ambitious use of its intrinsic "freedom," in others clinging to the security of previously elaborated repertories of "form."[2]

Even within the same age, a decision by the artist to recast the same work in a different medium—to move from the stage, say, to the cinema, as in the case of Eliot's *The Film of Murder In The Cathedral*—raises similar problems with respect to reality. Says Eliot in his "Preface" to *The Film*: "The first and most obvious difference, I found, was that the cinema (even where fantasy is introduced) is much more realistic than the stage. . . . In looking at a film, we are much more passive; as audience, we contribute less. We are seized with the illusion that we are observing the actual event, or at least a series of photographs of the actual event; and nothing must be allowed to break this illusion." Continues Eliot:

> The difference between stage and screen in respect of realism is so great, I think, as to be a difference of kind rather than degree. It does not indicate any superiority of either medium over the other: it is merely a difference. It has further consequences. The film, standing in a different relation to reality from that of the stage, demands rather different treatment of *plot*. An intricate plot, intelligible on the stage, might be completely mystifying on the screen. . . . The observer is, as I have said, in a more passive state. The film seems to me to be nearer to narrative and to depend much more upon the episodic. And, as the observer is in a more passive state of mind than if he were watching a stage play, so he has to have more explained to him. . . .

Thus our dilemma about the function of art arises in the first place not because Eliot in any way perceives art to lack "its own function," but rather because the functions of art are polymorphous. Furthermore, because Eliot feels the very essence of this multiplicity of functions lies not chiefly in its "intellectual but emotional" character, the function of art is mostly incapable of being "defined adequately in intellectual terms."[3] But when Eliot *does* chance to embark on explanation, he most often will attempt to overcome this difficulty by invoking what may be termed his doctrine of perspective. By "perspective" or "point of view" Eliot generally means some selection of reality that has been claimed by the artist's feelings and incarnated successfully in a work of art. In other words, art is an attempt to fix the artist's unique perspective in a particular medium; therefore, it can diminish or aggrandize everyday reality. In one direction art can move toward realism, comedy and satire (genres whose chief function is to render the outlines of a distinctive norm, habit or type) either by muting our own feelings, or by extracting all feeling from reality in order to reduce it ("simplification," "reduction," "stripping" and "caricature" are the words used by Eliot[4]) to a mere show of puppet-like creatures which dance to the mechanical beat of automata.[5] In the opposite direction art rediscovers the mystery of reality by reawakening our feelings, sweeping aside the veil of custom that hinders art from exercising its traditionally noetic function.

Perspective and the Function of Art

Art offers, if not other worlds, the possibility of an infinity of new perspectives upon the same landscape, so that potentially we inhabit an array of perspectives that range from total intellectual belief and emotional "devotion" to "conscious and critical" detachment. At one moment we can seek the security of becoming "more spectators and less participants,"[6] while in the next we can throw ourselves open to reality. Art thrives on this delicate balance between detachment and openness, between the distance afforded by a "consciousness of language" or "style," and the tendency toward a complete sympathetic participation in "the subject matter," between the "double" perspective of a mutual awareness of "the way in which . . . [a story] is told" and "interest in a story for its own sake." Eliot puts it succinctly in the following proposition. "A complete unconsciousness or indifference to the style at the beginning, or to the subject matter at the end, would," he declares, "take us outside of poetry altogether: for a complete unconsciousness of anything but subject matter would mean that for that listener poetry had not yet appeared; a complete unconsciousness of anything but style would mean that poetry had vanished."[7]

A more telling example of this axiom is the "*confusion des genres*" which results when we fail to distinguish between the depths of meaning that flow from devout participation in celebration of the Christian Mass and the profoundly different, "almost orgiastic" degree of "satisfaction" that may be drawn from a narrowly aesthetic interest in the "Art of the Mass," where the *spectator's* "attention was not on the meaning of the Mass, for he was not a believer" but on the panoply and spectacular "drama of it." Not only will a "devout person, in assisting at Mass," not be "in the frame of mind of a person attending a drama, for he is *participating*," but he will only "be aware of the Mass as art, in so far as it is badly done and interferes with . . . [his] devotion."[8]

Hence Eliot's superb refusal to be bound to a single definition of art; art recreates itself anew in every time and place. Art may see its basic duty as offering us versions of reality reduced to a lesser scale, a middle ground between the supernatural and the trivial. Art offers those photographic "representations" we "crave" of "human realities,"[9] while it also offers those equally necessary (and perhaps not wholly licit) realms of ostentation and fancy that appear to some the stepchildren of art. It even offers those blatant flights of "as if" which quench our desire for what Wallace Stevens so aptly termed "the *exhilarations* of changes"—that necessary delight in transformation and metamorphosis that helps to stave off the terror of directly confronting "The weight of primary noon,/ The ABC of being."[10] Yet art must periodically return from the realms of fancy to forge anew its bond to reality: for unless art points beyond itself to a greater reality, it must eventually collapse into meaninglessness. "No symbol," Eliot stoutly maintains in language that hearkens back to Coleridge, "is ever a mere symbol, but is continuous with that which it symbolizes."[11] What does Eliot mean by symbolism?

Symbolism is that to which the word tends both in religion and in poetry; the incarnation of meaning in fact; and in poetry it is the tendency of the word to mean as much as possible. To find the word and give it the utmost meaning, in its place; to mean as many things as possible, to make it both exact and comprehensive, and really to *unite* the disparate and remote, to give them a fusion and a pattern with the word, surely this is the mastery at which the poet aims; and the poet is distinguished by making the word do more *work* than it does for other writers. Of course one can "go too far" and except in directions in which we can go too far there is no interest in going at all; and only those who will risk going too far can possibly find out just how far one can go. . . . And the poet who fears to take the risk that what he writes may turn out not to be poetry at all, is a man who has surely failed, who ought to have adopted some less adventurous vocation.[12]

To invoke yet another avenue of explanation, we may conclude that any logic of art must almost inevitably founder on the shoals of mystery as it ventures to explain the nature of belief. For no theory of artistic belief, of which dramatic illusion is but a single department, can succeed unless it comprehends all "species of religious, philosophical, scientific . . . as well as that of everyday belief"[13] which must fall at least obliquely under its purview. And if art is held to be polymorphous and its ontological status is acknowledged to be uncertain, and perhaps everchanging, the best Eliot is able to do is to recognize—like Coleridge before him—that artistic belief may involve a number of contradictory attitudes held simultaneously, or else a very special attitude so complex in its perpetual hovering between detached skepticism and total belief as to be "probably quite insoluble."[14] Hence Eliot's glancing reference to the latter-day heirs of Romantic aesthetic theory, the philosophic school of Phenomenology whose followers, like spectators at a play, urge suspension of "belief in the reality of the immediately given"[15] phenomena in order fully "to intuit . . . [and] describe the data of direct experience in a fresh and systematic manner. . . . "[16] When, on one occasion, Eliot tries to demarcate the boundaries of art, he is forced to concede that

What I have said could be expressed more exactly, but at much greater length, in philosophical language: it would enter into the department of philosophy which might be called the Theory of Belief (which is not psychology but philosophy, or phenomenology proper)—the department in which Meinong and Husserl have made some pioneer investigation; the different meanings which belief has in different minds according to the activity for which they are oriented.[17]

In fact, the richest moments of experience subsume a fusion of "actual experience . . . *and* intellectual and imaginative experience (the experience of thought and the experience of dream) as its materials" so as to become "a third kind" of experience which cannot be classed "either as 'truth' or 'fiction.' "[18]

From Convention to Exploration

With respect to the actual nature of form in art, Eliot refers to the necessary task of "draw[ing] a circle" around some "circumscribed" portion of reality with a vocabulary of conventions or some agreed-upon "conventional scheme," imposed by "an individual dramatist" or, better still, by "a number of dramatists working in the same form at the same time." By convention or "conventional scheme" Eliot means any "selection or structure or distortion in subject matter or technique" by which "form or rhythm [is] imposed upon the world." In short, art for the most part must confine its search, according to the first premise of Eliot's definition, to the discovery of convention or "form to arrest . . . the flow" of aimless existence "before it . . . ends its course in the desert of exact likeness to [a] . . . reality," as underscored by Eliot's choice of metaphor, almost totally barren of meaning to the "commonplace mind."[19] On the other hand, an art which ventures little more than spinning of arbitrary convention, or projecting fictive patterns across the surface of existence dooms itself to eliciting from reality no answering response, but only the confusion and terror of silence. Such art is the opposite of noetic art, leaving us, as Sartre notes ruefully, with a bitter legacy: the conviction that we are utterly "superfluous," and can only "live in music."[20] But for Sartre, the symbol of music partakes of a sterile aestheticism, an impossible and thus infinitely alluring world "on the other side of existence, in this other world which you can see in the distance, but without ever approaching it," a dangerous world of inverted values where humanity is subdued in the feverish attempt "to drive existence out . . . to rid the passing moments of their fat, to twist them, dry them, purify" them into the outlines of a world "so hard, so brilliant," so remote from the contingency of process in "its metallic transparency," that it is transformed into an eternal present "without a past, without a future . . . [where] . . . melody stays the same, young and firm, like a pitiless witness." But Sartre's rapture "I am in the music" reverses almost instantly into elegy, and his obsessive pursuit of "another time" and "another happiness" whose siren "music . . . traverses our time through and through, rejecting it" to preserve inviolate the fiction of its own escapist world of make-believe where "the moments of . . . life . . . follow and order themselves like those of a life remembered"[21] ends in a futile but tantalizing naught.

From the outset the case is sharply different for Eliot, different and significantly more complex. His quest after adequation attests to Eliot's refusal to allow despair to become a refuge from life, a means of permanently escaping the flux of experience. Deliberately to cast one's self among the "legion of the hopeless" through a passive and dispirited acquiescence to present despair would itself, Eliot says, prove a form of "deception."[22] For

Eliot the moment of musical rapture, "you are the music/ While the music lasts,"[23] tempts the artist not into despair but leads him to a reaffirmation of art as struggle, a conception of art that reflects the wisdom that "to arrive at the condition of music would be the annihilation of poetry."[24] Although in actual practice recognized to be virtually "an unattainable ideal," it is nevertheless for the "dim outline" of this elusive "ideal" that the poet must continually seek, the ideal vision of an art capable of discovering and rendering visible the "design of human action and of words" by fusing together the largely formless contingency of existence and the intuited world of "musical order."[25]

Thus a vision of reality as process emancipates and vivifies the artist and the man. It evokes and nourishes an illuminating vision of steady exploration as the artist's true calling, urging an acceptance of life and art as tentative and ongoing, presenting a vision of life as caught between the ecstacy of a full revelation of meaning and the void of no meaning.

A similar attitude toward existence, displaying a like assent to flux and uncertainty, may be found in the philosopher Michael Polanyi's observation that "the explorer's fumbling progress is a much finer achievement than the well-briefed traveller's journey."[26] Only by dwelling among "a society of explorers [does] man [remain] . . . *in thought*,"[27] suggests Polanyi, a society that eschews the false stability of the merely habitual or quotidian, a society that fights to remain open to the strange loomings and shifting perspectives of reality, attracting "our attention by clues which harass and beguile our minds into getting ever closer to it . . . [while promising to continue] always [to] manifest itself in still unexpected ways."[28]

Hence to speak of art as escape, no matter what the guise of decorative theories, is to capitulate to the horror of life envisioned as waste and void. Redemption for the artist consists in the struggle "to learn to use words" in a world where "each venture" proves "a new beginning, a raid on the inarticulate/ With shabby equipment always deteriorating/ In the general mess of imprecision of feeling,"[29] and the imposing sum of our "articulate equipment turns out . . . merely a tool-box," a shabby and pitiful array of tools for capturing briefly and ultimately unsuccessfully the underlying mystery of the "inarticulate."[30] Art is fraught with pain and anguish, but may indeed vouchsafe "some perception of an order in life " by first "imposing an order upon [reality]."[31] Yet if unaccompanied by an acceptance of metaphysical limit afforded only by religious doctrine, the acceptance of process alone is meaningless, a reversion to stoicism or outright refuge in an escapist doctrine. In other words, the act of struggle toward an assent to process must, upon closer scrutiny, also be found to contain within itself a complementary struggle to hold fast to an encompassing framework of religious belief. In the words of the Romantic thinker Friedrich Schlegel

"It is equally fatal intellectually to have a system and to have none. One must decide to combine both."[32] Eliot's mature vision of existence teaches that life, no less than art, must consist in a dynamic "state of tension" or "opposition between free and strict"[33] which governs the reciprocal struggle between the "freedom" of changing experience and the encircling contours of "form."[34] For Eliot any path—aesthetic or moral—to a reconciliation of the timeless agony of life must itself pass through time, through a world "not . . . ready-made . . . [but always] constructing itself"[35] anew; for it is "only through time [that] time is conquered."[36]

III

The Search for Form

8

Trying Out Useable Forms
in Some Specific Texts

From Voice to Drama to Music

When, in his final lecture in 1933 as Charles Eliot Norton Professor of Poetry at Harvard, T.S. Eliot observed that "our lives are mostly a constant evasion of ourselves, and an evasion of the visible and sensible world," he was reiterating the question that had and would continue to shape his life's work. In a universe radically temporal and contingent, how does the poet evolve a poetics—a guiding conception of the nature and possibilities of language, adequate to rendering on paper *and* exhibiting on stage the many shapes of self?

Having once asked the question, Eliot here, as elsewhere, proceeds to evade it. It would be accurate to say that much of Eliot's criticism consists of tactical manoeuvres that allow the poet to raise questions about selfhood while evading sustained exploration. Take, for example, the phrase cited above. Perhaps taking his cue from Coleridge ("the sad ghost of Coleridge beckons to me from the shadows"), the implications of the word "evasion," once dwelt upon in context, skirt nearer and nearer the frontiers of philosophy and theology. For the self we evade, "the substratum of our being," is neither a metaphysical unity nor a solid identity, but a flux of "deeper, unnamed feelings." No sooner does Eliot raise this central mystery of selfhood than he veers away from serious discussion. In fact, the method involved is designed to give the appearance of accelerating movement from topic to topic (first poetry, then epistemology, finally metaphysics), the same method used in "Tradition and the Individual Talent," where Eliot edges discussion away from poetics, the ostensible subject ("the relation of the poem to its author"), impels it towards the bounds of philosophy proper (whence the sudden attack on "the metaphysical theory of the substantial unity of the soul"), until the pressing need to draw a conclusion—a significant conclusion—compels a retreat "at the frontier of metaphysics or mysticism" to more tractable matter at hand. Speeding the reader from the outposts of one discipline to those of a second or third leaves Eliot free to chart a course for safer territory. Eliot's method here is irony, a term he himself applied to F.H. Bradley. And Eliot's words in defense of Bradley, "he perceived the contiguity and continuity of the various provinces of thought," are clearly intended to apply to himself as well.

Thus, in his life-long oscillation between poetry and its alternatives, between the impulse to render concretely the nuances of felt experience and the desire to transcend experience entirely by circumscribing it within the settled categories of expository reason, Eliot is typical of an important pattern within the larger movement of nineteenth- and twentieth-century thought. And although he repeatedly abjured philosophic exposition ("the attempt to use language in the most abstract way possible")[1] in favor of poetry, Eliot's hunger for general truths remained unabated; only he sought them as poet, "the least abstract of men, because . . . the most bound by his own language,"[2] a man who can hope to "express a general truth," as Eliot declares in his warm praise of Yeats, only by "retaining all the particularity of his experience," and thereby transforming it into a "general symbol."[3]

But in three of Eliot's essays, "at the back of his mind, if not as his ostensible purpose," Eliot is clearly "trying to defend the kind of poetry he is writing, or to formulate the kind that he wants to write."[4] In the course of tackling circumscribed questions, Eliot moves beyond the advance-and-retreat of irony to engage the question of how best can the poet render the shapes of self. In his essay on "Poetry and Drama," he takes up the question of the apparent incompatibility of dramatic poetry and poetic drama, hitting upon the paradox at the very heart of Eliot's quest for adequation. Of the three essays, this is perhaps the most important. Second, the argument of "The Three Voices of Poetry" confirms voice as the key structural element in Eliot's own poetry, making possible our inference that consciousness itself is experienced, and thus rendered on paper, as dialogic—an unending dialogue among the self's many voices. The third essay, "The Music of Poetry," written a decade earlier, provides the basis for asserting that music became for Eliot a metaphor to describe what we now call a field theory of consciousness. Thus, I argue for reading Eliot's development, in part, as a conflict between rendering voice directly on paper or attempting to exhibit it mediated by character on stage, a conflict that resolves itself, after *Burnt Norton*, with the decision to continue in the musical mode of *Four Quartets*.

An incompatibility between dramatic poetry and poetic drama is the paradox at the heart of T.S. Eliot's quest for adequation. Although the quest for adequation is, by definition, intensely dramatic, rarely has it yielded successful drama. That is why revaluing the usual distinction between "drama" and the "dramatic" sheds considerable light on the curve of Eliot's development. In fact, the true achievement of Eliot's poetry of adequation cannot be grasped apart from the monumental problems of metaphysical intention and structural design that undermine his plays.

Reasons are not far to seek. With regard to Eliot's plays, the truth of Thomas Hardy's prophetic warning that "mental performance alone may . . . eventually be the fate of all drama other than that of contemporary or frivolous life" is, I think, indisputable. Helpful, too, is George Steiner's conjecture (in *The Death of Tragedy*) that although the "origins of the romantic movement" may be sought in its "explicit attempt to revitalize the major forms of tragedy," the "romantic imagination injects into experience a central quality of drama and dialectic"—dialectic between language and experience that gives rise in the end *not* to poetic drama but to the highly dramatic poetry of adequation.

This fact is confirmed, it seems to me, in "Poetry and Drama" and "The Three Voices of Poetry," collected back-to-back in *On Poetry and Poets*, although it is a confirmation hedged by irony and humor. The closing paragraph of "Poetry and Drama" holds out to us in "dim outline the ideal towards which poetic drama should strive." But, at least in Eliot's case, this ideal turns out to be "unattainable" precisely because it is an accurate and succinct description of what Eliot has already attained: a poetry of adequation. An occasion for lamenting what lay beyond his reach turns out, on closer inspection, to be a celebration and definition of what Eliot did in fact achieve.

> It seems to me that beyond the nameable, classifiable emotions and motives of our conscious life when directed towards action—the part of life which prose drama is wholly adequate to express—there is a fringe of indefinite extent, of feeling which we can only detect, so to speak, out of the corner of the eye and can never completely focus; of feeling of which we are only aware in a kind of temporary detachment from action.[5]

And in "The Three Voices of Poetry," which closes with reverent praise for Shakespeare, Eliot explicitly describes poetry of the first voice, which is "the voice of the poet talking to himself—or to nobody"—the voice that most typifies both the process and the poetry of adequation—as something germinating in the poet "for which he must find words; but he cannot know what words he wants until he has found the words; he cannot identify this embryo until it has been transformed into an arrangement of the right words in the right order."

In other words, the poet "is oppressed by a burden which he must bring to birth in order to obtain relief." Then, shifting into one of his most telling figures of speech, Eliot likens the poet of adequation to a person "haunted by a demon, a demon against which he feels powerless, because in its first manifestation it has no face, no name, nothing; and the words, the poem he makes, are a kind of form of exorcism of this demon."[6]

Journey of the Magi: A Paradigm

The narrator of *Journey of the Magi*[7] is haunted by just such a demon. The first stanza, a retrospective tale told from memory, is likely to mislead, at least on a first reading, because the minutely detailed, pleasurably unhurried recounting by the Magus of his journey, combined with his air of cultivation, his urbane detachment, and his self-consciously literary affectation of inverting adjectives ("cities *hostile*" and "towns *unfriendly*"), all seem to promise an adventure located in the recent—if not immediate—past.

> "A cold coming we had of it,
> Just the worst time of the year
> For a journey, and such a long journey:
> The ways deep and the weather sharp,
> The very dead of winter."
> And the camels galled, sore-footed, refractory,
> Lying down in the melting snow.
> There were times we regretted
> The summer palaces on slopes, the terraces,
> And the silken girls bringing sherbet.
> Then the camel men cursing and grumbling
> And running away, and wanting their liquor and women,
> And the night-fires going out, and the lack of shelters,
> And the cities hostile and the towns unfriendly
> And the villages dirty and charging high prices:
> A hard time we had of it.
> At the end we preferred to travel all night,
> Sleeping in snatches,
> With the voices singing in our ears, saying
> That this was all folly.

But urbane travelogue transforms itself into disquieting mystery, as "the voices singing in our ears, saying/ That this was all folly" compels us to reconsider our first impression of the Magus, and of the reasons, heretofore obvious, for this journey. This is especially so because of the ambiguous referent of "saying": *who* says it was folly—the "voices" or the dispirited band of travellers—and *what* are these voices, uncapitalized (and thus wrenched from their accustomed theological context), that intrude upon our expectations of a divinely sanctioned pilgrimmage?

> Then at dawn we came down to a temperate valley,
> Wet, below the snow line, smelling of vegetation,

With a running stream and a water-mill beating the darkness,
And three trees on the low sky.
And an old white horse galloped away in the meadow.
Then we came to a tavern with vine-leaves over the lintel,
Six hands at an open door dicing for pieces of silver,
And feet kicking the empty wine-skins.
But there was no information, and so we continued
And arrived at evening, not a moment too soon
Finding the place; it was (you may say) satisfactory.

The sharply etched, chiaroscuro-like descriptions of the second stanza, ominous in their understated progression ("Then . . . And . . . And . . . Then . . . And. . . "), and ominous, too, for the atmosphere of impending doom they evoke, seem to invite comparison to Biblical events (the casting of dice for Christ's garments, the three trees on the low sky recalling Golgotha); but we never learn whether these are valid prefigurations or whether the Magus, confused by age or pent-up emotion, has not inadvertently dislocated the narrative, inserting events into the temporal sequence that were not to take place until many years later.

Moreover, as in the first stanza, we are surprised by the abrupt asymmetry between the meticulously visual character of the second stanza's first eight lines; the self-amused, perhaps mocking tone of "it was (you may say) satisfactory"; the pun, whether contrived by the Magus or lodged there by Eliot, on the theological notion of satisfaction as atonement (*satisfactio operis*)—and the neutral, nondescript "place" to denominate the location of Christ's Birth. Why lavish twenty-eight, eloquence-wrought lines on the preliminaries, when only three lines, cast in flat, possibly misinformative language, are devoted to the fact itself? In other words, why does the Magus suddenly find himself forsaken by his resources of style, his powers of description, his cherished articulateness?

All this was a long time ago, I remember,
And I would do it again, but set down
This set down
This: were we led all that way for
Birth or Death? There was a Birth, certainly,
We had evidence and no doubt. I had seen birth and death,
But had thought they were different; this Birth was
Hard and bitter agony for us, like Death, our death.
We returned to our places, these Kingdoms,
But no longer at ease here, in the old dispensation,
With an alien people clutching their gods.
I should be glad of another death.

The reason is made explicit in the third stanza. The Magus cannot understand the experience of Christ or Christ's Birth, cannot yet comprehend what has unfolded before his eyes. From his perspective, divine transformation is inextricably bound up with chaotic upheaval. And the Magus can find no language, no vocabulary, no system of meaning, no frame of reference either logical or theological, in which to set forth his experiences.

Save for the poem's title, its frame, so to speak, could *we* know, with any certainty, the subject of this poem? Because text—the experience itself— searches futilely for context, there arises a radical disjunction between experience and meaning. This is the reason that the last stanza appears so sparse and abstract, bereft of the sort of minute observation that is as important to the Magus as it is inconsequential to history. His repetitiveness here born of an urgent quest for meaning (" . . . but set down/ This set down/ This"), he fumbles with abstractions like "Birth" and "Death," "birth" and "death," none of which is explored at length for its infinite ramifications. Instead, the Magus focuses on his own "agony," struggling to preserve his old self as his control, once so seemingly assured and un- shakable, ebbs into despair. The verbal reenactment of that lost past, that old self, a reenactment so willingly undertaken to flee a present in which, with characteristic understatement, he "no longer" feels "at ease," cannot be sustained into the present; and the style of the last stanza, his style, which mirrors a self that is now dead, changes accordingly.

Radical Temporality: The Missing Present

Above all, the poetry of adequation is a poetry of radical temporality striving to capture the multiple realities of experience. In other words, its obsession with time and experience are really two sides of the same coin. If we imagine a graph with one axis representing time (past, present, and future), and the other designating the broadest imaginable spectrum of experience, it would be possible, at least in theory, to plot both the structure and movement of every poem and play that Eliot wrote. In exploring the major characteristics of Eliot's poetry of adequation, my aim is above all to highlight common structural elements. The poetry of adequation is always a poetry of radical temporality. As is true of all Eliot's works, *Journey of the Magi* is a temporal drama in two senses: it is a poem about time, and it uses tense and other verbal devices to enact the treacheries and consolations of time. The dramatic quality of *Journey of the Magi* arises when the Magus's identity, thrown into question by a new experience, becomes problematic to itself. At the conclusion of the monologue, for example, the Magus declares himself "no longer at ease *here*, in the old dispensation."

Isolated in a bleak present, he can no more turn to the past for consolation than he can embrace the future with hope or belief. Describing a like case, Samuel Taylor Coleridge describes a self that now "exist[s]" in fragments. Annihilated as to the Past," the self is "dead to the Future, or seek[s] for the proofs of it everywhere, only not (alone where they can be found)," in himself. "I should be glad of another death," cries the Magus, voicing a sentiment parallel to Sartre's lament, "I am cast out, forsaken in the present: I vainly try to rejoin the past. . . . " Grounded in the experience of a shattered identity, the drama of radical temporality begins at the moment when meaning is no longer perceived to be adequate to experience. Identity then dissolves into a temporal perspective marked by disjunction and discontinuity, a perspective whose segments fail to cohere.

Speaking to Harry in *The Family Reunion*, Agatha puts the problem this way. "I can guess about the past and what you mean about the future," she says. "But a present is missing, needed to connect them."[8] Throughout Eliot's oeuvre, the adverb *here* almost always signals this dilemma of a missing present needed to connect past and future, a present that cries out for a decision or a commitment. "*Here* I am," begins Gerontion, "an old man in a dry month."[9] And the missing present as wasteland is a theme sounded regularly. It appears in "What the Thunder Said," the fifth section of *The Waste Land*:

> *Here* is no water but only rock
> Rock and no water and the sandy road
> The road winding above among the mountains
> Which are mountains of rock without water.[10]

And it reappears as theme incarnate of *The Hollow Men*:

> This is the dead land
> This is cactus land
> *Here* the stone images
> Are raised, *here* they receive
> The supplication of a dead man's hand
> Under the twinkle of a fading star.[11]

In its most extreme form, the drama of the missing present—Matthew Arnold's "hot prison of the present"—is pictured by the Chorus in *Murder in the Cathedral* as:

> The horror of the effortless journey, to the empty land
> Which is no land, only emptiness, absence, the Void,
> Where those who were men can no longer turn the mind
> To distraction, delusion, escape into dream, pretence,
> Where the soul is no longer deceived, for there are no
>   objects, no tones,

> No colours, no forms to distract, to divert the soul
> From seeing itself, foully united forever, nothing with
>   nothing,
> Not what we call death, but what beyond death is not death,
> We fear, we fear.[12]

In *Burnt Norton* Eliot portrays the desolation of here as "a place of disaffection," a state of alienation and estrangement that is "Neither plenitude nor vacancy," sounding each term in its full theological and philosophical splendor. "*Here* is a place of disaffection," he begins,

> Time before and time after
> In a dim light: neither daylight
> Investing form with lucid stillness
> Turning shadow into transient beauty
> With slow rotation suggesting permanence
> Nor darkness to purify the soul
> Emptying the sensual with deprivation
> Cleansing affection from the temporal.
> Neither plenitude nor vacancy.

Here is a place that offers neither the plenitude of art, which is the memory of a fiction suggesting permanence (" . . . as a Chinese jar still/ Moves perpetually in its stillness"), nor the vacancy of spiritual asceticism, involving descent

> Into the world of perpetual solitude,
> World not world, but that which is not world,
> Internal darkness, deprivation
> And destitution of all property,
> Desiccation of the world of sense
> Evacuation of the world of fancy,
> Inoperancy of the world of spirit;

Embracing "the one way" (the plenitude of nature captured through art) or "the other" (the vacancy achieved through self-abnegation and denial of the senses) are the only escape from the "horror of the effortless journey." But each requires an act of decision. Here is

> Only a flicker
> Over the strained time-ridden faces
> Distracted from distraction by distraction
> Filled with fancies and empty of meaning
> Tumid apathy with no concentration
> Men and bits of paper, whirled by the cold wind
> That blows before and after time,

> Wind in and out of unwholesome lungs
> Time before and time after.
> Eructation of unhealthy souls
> Into the faded air, the torpid
> Driven on the wind that sweeps the gloomy hills of London,
> Hampstead and Clerkenwell, Campden and Putney,
> Highgate, Primrose and Ludgate.[13]

Only when the use of memory and history are understood can the world of the present emerge in the fullness of its triumph, as in the conclusion to *Little Gidding*:

> Quick now, *here*, now, always—
> A condition of complete simplicity
> (Costing not less than everything)
> And all shall be well and
> All manner of thing shall be well
> When the tongues of flame are in-folded
> Into the crowned knot of fire
> And the fire and the rose are one.[14]

Multiple Realities

> Forlorn! the very word is like a bell
>   To toll me back from thee to my sole self!
> Adieu! the fancy cannot cheat so well
>   As she is famed to do, deceiving elf.
> Adieu! adieu! thy plaintive anthem fades
>   Past the near meadows, over the still stream,
>   Up the hill-side; and now 'tis buried deep
>   In the next valley-glades:
> Was it a vision, or a waking dream?
>   Fled is that music:—Do I wake or sleep?

With these questions at the conclusion of his *Ode to a Nightingale* did Keats chart the course for nineteenth-century poets and their twentieth-century heirs. Brooded upon at length, these questions induced the particular despair that the romantics termed "dejection": the inability either to recover a past experience or to discover its larger meaning. And "dejection" led to what Eliot called "the rending pain of reenactment," a punishment suffered equally by Coleridge's Ancient Mariner and Eliot's Magus. "We had the experience but missed the meaning, / And approach to the meaning restores the experience / In a different form, beyond any meaning / We can assign to happiness." These words I take to be Eliot's reply to Keats, as well as a suitable starting point to explain how adequation works.

Eliot's doctoral dissertation, *Knowledge and Experience*, is built on the premise that our knowledge of the world is existential, intentional: the self is known only through experience, and since subject and object arise together from experience, the complexity of the universe is indissolubly linked to the growth of interiority. "The objecthood of an object, it appears," says Eliot, "is the fact that we intend it as an object: it is the attending that makes the object, and yet we may say with equal truth that if there were no object we could not attend."[15] Instead of knower and known it is more correct to speak of points of view; we occupy "more than one point of view at the same time, an attitude which gives us our assumptions, our half-objects, our figments of imagination; we vary by self-transcendence. . . . Ours is the painful task of unifying (to a greater or less extent) jarring and incompatible [worlds] . . . and passing, when possible, from two or more discordant viewpoints to a higher which shall somehow include and transmute them."[16] Moreover, this process, admittedly dialectical, is impossible without language: "Without words, no objects."[17] Words can reconcile jarring and incompatible worlds because words are symbols, and "the symbol and that which it symbolizes . . . [are] continuous. The reality without the symbol would never be known, and we cannot say that it would even exist . . . but on the other hand the symbol furnishes proof of the reality. . . . "[18] Thus the development of a self is "organic": it "may be said both to be already present at the moment of conception, and on the other hand to develop at every moment into something new and unforseen. . . ."[19]

This notion of reconciling discordant worlds into meaningful wholes has been most clearly developed by the philosopher and phenomenologist, Alfred Schutz, who articulates the rich density and texture of our experience into "multiple realities." Whereas William James "had spoken of a 'sense of reality' which can be investigated in terms of a psychology of belief and disbelief,"[20] Schutz undertook to free himself from James's restriction by preferring to speak:

> . . . instead of many subuniverses of reality of *finite provinces of meaning* upon each of which we may bestow the accent of reality. We speak of provinces of *meaning* and not of subuniverses because it is the meaning of our experiences and not the ontological structure of the objects which constitutes reality.

Schutz continues:

> Each of these multiple realities, or finite provinces of meaning, has its own degree of tension of consciousness and *attention à la vie*. Each may be reached from any other one by a modification of either of the latter—a modification which is subjectively experienced as a shock or leap.[21]

To describe the movement from, say, a "vision" or a "waking dream"—each a different reality—back to what Keats called "my sole self," Schutz borrows from "the structure of music" to illustrate the "counterpointal structure" of self:

> What I have in mind is the relationship between two independent themes simultaneously going on in the same flux or flow of music; or, more briefly, the relationship of counterpoint. The listener's mind may pursue one or the other, take one as the main theme and the other as the subordinate one, or vice versa: one determines the other, and nevertheless it remains predominant in the intricate web of the whole structure.[22]

In these passages, Schutz offers the reader of Eliot three heuristic tools.

In the first instance, he provides us with a description of how the mind works, a description that is remarkably close to that offered in "Poetry and Drama" where Eliot states that "a mixture of prose and verse in the same play is generally to be avoided: each transition makes the auditor aware, with a jolt, of the medium." Adds Eliot:

> It is, we may say, justifiable when the author wishes to produce this jolt: when, that is, he wishes to transport the audience violently from one plane of reality to another.[23]

The idea of this passage is echoed in lines from *The Family Reunion*:

> It's only when they see nothing
> That people can always show the suitable emotions—
> And so far as they feel at all, their emotions are suitable.
> They don't understand what it is to be *awake*,
> *To be living on several planes at once*
> *Though one cannot speak with several voices at once.*
> I have all of the rightminded feeling about John
> That you consider appropriate. Only, that's not the language
> That I choose to be talking. I will not talk yours.[24]

Second, picturing the eddying flux of consciousness as shifts or transitions among multiple realities—or multiple realms of meaning— provides us with a poetics for explaining how and why Eliot's poetry comes to be written. The operative premise is that every nuance and jolt of reality calls forth—or will cause a struggle in the poet to elicit—a different style or repertory of styles. In theory, each and every experience can speak to us with a new—and possibly unique—voice, because each can signal the appearance of a new realm of meaning. In fact, the struggle to accommodate diverse experiences within larger frameworks of meaning is another way of defining the process of adequation. And that is why the profusion of styles, stanzaic arrangements, and typographic devices in Eliot's oeuvre are all important and worthy of detailed exploration: they are a critical part of Eliot's ongoing attempt to elevate style—the experience of voice—to the level of form, and to extract adequate meaning from this repertory of forms.

Third, it helps to explain why Eliot sought from the world of music a metaphor more adequate to the task of rendering the shapes of self. His most complete discussion occurs in "The Music of Poetry":

> I think that a poet may gain much from the study of music: how much technical knowledge of musical form is desirable I do not know, for I have not that technical knowledge myself.

"But," continues Eliot:

> . . . I believe that the properties in which music concerns the poet most nearly, are the sense of rhythm and the sense of structure. I think that it might be possible for a poet to work too closely to musical analogies: the result might be an effect of artificiality; but I know that a poem, or a passage of a poem, may tend to realize itself first as a particular rhythm before it reaches expression in words, and that this rhythm may bring to birth the idea and the image; and I do not believe that this is an experience peculiar to myself. The use of recurrent themes is as natural to poetry as to music. There are possibilities for verse which bear some analogy to the development of a theme by different groups of instruments; there are possibilities of transitions in a poem comparable to the different movements of a symphony or a quartet; there are possibilities of contrapuntal arrangement of subject-matter.[25]

Possibilities of contrapuntal arrangement, of sudden transitions, of recurrent themes, of theme and variations—all these provide an analogy for ordering and rendering the multiple realities of experience through which adequation operates. That may well explain Eliot's statement that it "is in the concert room, rather than in the opera house, that the germ of a poem may be quickened."

All of these points converge in Eliot's definition of what he means by the music of a word:

> The music of a word is, so to speak, at a point of intersection: it arises from its relation first to the words immediately preceding and following it, and indefinitely to the rest of its context; and from another relation, that of its immediate meaning in that context to all the other meanings which it has had in other contexts, to its greater or less wealth of association. Not all words, obviously, are equally rich and well connected . . . for it is only at certain moments that a word can be made to insinuate the whole history of a language and a civilization. This is an "allusiveness" which is not the fashion or eccentricity of a peculiar type of poetry; but an allusiveness which is in the nature of words, and which is equally the concern of every kind of poet.[26]

Because consciousness is intentional, and because it fulfills itself in and through language, it is Eliot's oeuvre as a whole—the poems and plays taken together—that constitutes the palimpsest of his self.

This is why a scrutiny of poem after poem cannot help but reveal a striking design in the work as a whole. Depicting self and process poses the ultimate dilemma and challenge of form for Eliot. The plays are a series of vital if ultimately unsuccessful experiments in poetic form, often intelligible only as chapters otherwise absent from the unfolding design of *Collected Poems.*

But only against the background of his work viewed as a whole do we recognize the degree to which Eliot found himself compelled, in the attempt to mediate between form and process, to rely on what James Olney, in his brilliant chapter on *Four Quartets* in *Metaphors of Self,* calls the "re-capitulation" and "recall"[27] of poetic elements—single words, phrases, grammatical usages, images, motifs, linguistic idiosyncracies, and themes of every kind—to produce in his work a tight-knit web of language in which allusion, cross reference, and resonance are unending. Eliot swiftly emerges as a poet fluent in at least a half-dozen major styles, each with its characteristic speaker, point of view, vocabulary, rhetorical stance, and level of awareness. Almost every major poem exhibits an ongoing internal strife between these competing styles and voices for poetic supremacy, and the long curve of Eliot's development betrays a similar oscillation between the felt power and perceived liabilities of first one style, then another.

For instance: with great frequency Eliot recurs to what I call a "poetry of the interrogative," in which the proliferation of interrogative pronouns and unanswerable queries constitutes both an attitude toward language (and the universe), and a sign of their "insidious intent"[28] to overwhelm the unwary individual. To ask a question, even to frame an ostensibly innocent query is, for Eliot, an act of inestimable significance. Questions overwhelm. They disturb the universe. They threaten the very routines of habitual life. Similarly, there is Eliot's strong attraction to what he describes as a poetry of "incantation,"[29] which turns up as a series of *Landscapes* (*New Hampshire, Virginia, Usk, Rannoch, by Glencoe,* and *Cape Ann*) at a strategic junction in the completed shape of the *Collected Poems,* but also constitutes the style chosen to explore themes that would be reworked for *Four Quartets* and, perhaps surprisingly, in the plays.

It has often been observed that throughout his poetry, Eliot relies on a group of related styles best characterized by what David Perkins calls a "poetry of 'vision,'"[30] a poetry in which the outlines of our accustomed world tremble, begin to blur, then dissolve completely, thrusting the reader into a world of nightmare, phantasmagoria or surreal experience whose meaning lurks beyond our reach. In fact, as we sort through the rich diversity of Eliot's poetry, the need to describe style in terms of its function and its significance to Eliot's larger purpose becomes urgent. We find Eliot at times turning to an extraordinarily telling "poetry of manners" (as in many of the poems in *Prufrock and Other Observations*—1917); a less successful "poetry of Augustan satire" (as in the excised long opening of *The Fire Sermon*, imitating Pope, in *The Waste Land: Facsimile and Transcript*);[31] a savagely reductive "poetry of marionnettes" (as in *Poems 1920, Gerontion* excepted), which turns on the relationship between puppet and puppeteer, surfacing momentarily as part of Harry's nightmarish, tropical wanderings in *The Family Reunion*;[32] a more complex and highly fluid "poetry of juxtaposition" (as in *The Waste Land*); a beleaguered and often despairing "poetry of the minimal" (as in *The Hollow Men*); a "poetry of interiority," (as in *Ash-Wednesday*), where introspection becomes posture, and grappling with the voices of the interior betrays an exterior world whose pull cannot be easily evaded; an almost uncharacterizable poetry which attempts a halting and perhaps unsuccessful transcription of moments of intense, luminous experience; and a "poetry of meditation or reflection" (strategically, a fusion of the *Landscapes* and *Ash-Wednesday*), as in *Four Quartets*.

The quest of Eliot's oeuvre is the quest for adequation—for the universal incarnated in the particular, for the meaning hidden in the experience. But the experience of knowing Eliot's works individually and as an evolving whole is, as James Olney eloquently puts it, the experience of a fabric woven of words whose goal is not simply "to discover truth and to present it, but to pursue and to create it, and not to create it outside the pursuit but within it. And in his re-creation, the reader, in effect, becomes the pursuit, the pondering, the process, the poem."[33]

The Imperative Voice: Reality and Monologue

The imperative voice breaking in upon consciousness: commanding, exhorting, entreating, enjoining—no dialogue is more characteristic in Eliot. Take, for example, the series of imperatives (Stand . . . Lean . . . Weave . . . Clasp . . . Fling . . . and turn . . . But weave, weave. . . .) that structure the first stanza of *La Figlia che Piange*.

> *Stand* on the highest pavement of the stair—
> *Lean* on a garden urn—
> *Weave, weave* the sunlight in your hair—
> *Clasp* your flowers to you with a pained surprise—
> *Fling* them to the ground *and turn*
> With a fugitive resentment in your eyes:
> But *weave, weave* the sunlight in your hair.[34]

Are these the commands of a stage director, as the immediacy of the present tense might well suggest on a first reading, or is this the voice of the speaker conjuring memory (or of memory relentlessly descending on the speaker) in a witting (or unwitting) Pre-Raphaelite parody of the poetic language of divine invocation? We see the stock props of melodrama: the highest pavement of the stair, a garden urn, clasped flowers flung to the ground, a gesture which precipitates the look of "fugitive resentment." We see a studied, Latinate, almost operatic overtone in the speech. And we hear, too, the tone of feigned detachment with which these imperatives issue from the speaker ("I should have lost a gesture and a pose," adds the speaker in the third stanza), even as we realize the haunting power that this trite scene of romantic parting will continue to exert over "The troubled midnight and the noon's repose." And finally, we ask why the command to "Weave, weave the sunlight in your hair—" is the only imperative to be repeated: "But weave, weave the sunlight in your hair." Does sunlight remain the only natural element in this otherwise artificial tableaux that remains beyond his control? Does the speaker sense that sunlight alone possesses the magic necessary to transform and transfigure these stock props? Is that why the final line of the first stanza follows a colon, so as to emphasize the importance of the natural sunlight?

> Stand on the highest pavement of the stair—
> Lean on a garden urn—
> Weave, weave the sunlight in your hair—
> Clasp your flowers to you with a pained surprise—
> Fling them to the ground and turn
> With a fugitive resentment in your eyes:
> But weave, weave the sunlight in your hair.
>
> So I would have had him leave,
> So I would have had her stand and grieve,
> So he would have left
> As the soul leaves the body torn and bruised,
> As the mind deserts the body it has used.
> I should find
> Some way incomparably light and deft,
> Some way we both should understand,
> Simple and faithless as a smile and shake of the hand.
>
> She turned away, but with the autumn weather
> Compelled my imagination many days,
> Many days and many hours:
> Her hair over her arms and her arms full of flowers.
> And I wonder how they should have been together!
> I should have lost a gesture and a pose.
> Sometimes these cogitations still amaze
> The troubled midnight and the noon's repose.

Now, suppose we mentally reorder the sequence of stanzas, beginning the poem with the first of the third stanza, and concluding the monologue with the last of the third stanza.[35] By framing the imperatives—the immediate experience or visionary text, so to speak—in a reflective or meditative context, the power of experience to haunt the speaker is decreased directly as the meditation becomes more adequate to render its meaning.

But offering a more traditional ordering of stanzas does violence to the speaker's experience precisely because it minimizes the conflict among the realities he experiences, and therefore the urgency of his quest for adequation. Conversely, we may assume that Eliot's recasting of a traditional nineteenth-century genre stems from the urgency of his quest for an adequate form. Just as *Journey of the Magi* employed three stanzas, each with its own signature of style, to underscore the failure of language to comprehend an experience pointed to by the title, so *La Figlia che Piange* distorts form to enact the quest for adequation.

Now, compare the imperatives of *La Figlia che Piange* with those in the first two stanzas of *Sweeney Erect*:

> Paint me a cavernous waste shore
>   Cast in the unstilled Cyclades,
> Paint me the bold anfractuous rocks
>   Faced by the snarled and yelping seas.
>
> Display me Aeolus above
>   Reviewing the insurgent gales
> Which tangle Ariadne's hair
>   And swell with haste the perjured sails.[36]

With obvious exceptions, many of the questions prompted by the imperatives of *La Figlia che Piange* are raised here as well. Drawn from Greek mythology and cast in the appropriate diction and mock-heroic style, there is no longer as pressing a sense of personal recollection or reminiscence on the part of the speaker. The subject matter is literary, bookish; but the tone is urgent, with an undercurrent of hysteria. Are these stanzas meant to convey the speaker's recurring nightmare? Except in the context of the whole poem, it is impossible to tell. But, except for the title's erotic pun, there is little in the first two stanzas of *Sweeney Erect* to prepare the reader for the abrupt transition to the new style—and the new dimension of reality—that begins the third stanza:

> Morning stirs the feet and hands
>   (Nausicaa and Polypheme).
> Gesture of orang-outang
>   Rises from the sheets in steam.

This withered root of knots of hair
   Slitted below and gashed with eyes,
This oval O cropped out with teeth:
   The sickle motion from the thighs

Jackknifes upward at the knees
   Then straightens out from heel to hip
Pushing the framework of the bed
   And clawing at the pillow slip.

Sweeney addressed full length to shave
   Broadbottomed, pink from nape to base,
Knows the female temperament
   And wipes the suds around his face.

Again, the seventh stanza marks a transition to another reality, an aside embodied in a literary reference to Emerson, enclosed in parentheses in a gesture that is almost deferential in its understatement:

(The lengthened shadow of a man
   Is history, said Emerson
Who had not seen the silhouette
   Of Sweeney straddled in the sun.)

Tests the razor on his leg
   Waiting until the shriek subsides.
The epileptic on the bed
   Curves backward, clutching at her sides.

After the ninth stanza, the speaker's perspective again changes, with the style subsiding from kinesthetic ferocity into singsong narrative that suggests bourgeois embarrassment:

The ladies of the corridor
   Find themselves involved, disgraced,
Call witness to their principles
   And deprecate the lack of taste

Observing that hysteria
   Might easily be misunderstood;
Mrs. Turner intimates
   It does the house no sort of good.

But Doris, towelled from the bath,
   Enters padding on broad feet,
Bringing sal volatile
   And a glass of brandy neat.

What is true of Eliot's other monologues is also true here: the quest for adequation is a desperate attempt to "pull together" the multiple realities— or selves—into a single persona that coheres.

Multiple Realities and the Polyphonic Poems

Each and every reality can speak to us with a new and unique voice. This argument can be carried from the unit of the stanza (or group of stanzas) to the unit of the single line. Certainly in the case of Eliot's polyphonic poems— *The Waste Land*, say, or *Coriolan*—each new line (or two) likely signals the appearance of a new voice, a new speaker, a new style, a new reality, as if the reader were overhearing voices from a crowded drawing room; or, at dusk, voices crowded onto the stage of history. Although banished from the final version of *The Waste Land*, the celebration of and delight in "voices" that lead Eliot to entitle the first two sections *He Do The Police In Different Voices*[37] is entirely characteristic. Arguably, the first two stanzas of *The Burial of the Dead* contain some dozen or so voices, from the lines of the aged Marie, remembering her youthful delight ("He said, Marie, / Marie, hold on tight. And down we went. / In the mountains, there you feel free") to the Old Testament prophet challenging the reader ("Son of man, / You cannot say, or guess, for you know only / A heap of broken images . . ."); and from the baleful resignation of the opening voice ("April is the cruelest month . . . mixing memory and desire . . .") to its embodiment in the inability of the self-centered hyacinth girl to guess at the fragmentary experience of her lover:

> —Yet when we came back, late, from the hyacinth garden,
> Your arms full, and your hair wet, I could not
> Speak, and my eyes failed, I was neither
> Living nor dead, and I knew nothing,
> Looking into the heart of light, the silence.

Polyphony alone proves insufficient. In shaping successive versions of the manuscript text and in adding the notorious notes to fill out the poem for book publication (the poem had appeared, with no notes, in *The Criterion*, October 1922, and *The Dial*, November 1922), Eliot had invoked a number of other aesthetic strategies. Until he was overruled by Pound, Eliot had considered employing *Gerontion* as a preface to *The Waste Land*; this, coupled with the famous statement in the notes ("Tiresias, although a mere spectator and not indeed a 'character', is yet the most important personage in the poem, uniting all the rest. . . . What Tiresias *sees*, in fact, is the substance of the poem"), suggests a strategy for framing the poem's many voices within a monologue superstructure. In the back of his mind, Eliot may have thought to transform an identifiable, socially delineated persona into shadowy, quasi-supernatural, historical figures whose challenge would be to make sense not simply out of a haunting moment of experience but out of the entire sweep of history.

"Here I am, an old man, in a dry month," begins Gerontion, *here*, isolated in the present. Gerontion then casts his memory back to the past, looks in vain to the future ("After such knowledge, what forgiveness?"), and returns to the present, dismissing his own meditations as "Thoughts of a dry brain in a dry season." The more traditional monologue's temporal structure serves here as a framing device, an attempt to invest a speaker, not otherwise susceptible of characterization, with definition and identity. Since Gerontion cannot bring order to history's chaos, he is himself a prisoner of the present, an eternal present, just as the Magus finds himself imprisoned in a *now*, a missing present, condemned to live out his years puzzling over past and future.

A related problem is evident in Eliot's hunt for adequate terms— spectator, character, personage—to describe the role of Tiresias in *The Waste Land*, terms whose inadequacy Eliot would confront more fully in his discussion of *The Family Reunion's* shortcomings in the essay "Poetry and Drama." As a spectator, Tiresias is passive. Nowhere does he define himself in and through an act of understanding, a moment of insight, a revelation. Like the Magus, "throbbing between two lives," Tiresias "Perceived the scene, and foretold the rest"—*perceived* denoting nothing active, *foretold* promising no end to the cyclicity of history. Like Coleridge's Ancient Mariner, Tiresias and Gerontion and Magus are doomed to suffer "the rending pain of reenactment" in default of understanding.

Chock full of mythology, the "Notes On The Waste Land" point to the same problem. In the way of mythology, Eliot is perhaps best known for his warm praise of James Joyce's *Ulysses*, writing that "manipulating a continuous parallel between contemporaneity and antiquity" had "the importance of a scientific discovery." Psychology, ethnology, and *The Golden Bough* together had transformed the possibilities open to art. "Instead of a narrative method," wrote Eliot, "we may now use the mythical method. It is, I seriously believe, a step toward making the modern world possible in art." But in conversation with Virginia Woolf, Eliot displayed serious reservations. "Bloom tells one nothing," he said. "Indeed, this new method of giving the psychology proves to my mind that it doesn't work. It doesn't tell as much as some casual glance from outside often tells."[38]

Here, then, is the crux of the matter. Prufrock may struggle to escape "The eyes that fix you in a formulated phrase," the casual glance, the Sartrean "stare" that confirm his inauthenticity. Yet these very exterior details—"My morning coat, my collar mounting firmly to the chin, / My necktie rich and modest, but asserted by a simple pin"—are what fix Prufrock in the reader's mind precisely because they are so richly suggestive of his inner nature. Likewise, it can be argued that the portrayal of hysteria in *A Game of Chess* is rendered most successfully through the social accents of the woman's voice:

> "My nerves are bad to-night. Yes, bad. Stay with me.
> "Speak to me. Why do you never speak. Speak.
> "What are you thinking of? What thinking? What?
> "I never know what you are thinking. Think."

And the same would hold true for the reductive verse and parodic portrayal of Eliot's "young man carbuncular":

> A small house agent's clerk, with one bold stare
> One of the low on whom assurance sits
> As a silk hat on a Bradford millionaire.
> The time is now propitious, as he guesses,
> The meal is ended, she is bored and tired.
> Endeavours to engage her in caresses
> Which still are unreproved, if undesired.
> Flushed and decided, he assaults at once;
> Exploring hands encounter no defence;
> His vanity requires no response,
> And makes a welcome of indifference.[39]

In short, two aesthetic strategies remain in perpetual conflict throughout *The Waste Land*. A polyphony of voices provides, from various angles, a thematic consideration of waste and void. But there also exists, as it were, a vestigial persona, a shadowy and dysfunctional point of view that Eliot relegated to—but never removed from—the poem's notes. So the poem as artifact is still, and still turning, depending on whether we view it as structured by controlling symbol (waste and void) or persona (Tiresias).

Coriolan

If anything, the polyphony of voices deployed in the two fragments of *Coriolan*[40] (*Triumphal March* and *Difficulties of a Statesman*) are more focused, more nuanced, and more carefully ordered according to a semi-schematic hierarchy of awareness. Moreover, if we adopt a psychological perspective (which the poem itself parodies), *Difficulties of a Statesman* proves to be an inverted image of *Triumphal March*. In the latter, the voices arise from a crowd gathered to watch Coriolanus's triumphal march, and at its midpoint the report we receive of Coriolanus's external appearance belies the existence of the voices that crowd into Coriolanus's consciousness in *Difficulties of a Statesman*, chipping away at his resolve. But the two fragments also rebut the psychological distinction between "public" and "private," "objective" and "subjective," much as Eliot does in his dissertation, especially in chapter 4. So, in *Difficulties of a Statesman*, the location of several of the voices remains ambivalent for the reader even as it does for Coriolanus himself.

Expressing a particular angle of vision hunkered low to the ground, the first voice of *Triumphal March* iterates, with numbing repetition, the "Stone, bronze, stone, steel, stone, oakleaves, horses' heels / Over the paving." Against the beat of this rhythmic monotone, we overhear the gossipy near-wonderment of the second speaker, whose eyes are raised over the heads of the crowd: "And the flags. And the trumpets. And so many eagles." "How many?" asks a third voice. "Count them," replies a fourth. "And such a press of people," continues the second voice, addicted to beginning each new phrase with the conjunctive "And." "We hardly knew ourselves that day, or knew the City," begins a fifth voice, striking both a note of irony (the absence of self-knowledge) and a shift in tense that suggests an attempt to view the present from the perspective of the future.

Several voices later, the excited exchange of information ("Here they come. Is he coming?") provides the foil for another voice to quote a single line from Edmund Husserl: "The natural wakeful life of our Ego is a perceiving." But the cinematic rush of voices allows little time to ponder either its significance here or other instances of "perceiving" in Eliot's oeuvre. "We can wait with our stools and our sausages," adds the fifth voice. "What comes first? Can you see? Tell us," queries the third voice. And then we are swept up in a catalogue of the passing spoils of war (ranging from "5,800,000 rifles and carbines" to "1,150 field bakeries").

Next comes the juxtaposition of two new voices focusing on Coriolanus himself; these voices represent the apex of awareness in this first part of the poem. The first voice describes Coriolanus's outward appearance and demeanor ("And the eyes watchful, waiting, perceiving, indifferent"), the passive "perceiving" (recall that Tiresias "perceived the scene") in sharp contrast to the agon which threatens Coriolanus's mind in *Difficulties of a Statesman*. The second voice, again unlocalized, is a cry of invocation ("O hidden under the dove's wing, hidden in the turtle's breast, / Under the palmtree at noon, under the running water / At the still point of the turning world. O hidden") whose agonized passion contrasts sharply with Coriolanus's mien of studied indifference, ". . . not the private man, but the public personage."[41] Then we are drawn back into the thick of the crowd, hearing about how "young Cyril" confused the bell rung in church at the elevation of the Host for that of a street vendor ("And they rang a bell / And he said right out loud, *crumpets*").

Difficulties of a Statesman begins with a Voice that intrudes upon Coriolanus's temporal authority, intrudes a second time, then continues to haunt his memory, until the poem ends with the ironic voice of the crowd, whose angry chant (RESIGN RESIGN RESIGN) puns the Christian resignation and relinquishment of pride that Coriolanus cannot bring himself to embrace. Although the opening Voice is based on Isaiah (40:6)

> A voice commands: "Cry!"
> and I answered, "What shall I cry?"
> —"All flesh is grass
> and its beauty like the wild flower's.
> The grass withers, the flower fades
> when the breath of Yahweh blows on them.
> (The grass is without doubt the people.)
> The grass withers, the flower fades,
> but the word of our God remains for ever."

Eliot's typography deliberately encourages ambivalence. Are we meant to infer that Coriolanus, not unlike the Magus, is uncertain of the voice's authority? Or does Coriolanus, sensing its import and message, engage in an unsuccessful struggle to push prophecy out of his mind? In other words, the poem's structure is twofold, dialogic, an epistemological variation on Arnold's "dialogue of the mind with itself" or, as Eliot would put it in *Little Gidding*: "So I assumed a double part, and cried / And heard another's voice cry: 'What! are *you* here?' / Although we were not." There is the initial appearance, triple recurrence, and final, ironic answer to the Voice by the crowd [italics added].

> *CRY what shall I cry?*
> All flesh is grass: comprehending
> The Companions of the Bath, the Knights of the British
>   Empire, the Cavaliers,
> O Cavaliers! of the Legion of Honour,
> The Order of the Black Eagle (1st and 2nd class),
> And the Order of the Rising Sun.
> *Cry cry what shall I cry?*
> The first thing to do is to form the committees:
> . . . .
> *What shall I cry?*
> Arthur Edward Cyril Parker is appointed telephone operator
> . . . .
> A committee has been appointed . . .
> . . . .
> A commission is appointed

. . . .
A commission is appointed
. . . .
What shall I cry?
Mother mother
. . . .
O mother
What shall I cry?
We demand a committee, a representative committee, a
  committee of investigation
      RESIGN   RESIGN   RESIGN

Note that it is the ironic reference to perpetual peace in line 22 that seems to unlock the door to the multitude of different voices that spill into his consciousness:

A commission is appointed
To confer with a Volscian commission
About perpetual peace: the fletchers and javelin-makers and
  smiths
Have appointed a joint committee to protest against the
  reduction of orders.

In the Coriolanus of Shakespeare, pride was snapped through the leader's attachment to his strong-willed mother. So here, the mention of peace seems to bend Coriolanus's thoughts to his mother:

Mother mother
Here is the row of family portraits, dingy busts, all
  looking remarkably Roman,
Remarkably like each other, lit up successively by the flare
Of a sweaty torchbearer, yawning.
. . . .
O mother (not among these busts, all correctly inscribed)
I a tired head among these heads
Necks strong to bear them
Noses strong to break the wind
Mother
May we not be some time, almost now, together,
If the mactations, immolations, oblations, impetrations,
Are now observed
May we not be
. . . .
O mother
What shall I cry?
We demand a committee, a representative committee, a
  committee of investigation
     RESIGN   RESIGN   RESIGN

With these thoughts come three other voices to harrow Coriolanus. First, there is the voice of memory, of the soldier-turned-statesman who longs to be back with his men ("Meanwhile the guards shake dice on the marches/ And the frogs (O Mantuan) croak in the marshes"), punctuated with the sudden thought of Virgil. Associated with the marches and marshes, we may assume, is the voice of the gifted observer of natural phenomena: "Fireflies flare against the faint sheet lightning" and, more elaborately,

> Come with the sweep of the little bat's wing, with the
>   small flare of the firefly or lightning bug,
> "Rising and falling, crowned with dust," the small creatures,
> The small creatures chirp thinly through the dust,
>   through the night.

Finally, there is the reappearance from *Triumphal March* of the religious invocation yearning for peace, the sentence fragments uncertain, the ellipses drawing attention to the mystery beyond language:

> O hidden under the . . . Hidden under the . . .
>   Where the dove's foot rested and locked for a moment,
> A still moment, repose of noon, set under the upper branches
>   of noon's widest tree
> Under the breast feather stirred by the small wind after
>   noon
> There the cyclamen spreads its wings, there the clematis
>   droops over the lintel
> . . . .
> O hidden
> Hidden in the stillness of noon, in the silent croaking night.

As Coriolanus yearns to be free of the present, "I a tired head among these heads" (recall Gerontion's "I an old man,/ A dull head among windy spaces"), his mind wanders from *here*, the present, to there, elsewhere in time and place, for "*There* the cyclamen spreads its wings, there the clematis droops over the lintel." As revealed in the brilliant polyphony of *Difficulties of a Statesman*, Coriolanus points ahead to the final humiliation of Lord Claverton in *The Elder Statesman*, a humiliation that allows Claverton to shed ". . . the self that pretends to be someone; And in becoming no one . . . begin[s] to live."

Adequation and Incantation: The Poetry of Landscape

Of the many episodes and images scattered throughout Eliot's oeuvre describing what it is like to have hope extinguished, none are more beautiful or evocative than Harry's words to Mary in *The Family Reunion*:

> The bright colour fades
> Together with the unrecapturable emotion,
> The glow upon the world, that never found its object;
> And the eye adjusts itself to a twilight
> Where the dead stone is seen to be batrachian,
> The aphyllous branch ophidian.

To which Mary replies:

> You bring your own landscape
> No more real than the other.[42]

In Eliot's oeuvre there occurs a small group of poems and passages from larger works which describe even as they enact the momentary rise and fall of hope. In these poems, the unrecapturable emotion seems, for a moment, recapturable; the glow upon the world seems, for a moment, about to discover its object; the twilight brightens, for a moment, and the eye delights in the landscape. These I call poems of incantation, for they resemble language used to enchant or produce a magical effect through word and sound. In the poetry of incantation—a designation inclusive of those poems gathered, in *Collected Poems*, under the rubric of *Landscapes*, as well as a number of other passages that dot Eliot's work—the sound is made to elicit feelings of ecstasy before the reader's mind can grasp the sense of failing conveyed by the words. While sound delays the mind from grasping sense, the reader's mind seems to tremble or hover on the brink of meaning.

It would be accurate to say that the poetry of incantation falls midway between Eliot's two other characteristic kinds of landscape. Compare, for example, the following lines from *Murder in the Cathedral* (1935), spoken by the First Tempter:

> Spring has come in winter. Snow in the branches
> Shall float as sweet as blossoms. Ice along the ditches
> Mirror the sunlight. Love in the orchard
> Send the sap shooting.[43]

to the opening lines of *Little Gidding*, first published in England in 1942:

> Midwinter spring is its own season
> Sempiternal though sodden towards sundown,
> Suspended in time, between pole and tropic.
> When the short day is brightest, with frost and fire,
> The brief sun flames the ice, on pond and ditches,
> In windless cold that is the heart's heat,
> Reflecting in a watery mirror
> A glare that is blindness in the early afternoon.
> And glow more intense than blaze of branch, or brazier,

Stirs the dumb spirit: no wind, but pentecostal fire
In the dark time of the year. Between melting and freezing
The soul's sap quivers. There is no earth smell
Or smell of living thing. This is the spring time
But not in time's covenant.[44]

While the lines spoken by the Tempter picture an observer removed from a scene—as in the case of *Ash-Wednesday*, where "a pasture scene" is viewed through "a slotted window bellied like the fig's fruit,"[45] itself a descendent of Keats's "Charm'd magic casements"—and therefore a scene whose description does not burden either the resources of sense or sound of the speaker's language, the passage from *Little Gidding* is exactly opposite. To the reader it rings with the conviction that all of the speaker's resources of language— alliteration, rhyme, tone, paradox, subversion of logical predication, temporal perspective, richness and depth of allusion (especially in matters sempiternal and theological), subject matter, range of diction, resonance of key words, and authority of tone—have been mustered and work harmoniously to build a whole in which complex sound and sense become intertwined and inseparable.

Eliot's poetry of incantation lies somewhere between these poles. "Poetry, of different kinds," says Eliot in "From Poe to Valéry," may be said to range from that in which the attention of the reader is directed primarily to the sound, to that in which it is directed primarily to the sense. With the former kind, the sense may be apprehended almost unconsciously; with the latter kind—at these two extremes—it is the sound, of the operation of which upon us we are unconscious. But, with either type, sound and sense must cooperate; in even the most purely incantatory poem, the dictionary meaning of the words cannot be disregarded with impunity."[46]

In Eliot's *Landscapes* the dictionary meaning of words, and the larger patterns of meaning they weave, are never disregarded. What happens is that the poem's technique—its extensive rhyme, its use of parataxis, and its elimination of normal grammar and syntax—arrests the reader's pursuit of sense, while immediately stirring the reader's feelings at a deep and primitive level through the use of sound. Techniques which promote difficulty but emphasize sound defeat the reader's expectations on first reading, requiring a more active or energetic pursuit of meaning even as the ear's enchantment by sound and rhyme retards this pursuit. In two of the *Landscapes* (*New Hampshire* and *Cape Ann*), sound and image initially promise ecstasy as they tremble on the brink of a meaning adequate to experience, only to fall back into resignation as sense (the meaning and pattern of words) is slowly deciphered. In the other three (*Virginia*, *Usk*, and *Rannoch, by Glencoe*) sound and image enact dullness and despair, but the sense of each poem transcends these feelings and points the direction of hope. The incantatory effect of the rhyme in *New Hampshire* may indeed be easily diagrammed, so straightforwardly does it work.[47] In the first four lines, the immediacy of the children's voices (heard, not seen), and the blur of color created by "Golden head, crimson head" (seen, not heard) are subverted by Eliot's characteristic use of "Between" (rhyme group a) to suggest that these images be viewed as poles that mark the passage of time and the progress of decay. Suddenly time intrudes into the pastoral, bringing with it a further paradox: the interval between "blossom- and the fruit-time" (a single season) is equated by means of the colon in line two with the interval "Between the green tip and the root" (the life of the orchard). The sense of these four lines is clear: the springtime of childhood passes as quickly as a single season of spring—yet the rhyme patterns continue to delight and look ahead to the final lines (rhyme group c), in which the children's idyll is now explicitly shadowed by the menace of time.

In line five "Black wing, brown wing, hover over," (rhyme groups c and d) the ominous suggestion of the wing, casting its unmentioned shadow, hovering over, enacts a meaning that is rendered more fully in the lyrical duet that takes place between Agatha and Harry in *The Family Reunion*.

> Agatha: I only looked through the little door
> When the sun was shining on the rose-garden:
> And heard in the distance tiny voices
> And then a black raven flew over.
> And then I was only my own feet walking
> Away, down a concrete corridor
> In a dead air.[48]

In this passage, the sequence of "And then . . . And then" implies a cause-and-effect relationship which is developed in line six of *New Hampshire*. Here, five lines of near-ecstatic imagery are capped by the voice of weary resignation ("Twenty years and the spring is over"), a line whose ambivalence and undercurrent of fear are made manifest in the first speech of the Chorus in *Murder in the Cathedral*:

> Seven years and the summer is over
> Seven years since the Archbishop left us,
> He who was always kind to his people.
> But it would not be well if he should return.[49]

Line six marks the explicit presence of the adult speaker, allowing for the possibility that the preceding five lines, although cast in the present tense, are really an evocation or a memory whose haunting power cannot be extinguished. Time is the enemy: "To-day," personified, "grieves"—does us harm (rhyme group e), affects us with grief or sorrow, as will "to-morrow," condemning us to no spoken possibility of escape from time's oppression. The arrival in line eight of autumn ("Cover me over, light-in-leaves"), as children's play, prefigures both the real burial that time inevitably brings, as well as the annual agony of seasonal rebirth ("April is the cruellest month . . . stirring/ Dull roots with spring rain./ Winter kept us warm, covering/ Earth in forgetful snow"). Along with this recognition comes the transformation of line three ("Golden head, crimson head") into line nine ("Golden head, black wing"), so that the visual image now accords with the reality of the adult's knowledge. The remaining verbs ("Cling, swing/ . . . sing,/ Swing up into the apple tree"), rhyme group c, describe the joyous motions of the children at play. But, in the wider context of Eliot's oeuvre, they also bring to bear more ominous connotations that derive from the "black wing" hovering over the scene. For example, "swing" and "wing" are put to a very different use in *Murder in the Cathedral*, as the Chorus cries out to Thomas:

> The Lords of Hell are here.
> They curl round you, lie at your feet, swing and wing
>   through the dark air.
> O Thomas Archbishop, save us, save us, save yourself that we
>   may be saved;
> Destroy yourself and we are destroyed.[50]

Yet the reader still delights in the image evoked by the final line, which is really a continuation of the poem's first line: "Children's voices in the orchard/. . . Swing up into the apple tree."

Again the incantatory effect being practiced by the poet in *Virginia* is a diagrammatically strong one.[51] Like the movement of the river itself, the last line of *Virginia* (rhyme group a) circles back to the first, enacting a continuity that is metaphor both for the languor and torpor afflicting the speaker's will, and for the inexorable movement of time. The long vowels themselves have an effect that is almost mesmerizing, inducing in the reader a condition of mind (and will) scarcely allowing for active thought.

Moreover, the speaker's choice of river as a metaphor of will (rhyme group c) is self-fulfilling: although a river's course is predetermined and unchanging, will can effect change, shaping its own course through decision unless it abandons the freedom vouchsafed to it. In the context of this landscape, the thought of the heat moving (rhyme groups b^1, c and d), or lifting, provides little sense of relief. If we accept the equation that "heat is silence," which entails a relinquishing of the powers of speech and hence of adequation, then the question really being raised by the speaker is whether the cycle of "Ever moving/ Iron thoughts [that] came with me/ And go with me" can be broken. The answer to this, of course, turns on the speaker's reply to a prior question: "Will heat move/ Only through the mocking-bird/ Heard once?"

In point of fact, "the mocking-bird/Heard once" is really the poem's only event, absent the continuous flow of time in both the river and the self. In other words, the poem is, in fact, a drama of decision, in which the speaker must decide between two courses of action. His question here parallels the question that launches *Burnt Norton*:

> Through the first gate,
> Into our first world, shall we follow
> The deception of the thrush?[52]

The alternative is the movement typified in the first three lines of *Ash-Wednesday*[53], each beginning with "Because I do not hope" ("Because" later transformed into "Although" by the anything-but-still will), but each concluding with a renunciation (actual or implied) of renunciation, of the *still will*. Turning and moving are characteristic of the active will: desiring, striving, attaining, followed by the return of new desire. But even "turning" contains within itself two opposite movements. Does the speaker renounce a spiritual turning toward God, or the very different turning of a line of poetry: "(Why should the agèd eagle stretch its wings?)/ Why should I mourn/ The vanished power of the usual reign?"

Loss of our first world, whether real or imagined ("the mocking-bird") with pun acknowledged, becomes an excuse, a rationale for inaction and indecision (rhyme groups c and e):

> Still hills
> Wait. Gates wait. Purple trees,
> White trees, wait, wait,
> Delay, decay.

But the anticipated conclusion is, to say the least, unsatisfactory. In choosing neither alternative, the speaker guarantees a continuation of the past into the future: "Ever moving/ Iron thoughts came with me/ And go with me," the triple repetition of "river" suggesting another step toward entropy and decay. But the poem's question remains unanswered even as the last line rounds back into the poem's first line, allowing the speaker's state of indecision to become the consuming condition—and event—of his life. As in Prufrock's case, the question is overwhelming, begetting no resolution. Even as the sounds of the poem enact movement that is retarded and arrested, making palpable an entropy that refuses to be surmounted, the question hangs in the air, a present possibility of hope, of decision.

The Common Matrix: Poetry and Plays

All scholars interested in Eliot's complete oeuvre are indebted to E. Martin Browne's important volume, *The Making of T.S. Eliot's Plays*,[54] which provides a detailed record of how the plays came to be written. This harvest of manuscripts traces the evolution of each play from earliest draft to final verison, affording us the opportunity to place side by side to compare the germinal ideas from which each of the plays spring.

The common matrix of ideas embodied in key phrases and passages that many of the plays—but especially *Murder in the Cathedral* and *The Family Reunion*—share in common with Eliot's poetry becomes clear. Eliot's dramatic repertory, far from being comprised of viable, self-contained plays, comes to seem a series of masterful if flawed experiments in poetic form—experiments which become meaningful only when viewed as chapters (otherwise absent) from the gradually unfolding design of the *Collected Poems*.

This critical perspective is basic to my application to Eliot's oeuvre of Sartre's statement that "fictional technique always relates back to . . . metaphysics." For, behind each of Eliot's successively different volumes of poetry lies an often invisible aesthetic strategy. Taken together these volumes portray Eliot's attempt to solve a specific metaphysical dilemma that shapes Eliot's experiments in dramatic form, driven by the problem of how best to *exhibit* on the stage—as opposed to suggesting or depicting on paper—the shape of self through time.

Ghosts. Or shadows. Or Eumenides or daemons. Or the shades of past selves. To both points they are the answer. "Nothing is more dramatic than a ghost," says Eliot in *Selected Essays*.[55] But in calling this remark "an illuminating technical insight" into Eliot's plays, Michael Goldman, in his fine essay on "Fear in the Way: The Design of Eliot's Drama," minimizes what is in my view a key insight into the theory and origins of Eliot's playwriting. Because all of Eliot's plays are what I call *symbolic dramas of possession or influence*—the dramatic counterpart to the poetry of adequation—it was necessary for Eliot to find a convention that would allow him to symbolize on stage the temporal continuity of the self from past to present through a dialectical process of possession or influence as recounted in his letter to Stephen Spender:

> [Y]ou don't really criticise any author to whom you have never surrendered yourself. . . . Even just the bewildering minute counts; you have [first] to give yourself up, and then recover yourself, and the third moment is having something to say, before you have wholly forgotten both surrender and recovery. Of course the self recovered is never the same as the self before it was given.[56]

Literary surrender then is but one instance of a far wider truth. Surrender, recovery, and the wresting of meaning from experience are three stages in the process of adequation. And, as Eliot says in *East Coker*: "In order to possess what you do not possess/ You must go by the way of dispossession." As a symbolic convention, ghosts must point beyond themselves to meaning that can be understood by the audience. Whether or not they can do so successfully is the question on which Eliot's success or failure as a dramatist hinges.

Murder in the Cathedral

"A man comes home, foreseeing that he will be killed, and he is killed"—that is how Eliot describes the play's "essential action" (or lack thereof) in "Poetry and Drama."[57] For all intents and purposes, the essential action of *Murder in the Cathedral* is contained in the third stanza of an ode in some undated pages of manuscript notes in the Houghton Library, Harvard University.

> What shall the slain gain
>   Between the temple and the altar
>   Ghosts wait
>   without the gate
>   The people wait
>   The sheep unfed
>   Rumours are bred. Shadows delate
>   Those who move between the missal and the psalter.
> Come happy December, who shall observe you who shall
>   observe you
> Who shall declare you. Shall
> The son of man be born again in the litter of scorn
> While the poor wait
>   outside the gate
> And the lord lies drunk in the hall
> And the king confers with advisers of State.[58]

Cast in the incantatory style that marks Eliot's landscape poems, this passage prefigures Thomas's lines immediately prior to the entrance of the First Tempter in the play's final version:

> Meanwhile the substance of our first act
> Will be shadows, and the strife with shadows.
> Heavier the interval than the consummation.
> All things prepare the event. Watch.[59]

Whereas Thomas finds no difficulty in resisting the ghosts of former desires who tempt his will, his real struggle arises from the Fourth Tempter's enticements to do the right thing for the wrong reason. "Shadows delate"— accuse, bring a charge against Thomas, attempt to impeach—by tempting him with his own desires. Tempted by a past self (a ghost, a shadow), the real action of the play is, to invoke two of Eliot's favorite terms, an *agon* (an inner contest or struggle) or a *patience* (a calm abiding of suffering).

But the agon proves dramatic here only because it is embedded in a religious play at a religious festival. Religion supplies the context and meaning just as the title of *Journey of the Magi* gives poignance to the lived experience of the Magus. "All things prepare the event," says Thomas, but the real question is whether the play is about murder (an event in the temporal sphere) or martyrdom (a religious action). And the ironic clash between experience and meaning is driven home when the Fourth Tempter seizes on and repeats Thomas's words:

> You know and do not know, what it is to act or suffer.
> You know and do not know, that *action* is suffering,
> And suffering action. Neither does the *agent* suffer
> Nor the patient act. But both are fixed
> In an eternal action, an eternal patience
> To which all must consent that it may be willed
> And which all must suffer that they may will it,
> That the pattern may subsist, that the wheel may turn
>   and still
> Be forever still.[60]

In the final version of the play, Eliot changed "acting" to "action" in the second line and "actor" to "agent" in the third, in order, I suspect, to underscore the religious frame of reference in two ways. He sought to eliminate the double and contradictory meanings of "actor" and "acting"; and he sought also to emphasize the meaning of "patient" as the correlative to agent ("A person or thing that undergoes some action, or to whom or which something is done by external agents," according to the O.E.D.).

Finally, the ironic clash between lived experience and divinely sanctioned meaning is driven home again at the end of the play through the speeches of the knights to the audience. As Eliot confirms in "Poetry and Drama," the knights are "quite aware that they are addressing an audience of people living eight hundred years after they themselves are dead," the point being to "shock the audience out of their complacency."[61] Here, the knights assume the role of tempters by reminding the audience that their acceptance in a play performed at a religious festival of Thomas's martyrdom likely would become in real life a psychological verdict of "Suicide While of Unsound Mind."

> From the moment he became Archbishop . . . he showed himself to be utterly indifferent to the fate of the country, to be, in fact, a monster of egotism. This egotism grew upon him, until it became at last an undoubted mania. I have unimpeachable evidence to the effect that before he left France he clearly prophesied, in the presence of numerous witnesses, that he had not long to live, and that he would be killed in England. He used every means of provocation; from his conduct, step by step, there can be no inference except that he had determined upon a death by martyrdom. . . . I think, with these facts before you, you will unhesitatingly render a verdict of Suicide While of Unsound Mind.[62]

The Family Reunion: The Limits of Dramaturgy

In 1927 Eliot had observed that the question of the "Theory of Belief" is a question involving "not psychology but philosophy, or phenomenology proper . . . the different meanings which belief has in different minds according to the activity for which they are oriented."[63] Just as *Murder in the Cathedral* concludes by pitting psychology against religion as suitable frames of reference for the phenomena we experience, so the 1937 typewritten scenario of *The Family Reunion* (Harvard draft, Houghton Library, FR/H) begins by raising the same question. The protagonist

> appears somewhat distraught, and peeps out of the window or draws the cur-
> *sees   tains hurriedly* (complaint from his mother at not leaving this to the maid).
> them?   Subsequent conversation shows that he thinks he is being followed, but is vague about the cause. Family perturbed, suspect nervous breakdown due to loss of wife. Gradually elicited that he pushed her overboard, or thinks he did. Mother suggests that he should go up and dress for dinner, and will feel better after a hot bath.[64]

This provides an opportunity for the family to discuss the protagonist's "mental condition. Suggestion that they should invite the Doctor to dinner and tip him off to form an opinion . . . [of his] condition." But when the family has dispersed to dress for dinner, a very different perspective on reality emerges, as the Eumenides make their first appearance. In scene 2, the protagonist's cousin, Mary,

> tries to persuade him however that his depression is only the shadows that he has brought with him. He refers obscurely to Furies. She endeavours to reassure him about all that past gloom and horror clearing up now that he has returned, and has almost succeeded when the Furies appear.[65]

In Part II, the Doctor conducts his examination.

Doctor evidently incredulous and believes him deranged. The Pursuit . . . had begun as he returned home, or a sense of pursuit, but he only SAW THEM for the first time before dinner. Doctor more and more convinced that the loss of his . . . wife has upset his mind, and brought out some latent sense of guilt from early years, which he has materialised in this way. Sympathetic. . . . [Harry] who first made the admission to the family as if it was torn out of him, becomes more and more explicit and emphatic about it as he finds that his story is not believed, and the horror of being thought insane grows upon him.[66]

The draft ends in a colloquy between the protagonist and his ELDEST AUNT.

Stage must be cleared so that ELDEST AUNT can talk to . . . [Harry] alone. She is recognised as the only one of the family who has any influence over him. Her attitude gradually changes. The EUMENIDES appear again to . . . [him]. Aunt pulls the curtains again. She agrees that . . . [he] must go to seek his purgation. He leaves. Companion enters. Aunt and Companion left alone on stage. They discuss . . . [him]. Finally Companion says to Aunt: "So *you* saw them too?"[67]

In seeking for an alternative to the psychological perspective, the question of what the EUMENIDES symbolize is central. And Eliot himself provides the answer in a scenario (in the Houghton Library collection) for the final section, written in manuscript.

Scene:	Harry and Agatha. My brothers will be going on the same as before— but I . . . Reverts to his wife. When *in*, he has no feeling of her being human being. When *out*, cannot connect. Stain, not guilt. But *here*, all horrors of childhood coming out and becoming legible. Never understood his childhood misery before. One thing led to another. Are we getting back to real source of trouble?
That is the process of de-possession	
Great uncle Harry was cursed by a witch?	Agatha on his father. Only looked through the little door. Harry realises or re-incarnates his father's feelings towards Agatha. Agatha is the de-possessed. She however wavers for a moment. The Eumenides appear again—scene corresponding to that in Act I. Harry decides to go and Agatha agrees.[68]

Because *The Family Reunion* is most clearly *a symbolic drama of possession or influence*, it took Eliot up to and, indeed, beyond the limits of his own dramaturgy, pointing the way back to poetry through the musical, meditative-reflective style of the *Four Quartets*, and shifting the emphasis of his future plays away from the *agon* suffered by the central character toward a lesser, more manageable treatment of the theme. Had Eliot made Celia's martyrdom the central theme of *The Cocktail Party*, we may conclude that he would have faced similar obstacles.

Indeed, Eliot has not generally received credit due him for the incisiveness of his own remarks about the structural techniques he employed in *The Family Reunion*, or about the insuperable problems they created both for author and audience, because neither Eliot's commentary nor the play itself has been duly recognized as an attempt to create a viable symbolic drama of possession or influence—a successful drama of adequation.

First, there is the dilemma of how to deal with the Furies. Says Eliot:

> They must, in future, be omitted from the cast, and be understood to be visible only to certain of my characters, and not to the audience. We tried every possible manner of presenting them. We put them on the stage, and they looked like uninvited guests who had strayed in from a fancy dress ball. We concealed them behind gauze, and they suggested a still out of a Walt Disney film. We made them dimmer, and they looked like shrubbery just outside the window. I have seen other expedients tried: I have seen them signalling from across the garden, or swarming on to the stage like a football team, and they are never right.[69]

Second, there is the overarching question of how to write a play based on the notion of a hierarchy of awareness among the different characters, and of the same character moving into and out of different states of awareness. How does the playwright exhibit on stage to an audience the existence of multiple realities, each with its own voice? With regard to the Chorus in *The Family Reunion*, continues Eliot,

> the device of using four of the minor personages, representing the Family, sometimes as individual character parts and sometimes collectively as chorus, does not seem to me very satisfactory. For one thing, the immediate transition from individual, characterized part to membership of a chorus is asking too much of the actors: it is a very difficult transition to accomplish. For another thing, it seemed to me another trick, one which, even if successful, could not have been applicable in another play.[70]

The problem grows more pressing in the case of Harry's two "lyrical duet[s]," as Eliot called them in "Poetry and Drama," the first with Mary in Part I, Scene II, and the second with Agatha in Part II, Scene II.[71] Roughly speaking, both correspond to climactic moments in the process of surrender and recovery that Eliot sketches in his letter to Stephen Spender. But, while imagery drawn from these passages would be further developed and recast in the very different—and nondramatic—lyrical, meditative, reflective mode of *Four Quartets*, their viability as a dramatic device was, in retrospect, open to serious question.

> . . . I had in two passages used the device of a lyrical duet further isolated from the rest of the dialogue by being written in shorter lines with only two stresses. These passages are in a sense "beyond character," the speakers have to be presented as falling into a kind of trance-like state in order to speak them. But they are so remote from the necessity of the action that they are hardly more than passages of poetry which might be spoken by anybody; they are too much like operatic arias. The member of the audience, if he enjoys

this sort of thing, is putting up with a suspension of the action in order to enjoy a poetic fantasia: these passages are really less related to the action than are the choruses in *Murder in the Cathedral*.[72]

The invocation of musical terms here—duet and operatic aria, for example—is no more accidental than in the case of *Four Quartets*. Music was for Eliot the analogy that would allow him to accomplish two aims. First, it allowed him to remain true to his experience of voice without becoming prisoner to the fictions of "character," "action," and "motivation" that were sine qua non to writing a play. Second, it allowed him to recognize voice for what it was: the signature of a particular reality, which, with a jolt, would be left behind for yet another voice and reality. In other words, music became the analogy that proved most adequate to the self's trancelike dance from reality to reality in its struggle to give voice—and meaning—to its experience.

For example, the words of the First Tempter in *Murder in the Cathedral* constitute the germ of *Little Gidding*:

> Thomas: You talk of seasons that are past. I remember
>   Not worth forgetting.
> Tempter: And of the new season.
>   Spring has come in winter. Snow in the branches
>   Shall float as sweet as blossoms. Ice along the ditches
>   Mirror the sunlight. Love in the orchard
>   Send the sap shooting. Mirth matches melancholy.[73]

Or, just prior to her "lyrical duet" with Harry, Agatha's description of being barred from the rose garden serves as a gloss on the action of *Burnt Norton*, published in 1935.

> Agatha. I only looked through the little door
>   When the sun was shining on the rose-garden:
>   And heard in the distance tiny voices
>   And then a black raven flew over.
>   And then I was only my own feet walking
>   Away, down a concrete corridor
>   In a dead air. . . .
> . . . .
> Harry. I was not there, you were not there, only our
>   phantasms
>   And what did not happen is as true as what did happen
>   O my dear, and you walked through the little door
>   And I ran to meet you in the rose-garden.[74]

As much as repetition and development of imagery in Eliot has become a common subject for study, little attention has been given to how the dialogue between "phantasms," as Harry puts it, throws light on the pronouns in *Burnt Norton*:

> Footfalls echo in the memory
> Down the passage which *we* did not take
> Towards the door *we* never opened
> Into the rose-garden. *My* words echo
> Thus, in *your* mind.
> . . . .
>   Other echoes
> Inhabit the garden. Shall *we* follow?
> Quick, said the bird, find them, find them,
> Round the corner. Through the first gate,
> Into *our* first world, shall *we* follow
> The deception of the thrush? Into *our* first world.
> There *they* were, dignified, invisible,
> Moving without pressure, over the dead leaves,
> In the autumn heat, through the vibrant air,
> And the bird called, in response to
> The unheard music hidden in the shrubbery,
> And the unseen eyebeam crossed, for the roses
> Had the look of flowers that are looked at.
> There *they* were as *our* guests, accepted and accepting.
> So *we* moved, and *they*, in a formal pattern,
> Along the empty alley, into the box circle,
> To look down into the drained pool.
> Dry the pool, dry concrete, brown edged,
> And the pool was filled with water out of sunlight,
> And the lotos rose, quietly, quietly,
> The surface glittered out of heart of light,
> And *they* were behind *us*, reflected in the pool.
> Then a cloud passed, and the pool was empty.
> Go, said the bird, for the leaves were full of children,
> Hidden excitedly, containing laughter.
> Go, go, go, said the bird: human kind
> Cannot bear very much reality.[75]

Without becoming overly schematic, I think it fair to suggest that the deceptive nature of the experience as it unfolds in *Burnt Norton* is related to Harry's words about "phantasms," and to note, also, that in the dramatic action of *Family Reunion*, Harry's momentary reluctance to heed Agatha's command ("You have a long journey") elicits the reappearance of the Eumenides:

> HARRY.   Not yet! not yet! this is the first time that I have
>   been free
>   From the ring of ghosts with joined hands, from the
>   pursuers,
>   And come into a quiet place.

Why is it so quiet?
Do you feel a kind of stirring underneath the air?
Do you? don't you? a communication, a scent
Direct to the brain ... but not just as before,
Not quite like, not the same ...
(The EUMENIDES appear)
                                        and this time
You cannot think that I am surprised to see you.
And you shall not think that I am afraid to see you.
This time, you are real, this time, you are outside me,
And just endurable. I know that you are ready,
Ready to leave Wishwood, and I am going with you.[76]

As Agatha puts it during their colloquy, the action of the play—of Harry's journey to and departure from Wishwood—". . . is not a story of detection, / Of crime and punishment, but of sin and expiation." Continues Agatha, extending to theology the formula of adequation:

It is possible that you have not known what sin
You shall expiate, or whose, or why. It is certain
That the knowledge of it must precede the expiation.
It is possible that sin may strain and struggle
In its dark instinctive birth, to come to consciousness
And so find expurgation. It is possible
You are the consciousness of your unhappy family,
Its bird sent flying through the purgatorial flame.
Indeed it is possible. You may learn hereafter,
Moving alone through flames of ice, chosen
To resolve the enchantment under which we suffer.[77]

These lines may suggest why Eliot left *Sweeney Agonistes*,[78] whose epigraph is drawn from the *Choephoroi* (Orestes: "You don't see them, you don't—but *I* see them: they are hunting me down, I must move on") unfinished, fragmentary. In the second fragment (*Fragment of An Agon*), an agon, Sweeney rehearses many of the themes that Eliot would embody in *The Family Reunion*: the inadequacy of language ("I gotta use words when I talk to you"); murder ("Any man has to, needs to, wants to / Once in a lifetime, do a girl in"); and isolation ("For when you're alone / When you're alone like he was alone") and rebirth ("That's all the facts when you come to brass tacks: / Birth, and copulation, and death. / I've been born, and once is enough. / You dont remember, but I remember, / Once is enough").

The insurmountable weakness of this language is the absence of the metaphor of family, which catalyzes the action in *The Family Reunion*, and the relatively low social station of Sweeney and his cohorts. In the Houghton Library typewritten scenario, the setting of *The Family Reunion* is pictured as "Just after tea. Present, in a conventional upper middle class drawing room: the MOTHER (widow) distinctly the head of the family (successful marriage, money, three sons). . . ."[79] A conventional upper middle class drawing room provided the rich matrix of conventions—the exquisite forms and rituals of social intercourse—to which all of Eliot's plays following *The Family Reunion* would be firmly anchored.

"You will understand," continues Eliot in "Poetry and Drama," "after my making these criticisms of *The Family Reunion*, some of the errors that I endeavoured to avoid in designing *The Cocktail Party*. To begin with, no chorus, and no ghosts."[80] But in abandoning the difficult conventions of chorus and ghosts Eliot was also forced to abandon lyrical duets as well as characters that speak "beyond character" in trancelike states. A full spectrum of levels of awareness (well known perhaps to Sir Henry Harcourt-Reilly, the psychiatrist) could no longer be exhibited on stage but would instead have to be hinted at in a variety of ways. A suggestion of mystery—or the mystery of suggestiveness—would replace the exhibition on stage of levels of awareness beyond those held to be typical of the drawing room. The martyrdom of Celia would have to be shunted off stage, where it could intrude suddenly at the play's end, a dark and stunning contrast to characters that aspire only to the shibboleths and conventions of drawing room comedy.

Thus Eliot's last plays—*The Confidential Clerk* and *The Elder Statesman*—would deal with the themes of possession and influence, but at a level that only occasionally rises above the schematic, and at a level that deals only with secular analogues to Eliot's early drama. In *The Confidential Clerk*, characters are haunted by loss and absence, as in Colby's overly thematic explanation to Sir Claude of the exhilaration produced by his present work:

> In a way, exhilarating.
> To find there is something that I can do
> So remote from my previous interests.
> It gives me, in a way, a kind of self-confidence
> I've never had before. Yet at the same time
> It's rather disturbing. I don't mean the work:
> I mean, about myself. *As if I was becoming*
> *A different person.*

Perhaps anticipating the role of Federico Gomez in *The Elder Statesman*, Colby continues:

> Just as, I suppose,
> If you learn to speak a foreign language fluently,
> So that you can think in it—you feel yourself to be

Rather a different person when you're talking it.
I'm not at all sure that I like the other person
That I feel myself becoming—though he fascinates me.
And yet from time to time, when I least expect it,
When my mind is cleared and empty, walking in the street,
Or waking in the night, then the former person,
The person I used to be, returns to take possession:
And I am again the disappointed organist,
And for a moment the thing I cannot do,
The art that I could never excel in,
Seems the one thing worth doing, the one thing
That I want to do. *I have to fight that person.*[81]

Much of the dialogue in *The Elder Statesman* turns on the just degree of responsibility that can be imputed to one character for influencing another, with characters—ghosts, really—from the past returning to exact a just accounting in the present.

For my purposes, Eliot's search for a useable form ceases after *The Family Reunion*: with this play he makes the decision to move in two different directions. On the one hand, he undertakes the completion of *Four Quartets*, with its pursuit of multiple realities and its quest for adequation through poetic form. On the other, he deliberately excises certain statements, certain impasses within dramatic form: in his final plays, *The Cocktail Party*, *The Confidential Clerk*, and *The Elder Statesman* Eliot chooses to deal only with radically circumscribed characters and situations. For Eliot, then, playwriting had served its central purpose. As he said in an interview:

> . . . writing plays (that is *Murder in the Cathedral* and *The Family Reunion*) made a dif-
> ference to the writing of the *Four Quartets*. I think that it led to a greater simplification of
> language and to speaking in a way which is more like conversing with your reader. I see
> the later *Quartets* as being much simpler and easier to understand than *The Waste Land*
> and *Ash-Wednesday*. Sometimes the thing I am trying to say, the subject matter, may be
> difficult, but it seems to me that I am saying it in a simpler way.[82]

But the poetic matrix of Eliot's dramatic work can still be glimpsed and felt in all of his later plays. This delimited world of voices and questions invading a twilight consciousness retains the power to move us, exemplifying as it often seems to the direction of the poet's own art and life.

A manuscript finale from *The Elder Statesman* most fittingly concludes this exploration of the poet's search for adequation in varying moral and aesthetic forms. Prefiguring the moment of Lord Claverton's death, we hear the voices in the dusk invading his consciousness, voices that rise movingly and suggestively against the dark and its doubts:

The Voices in the Dusk

Michael ⎫ each remind him of some moment in the past
Gomez ⎬ (not hitherto mentioned) and taunt him
Mrs. C. ⎭

Lord C. answers. He rises. It is now almost dark.
He takes a few paces and collapses.

Enter A. and Charles. Love duet finale.[83]

There were to be no more playwriting rehearsals. *The Voices in the Dusk* is a telling description of the complex matrices of poetic form in Eliot, as well as a lyrical sobriquet to his achievement in art.

The Invisible Genre: Social Criticism

The future is likely to bring no lessening of the controversy that has surrounded Eliot's views as social critic. Nor are we likely to witness any abatement in the number of apologies or attacks elicited by Eliot's various commentaries on social, political, or religious issues. To Russell Kirk, author of *The Conservative Mind: From Burke to Eliot,* and of the more recent *Eliot and His Age,*[84] Eliot is, without question or qualification, "the principal champion of the moral imagination in the twentieth century."[85] Critics, on the other hand, have proved far less generous, alleging on Eliot's part reactionism, feudal attitudes, clerico-Fascist tendencies, acute eccentricity, and an extreme ignorance of the realities of economic man.

In this study, however, I am far less concerned with vindicating Eliot's views on social issues than I am with the larger question of understanding the underlying motives which compelled Eliot to enter the fray as social critic in the first place, and in assessing whether these motives radiate from Eliot's chosen vocation as poet. The fact is, Eliot's labors as social critic stem *directly* from his vocation as poet; far from being independent of each other, the two activities are virtually inseparable, both kindled and spurred by his quest for adequation.

You will recall from the Preface that Eliot's later or more mature view of adequation gave rise to his three-stage or tripartite model of interpretation. First, there is "surrender" to—or "possession" by—the "bewildering minute" of experience. Second, there is the hoped-for moment of "recovery" from that experience, what Eliot would call during his writing of *The Family Reunion* the "process of depossession." And finally, there is the quest of discovery for "meaning," the painful coming to consciousness of "pattern."

Theology follows epistemology: ". . . sin," says Eliot, "may strain and struggle / In its dark instinctive birth, to come to consciousness / And so find expurgation." In the preceding pages, I have discussed why I believe that, both in form and in theme, Eliot's most significant experiment in drama, *The Family Reunion*, and his supreme poetic achievement, *Four Quartets*, are fully understandable only as symbolic dramas of "influence" or "possession" and "depossession." Here I assert that Eliot's social criticism springs directly from the third moment of this interpretive scheme: the need for an adequate framework of theology and belief to anchor those bewildering minutes both in the poet's own life and on the stage of history as they rushed by on the currents of time.

It may prove a law of language (or hermeneutics) generally, and certainly a fact of literature from the Romantics on down to Eiot's own contemporaries, that the farther the poet penetrates into the recesses of his self, the more desperately is he in need of a sheet-anchor—a creed, a view of history, a dogma—to tether him to an encompassing view of reality. For the man of action, the complexity of the world of events moves to the forefront, while introspection and a fascination with the minutiae of experience are, if present at all, of secondary importance. But for the poet who also writes social criticism, language is tugged in at least two different directions. There results what Eliot himself, in *After Strange Gods*, acknowledges to be ". . . an apparent incoherence between my verse and my critical prose," adding that ". . . in one's prose reflexions one may be legitimately occupied with ideals, whereas in the writing of verse one can only deal with actuality."[86] The split between actuality and verse, on the one hand, and ideals and prose reflection, on the other, corresponds to the primacy of the "bewildering minute" for the poet, and the preoccupation with "ideals" for the moralist.

After Strange Gods plays a role as *compensatory myth* that is closely tied to the parallel role played by *Selected Essays*. The two volumes are two separate versions of the same argument, with one overwhelming difference. *Selected Essays* deals with the *literary myth* of a Second Fall of Man; *After Strange Gods* focuses directly on the dogma of Original Sin itself. Whereas *Selected Essays* deals with the myth of adequation from a more or less literary perspective, *After Strange Gods* confronts the failure of adequation at its theological moment of inception. Belief in Original Sin accounts for the primary inadequacy of language, the analogous nature of all theological propositions, the dilemma which Negative Theology poses for the poet, the double remove at which Eliot here finds himself in his attempt to find words adequate to his own experience, to find "meaning" or "pattern" in the fallen world adequate to a full understanding of the mysteries of dogma.

This helps to explain both the tone and subject of *After Strange Gods*. Its tone is that of the despairing "moralist" who wishes to "preach . . .

primarily to those who . . . are possibly convertible."[87] Its subject is the burning need of the "moralist" to emphasize the "ideal," to underscore the importance of the third moment in his interpretive scheme—the pursuit of meaning and pattern—by denigrating and relegating to secondary importance the role of the "bewildering minute":

> At this point I shall venture to generalise, and suggest that with the disappearance of the idea of Original Sin, with the disappearance of the idea of intense moral struggle, the human beings presented to us both in poetry and in prose fiction to-day, and more patently among the serious writers than in the underworld of letters, tend to become less and less real.

Continues Eliot:

> It is in fact in moments of moral and spiritual struggle depending upon spiritual sanctions, rather than in those "bewildering minutes" in which we are all very much alike, that men and women come nearest to being real.[88]

To illustrate this point, Eliot the moralist then proceeds to an examination of the writings of several of his distinguished contemporaries. In comparing "the differences of moral implication" in Katherine Mansfield's *Bliss*, D. H. Lawrence's *The Shadow in the Rose Garden*, and James Joyce's *The Dead*, Eliot concludes that Mansfield's short story "is limited to . . . [a] sudden change of feeling," with "moral and social ramifications . . . outside of the terms of reference"; Eliot finds in the relations of "Lawrence's men and women . . . the absence of any moral or social sense"; and only in Joyce does Eliot find "orthodoxy of sensibility," calling him "the most ethically orthodox of the more eminent writers of my time. . . ."[89]

But these texts turn out to be illustrations of a more general argument, which ties together *After Strange Gods* and *Selected Essays* by reiterating the proper relation of orthodoxy to tradition:

> What I have been leading up to is the following assertion: that when morals cease to be a matter of tradition and orthodoxy—that is, of the habits of the community formulated, corrected, and elevated by the continuous thought and direction of the Church—and when each man is to elaborate his own, then *personality* becomes a thing of alarming importance.[90]

> I hold—in summing up—that a *tradition* is rather a way of feeling and acting which characterises a group throughout generations; and that it must largely be, or that many of the elements in it must be, unconscious; whereas the maintenance of *orthodoxy* is a matter which calls for the exercise of all our conscious intelligence. The two will therefore considerably complement each other. Not only is it possible to conceive of a tradition being definitely bad; a good tradition might, in changing circumstances, become out of date.

In conclusion, Eliot declares:

> Tradition has not the means to criticise itself; it may perpetuate much that is trivial or of transient significance as well as what is vital and permanent. And while tradition, being a matter of good habits, is necessarily real only in a social group, orthodoxy exists whether realised in anyone's thought or not. Orthodoxy also, of course, represents a consensus between the living and the dead: but a whole generation might conceivably pass without any orthodox thought; or, as by Athanasius, orthodoxy may be upheld by one man against the world. Tradition may be conceived as a by-product of right living, not to be aimed at directly. It is of the blood, so to speak, rather than of the brain: it is the means by which the vitality of the past enriches the life of the present. In the co-operation of both is the reconciliation of thought and feeling.[91]

Reconciliation of thought and feeling, explicitly the formula for achieving adequation, is therefore, a matter of theology; the quest for adequate form is, ultimately, a plea for an understanding of mysteries that comes only through the illumination of faith.

As its subtitle, *A Primer of Modern Heresy*, indicates, *After Strange Gods* is a statement of belief, a backup to *Selected Essays*, a necessary foundation in religion to anchor ever more firmly his *compensatory myth* in literature. Both volumes ought to be viewed as a measure of the anxiety attendant on Eliot's pursuit of his craft, of the quest for certitude that results from confronting the "bewildering minute" in experience. In this way, all of Eliot's social criticism—early and late—constitutes an invisible genre in Eliot's artistic development, a necessary counterpoise to his artistic experimentation. Like matter and antimatter, each presupposes and makes possible the other. Due in large measure to its strident, bristling tone, *After Strange Gods* has not received recognition for what it is: a religious *compensatory myth*, rooted in the need to believe, and cast in the form of a jeremiad justified on grounds of sincerity. In a society such as his own, says Eliot, "wormeaten with Liberalism, the only thing possible for a person with strong convictions is to state a point of view and leave it at that."[92] Moreover, *After Strange Gods* embodies in its substance, if not its tone, the whole impulse behind Eliot's social criticism: the need to define self and society within an encircling absolute, the passionate quest for a society that is, to invoke Karl Popper's frame of reference, closed.[93] Translating Eliot's social criticism into a typology discloses a pattern not unlike the two models of society proposed by Charles Lindblom: "Model 1," a vision of "harmony," guided by an "elite," an "ideal society ... knit together by consensus," and "Model 2," a "conflict-ridden society," one that is "preference-guided or volition-guided," and for which no "synoptic theory exists,"[94] a society that, in Eliot's words, ". . . moves/ In appetency, on its metalled ways / Of time past and time future."

Both *The Idea of a Christian Society* and *Notes towards the Definition of Culture* limn a vision of a conservative society—hierarchic, telic, and organic in structure—that accords with Lindblom's Model 1. Like *After Strange Gods*, *The Idea of a Christian Society* springs from an act of personal witness in September 1938, a "feeling of humiliation, which seemed to demand an act of personal contrition, of humility, repentance and amendment."[95] Throughout its pages it echoes the thinking of Coleridge:

> In using the term "Idea" of a Christian Society I do not mean primarily a concept derived from the study of any societies which we may choose to call Christian: I mean something that can only be found in an understanding of the end to which a Christian Society, to deserve the name, must be directed. I do not limit the application of the term to a per-fected Christian Society on earth; and I do not comprehend in it societies merely because some profession of Christian faith, or some vestige of Christian practice, is retained. My concern with contemporary society, accordingly, will not be primarily with specific defects, abuses or injustices but with the question, what—if any—is the "idea" of the society in which we live? to what end is it arranged?[96]

Answering his own question, Eliot specifies that it ". . . would be a society in which the natural end of man—virtue and well-being in community—is acknowledged for all, and the supernatural end—beatitude—for those who have the eyes to see it."[97] Since such a society would be knit together by ". . . a unified religious-social code of behavior," the product of a continuity between tradition and orthodoxy, there should be no need ". . . for the ordinary individual to be wholly conscious of what elements are distinctly religious and Christian, and what are merely social and identified with his religion by no logical implication."[98] Modifying Coleridge's concept of a "clerisy," Eliot proposes in its place a "Community of Christians":

> My Community of Christians, then, in contrast to Coleridge's clerisy, could hardly include the whole of the teaching body. On the other hand, it would include, besides many of the laity engaged in various occupations, many, but not all, of the clergy. A national clergy must of course include individual priests of different intellectual types and levels; and, as I suggested before, belief has a vertical as well as a horizontal measurement: to answer fully the question "What does *A* believe?" one must know enough about *A* to have some notion of the level on which he is capable of believing anything. The Community of Christians—a body of very nebulous outline—would contain both clergy and laity of superior intellectual and/or spiritual gifts. And it would include some of those who are ordinarily spoken of, not always with flattering intention, as "intellectuals."[99]

Contemplation of such an "Idea" must also lead to an indictment of

> the hypertrophy of the motive of Profit into a social ideal, the distinction between the *use* of natural resources and their exploitation, the use of labour and its exploitation, the advantages unfairly accruing to the trader in contrast to the primary producer, the

> misdirection of the financial machine, the iniquity of usury, and other features of a
> commercialised society which must be scrutinised on Christian principles.[100]

"We are being made aware," adds Eliot,

> that the organization of society on the principle of private profit, as well as public
> destruction, is leading both to the deformation of humanity by unregulated industrialism,
> and to the exhaustion of natural resources, and that a good deal of our material progress
> is a progress for which succeeding generations may have to pay dearly. . . . For a long
> enough time we have believed in nothing but the values arising in a mechanised,
> commercialised, urbanised way of life: it would be well for us to face the permanent
> conditions upon which God allows us to live upon this planet. . . . We need to know how
> to see the world as the Christian Fathers saw it; and the purpose of reascending to origins
> is that we should be able to return, with greater spiritual knowledge, to our own situation.
> We need to recover the sense of religious fear, so that it may be overcome by religious
> hope.[101]

And anticipating the argument of *Notes towards the Definition of Culture*,
Eliot goes on to emphasize

> the steady influence which operates silently in any mass society organised for profit, for
> the depression of standards of art and culture. The increasing organization of advertise-
> ment and propaganda—or the influencing of masses of men by any means except through
> their intelligence—is all against them. The economic system is against them; the chaos of
> ideals and confusion of thought in our large scale mass education is against them; and
> against them also is the disappearance of any class of people who recognise public and
> private responsibility of patronage of the best that is made and written.[102]

In his "Introduction" to *Notes towards the Definition of Culture*, Eliot
observes that in general, "the word culture is used in two ways: by a kind of
synecdoche . . . or . . . as a kind of emotional stimulant—or anaesthetic." As
a synecdoche, it is used "when the speaker has in mind one of the elements or
evidences of culture—such as 'art.' "[103] Yet as one of four "master tropes,"[104]
the synecdoche (or synecdochic form), which subsumes such relationships as
"part for the whole," "sign for the thing signified," "symbol for that which is
symbolized," and "microcosm for macrocosm," remains for Eliot what it had
been throughout his social criticism: the paradigm for any discussion of
culture. Keeping in mind that, in Eliot's ideal society, hierarchic organization of class corresponds to class structure, degrees of education or levels of
awareness, and continuity of tradition and orthodoxy, it is inevitable that he
begins by discussing the three senses of culture: development of the
"individual," "the group or class," and "the whole society." Here, as well as
throughout the remaining five chapters, Eliot's method is to identify the
symbolic or synecdochic relationships among and between these elements.
His emphasis, for example, on culture as a whole way of life simply reiterates
once again his organic, telic, and hierarchic vision of society:

> Taking now the point of view of identification, the reader must remind himself, as the author has constantly to do, of how much is here embraced by the term *culture*. It includes all the characteristic activities and interests of a people: Derby Day, Henley Regatta, Cowes, the twelfth of August, a cup final, the dog races, the pin table, the dart board, Wensleydale cheese, boiled cabbage cut into sections, beetroot in vinegar, nineteenth-century Gothic churches and the music of Elgar. The reader can make his own list. And then we have to face the strange idea that what is part of our culture is also a part of our *lived* religion.[105]

His defense of "class" and "elite" rests on the importance to the "structure of society ... from "top" to "bottom" ... [of] a continuous gradation of levels":

> it is important to remember that we should not consider the upper levels as possessing *more* culture than the lower, but as representing a more conscious culture and a greater specialisation of culture. I incline to believe that no true democracy can maintain itself unless it contains these different levels of culture.[106]

In the third chapter, "Unity and Diversity: The Region," Eliot argues the importance of "regionalism" and "local cultures"; in the fourth chapter, "Unity and Diversity: Sect and Cult," he points out that in religion a similar need exists for maintaining the balance between "universality of doctrine with particularity of cult and devotion."[107]

What I find most significant about *Notes towards the Definition of Culture* is Eliot's shift in aesthetic strategy away from the strident polemic that marked *After Strange Gods* to the master dialectician's use of the prose of definition or denotation. This is, of course, an outgrowth of a more general characteristic of Eliot's prose style, its dependence on "What Precisely / And If and Perhaps and But,"[108] its preoccupation with topology, with boundary and frontier, its attempts to narrow down or fix meaning even temporarily, its struggles to pin down the coordinates of definition within a field of meaning which at every moment threatens to transform itself into a minor province of some larger, more comprehensive domain of meaning. You will recall that in "The Music of Poetry," Eliot defined the "music of a word" as occuring at "a point of intersection: it arises from its relation first to the words immediately preceding and following it, and indefinitely to the rest of its context; and from another relation, that of its immediate meaning in that context to all the other meanings which it has had in other contexts, to its greater or less wealth of association. . . . This is an 'allusiveness' . . . which is in the nature of words, and which is equally the concern of every kind of poet."[109]

By contrast, Eliot's prose style here is deliberately antimusical. It attempts to arrest the movement towards "allusiveness" which can take place at any "intersection" where a new relation can suddenly bridge the gap between two words in different contexts. As a consequence, this prose demands of the reader both patience and participation. Since each definition presupposes a prior or posterior level of meaning, requiring further attention to articulate what has been left unsaid, Eliot's method is to lead the reader from one definition to the next, step by step, peeling away layers of meaning. And Eliot's method is deliberate. *Notes towards the Definition of Culture* boasts an epigraph drawn from the Oxford English Dictionary: "DEFINITION: 1. The setting of bounds; limitation (rare)—1483."[110] Moreover, the leisurely pace of the dialectic is governed by the subject matter itself: the synecdoche, the synecdochic model of society. Within the bounds of this model, Eliot's task is to draw forth and render explicit relationships that by definition already inhere in the synecdoche—relationships of part to whole, of signifier to that signified, of microcosm to macrocosm, of lower level to higher level as consciousness spirals upwards towards complexity or sinks downwards towards unity. As a model of a consubstantial cosmos, the synecdoche provides Eliot an opportunity to trace the kinds of continuity that would characterize an ideal cosmos.

Let several examples suffice. On one occasion, Eliot calls attention to the balance between unity and diversity, the need being to maintain this balance by preserving distance between part and whole.

> At this point I introduce a new notion: that of the vital importance for a society of *friction* between its parts. Accustomed as we are to think in figures of speech taken from machinery, we assume that a society, like a machine, should be as well oiled as possible, provided with ball bearings of the best steel. We think of friction as waste of energy. I shall not attempt to substitute any other imagery: perhaps at this point the less we think in analogies the better. . . . So, within limits, the friction not only between individuals but between groups, seems to me quite necessary for civilisation. The universality of irritation is the best assurance of peace.[111]

On another occasion, Eliot demonstrates why the logical term of relations between two entities ("cultures") must be maintained as a limiting case, although unimaginable in actuality.

> European culture has an area, but no definite frontiers: and you cannot build Chinese walls. The notion of a purely self-contained European culture would be as fatal as the notion of a self-contained national culture: in the end as absurd as the notion of preserving a local uncontaminated culture in a single county or village of England. We are therefore pressed to maintain the ideal of a world culture, while admitting that it is something we cannot *imagine*. We can only conceive it, as the logical term of relations between cultures.[112]

Or, to comprehend the dynamic opposition of centrifugal and centripetal forces that energize and hold together his synecdochic model of society, Eliot will find himself ". . . obliged to maintain two contradictory propositions:

that religion and culture are aspects of one unit, and that they are two different and contrasted things." Depending on our point of view, the dialectic moves in either of two directions. Adds Eliot:

> I wish to maintain *both* these points of view. We do not leave the earlier stage of development behind us: it is that upon which we build. The identity of religion and culture remains on the unconscious level, upon which we have superimposed a conscious structure wherein religion and culture are contrasted and can be opposed. The *meaning* of the terms "religion" and "culture" is of course altered between these two levels. To the unconscious level we constantly tend to revert, as we find consciousness an excessive burden. . . . Totalitarianism appeals to the desire to return to the womb.[113]

Like an Anglican divine delivering a sermon on the meanings which repose in a religious icon, Eliot then offers by way of further explanation what is, in effect, a sermon in miniature, a compact morality play: the *strain* of diverging religion and culture, the price of a more highly developed civilization, leads us to *indulge* in alcohol as an *anodyne*, a false solution against which we must struggle through *unremitting effort*.

> The contrast between religion and culture imposes a strain: we escape from this strain by attempting to revert to an identity of religion and culture which prevailed at a more primitive stage; as when we indulge in alcohol as an anodyne, we consciously seek unconsciousness. It is only by unremitting effort that we can persist in being individuals in a society, instead of merely members of a disciplined crowd. Yet we remain members of the crowd, even when we succeed in being individuals.[114]

Or, Eliot will focus directly on epistemology, pressing home the congruence between the hierarchies of understanding and culture in mankind's quest for higher consciousness. Just as "culture can never be wholly conscious—there is always more to it than we are conscious of . . . ,"[115] so "understanding involves an area more extensive than that of which one can be conscious. . . ."[116] Both culture and consciousness are pictured as vast fields upon which we focus attention as we would a narrow beam of light; beyond that beam is penumbra, surrounded by infinite darkness. There is much to be said for the view that *Notes towards the Definition of Culture* is a bravura exercise in veneration of a religious icon: a synecdochal, sacramental model of culture, cosmos, and society. My point here is that Eliot has figured forth a model of a consubstantial universe, a *compensatory vision* of a Christian Society through a fruitful dialectic between the prose of definition and the figure of the synecdoche.

There is perhaps no better way to conclude than to come full circle back to the passage from *After Strange Gods* in which Eliot points to the inner strain produced when ". . . one's prose reflexions . . . [are] legitimately occupied with ideals, whereas in the writing of verse one can only deal with actuality."[117] And there is a famous passage from Wallace Stevens that drives home to me the importance of Eliot's social criticism as a precarious yet indispensable *compensatory vision* in Eliot's struggle to maintain his vocation as a poet. Writes Wallace Stevens:

> To see the gods dispelled in mid-air and dissolve like clouds is one of the great human experiences. It is not as if they had gone over the horizon to disappear for a time; nor as if they had been overcome by other gods of greater power and profounder knowledge. It is simply that they came to nothing. Since we have always shared all things with them and have always had a part of their strength and, certainly, all of their knowledge, we shared likewise this experience of annihilation. It was their annihilation, not ours, and yet it left us feeling that in a measure, we, too, had been annihilated. It left us feeling dispossessed and alone in a solitude, like children without parents, in a home that seemed deserted, in which the amical rooms and halls had taken on a look of hardness and emptiness. . . . At the same time, no man ever muttered a petition in his heart for the restoration of those unreal shapes. There was always in every man the increasingly human self, which instead of remaining the observer, the non-participant, the delinquent, became constantly more and more all there was or so it seemed; and whether it was so or merely seemed so still left it for him to resolve life and the world in his own terms.

Therefore, Stevens contends that ". . . in an age of disbelief, when the gods have come to an end, when we think of them as the aesthetic projections of a time that has passed, men turn to a fundamental glory of their own and from that create a style of bearing themselves in reality." As a result,

> In an age of disbelief, or, what is the same thing, in a time that is largely humanistic, in one sense or another, it is for the poet to supply the satisfactions of belief, in his measure and in his style.[118]

Stevens's path is the other path, the path not chosen by Eliot, the path towards celebration of an art that springs from humanism, an art that figures forth supreme fictions. Eliot's path is the path towards participation in the symbolic, towards affirming and reaffirming its reality, towards a chastening acceptance of those dogmas that mediate the abyss between "actuality" and "ideals." In calling Eliot's social criticism an invisible genre, always and everywhere part of his life (though scorned by critics or contemporaries), I mean also to reemphasize its purpose as a continuing affirmation of an invisible universe of faith, an overarching canopy of meaning that compensates for (but is congruent with) the world as portrayed in Eliot's poetry of the actual.[119]

If Eliot's poetry aspires to music, his social criticism checks that aspiration by reining in language. If Eliot's poetry enacts the bewildering minutes when demonic voices invade consciousness, his social criticism attacks the "inner voice" that promotes Liberalism, imperils social order, nourishes heresy, tolerates self-annointed leaders. If Eliot's poetry turns on the fits and starts of illumination, his social criticism anchors conversion firmly in God's unfolding revelation. If Eliot's poetry portrays the chaos of pluralism, his social criticism posits a "Community of Christians" to chart society's course. If Eliot's poetry struggles with appetite and desire, his social criticism rails at the motive of Profit. If Eliot's poetry struggles to draw the shapes of self in a universe of process, his social criticism counters with a Christian vision of self and soul. If we fail to take seriously Eliot's struggle to balance the "ideal" against the "actual," we forfeit understanding of the achievement of Eliot's art. We forfeit as well comprehension of one of two polar moments possible to the modern mind.

Abbreviations Used in Notes

ASG	Eliot, T. S. *After Strange Gods: A Primer of Modern Heresy*. London: Faber and Faber, 1934.
Browne	Browne, E. Martin. *The Making of T. S. Eliot's Plays*. Cambridge: The University Press, 1969. Browne's own reference signs to Eliot's manuscripts are given within [ ]. For a complete listing, see Browne, List of Manuscripts, pp. xiii-xv.
Cats	Eliot, T. S. *Old Possum's Book of Practical Cats*. New York: Harcourt, Brace & World, Harbrace Paperbound Library, 1967.
CC	Eliot, T. S. *The Confidential Clerk*.
Concord	Weinblatt, Alan, ed. "A Computerized Concordance to the Poems and Plays of T. S. Eliot." (Unpublished.)
CP	Eliot, T. S. *The Cocktail Party*.
ES	Eliot, T. S. *The Elder Statesman*.
Film	Eliot, T. S. *The Film of Murder in the Cathedral*. New York: Harcourt, Brace & Co., 1952.
FLA	Eliot, T. S. *For Lancelot Andrewes: Essays on Style and Order*. London: Faber & Gwyer, 1928.
FR	Eliot, T. S. *The Family Reunion*.
Gallup	Gallup, Donald. *T. S. Eliot: A Bibliography*. Revised and Extended ed. New York: Harcourt, Brace & World, 1969.
Idea	Eliot, T. S. "The Idea of a Christian Society." In *Christianity and Culture*. New York: Harcourt, Brace & World, 1949.
KE	Eliot, T. S. *Knowledge and Experience in the Philosophy of F. H. Bradley*. New York: Farrar, Straus & Co., 1964.
MC	Eliot, T. S. *Murder in the Cathedral*.
Notes	Eliot, T. S. "Notes towards the Definition of Culture." In *Christianity and Culture*. New York: Harcourt, Brace & World, 1949.
OPP	Eliot, T. S. *On Poetry and Poets*. New York: Farrar, Straus & Giroux, Noonday Press, 1957.
Plays	Eliot, T. S. *The Complete Plays of T. S. Eliot*. New York: Harcourt, Brace & World, 1967.
Poems	Eliot, T. S. *Collected Poems 1909-1962*. New York: Harcourt, Brace & World, 1963.
Rock	Eliot, T. S. *The Rock: A Pageant Play*. New York: Harcourt, Brace & Co., 1934.
SE	Eliot, T. S. *Selected Essays*. New ed. New York: Harcourt, Brace & World, 1964.

SW	Eliot, T. S. *The Sacred Wood: Essays on Poetry and Criticism.* 7th ed. London: Methuen & Co., 1950; University Paperback, 1960.
TCC	Eliot, T. S. *To Criticize the Critic and Other Writings.* New York: Farrar, Straus & Giroux, 1965.
UPUC	Eliot, T. S. *The Use of Poetry and the Use of Criticism: Studies in the Relation of Criticism to Poetry in England.* London: Faber & Faber, 1964.
Waste Land MS	Eliot, T. S. *The Waste Land: A Facsimile and Transcript of the Original Drafts Including the Annotations of Ezra Pound.* Edited by Valerie Eliot. New York: Harcourt Brace Jovanovich, 1971.
Youth	Eliot, T. S. *Poems Written in Early Youth.* New York: Farrar, Straus & Giroux, 1967.

Notes

I: The Quest

Chapter 1

1. FR, p. 66 (Italics added.)

2. Søren Kierkegaard, *Fear and Trembling*, trans. Walter Lowrie (Princeton: Princeton University Press, 1941; 1954), p. 124; p. 122.

3. Jean-Paul Sartre, *Nausea*, trans. Lloyd Alexander (New York: New Directions, 1964), pp. 168–69.

4. OPP, p. 8.

5. Eliot, "Donne in Our Time," in *A Garland for John Donne*, ed. Theodore Spencer (Cambridge: Harvard University Press, 1931), p. 8. [Gallup entry B19]

6. F. H. Bradley, *Appearance and Reality*, 2nd ed. (London: Oxford University Press, 1897, 1946), p. 150.

7. KE, p. 136.

8. Eliot, *Syllabus of a Course of Six Lectures on Modern French Literature* (Oxford: Oxford University Press, 1916), quoted in John D. Margolis, *T. S. Eliot's Intellectual Development 1922–1939* (Chicago: University of Chicago Press, 1972), p. 10.

9. *Syllabus*, quoted in Margolis, pp. 10–11.

10. "Rhapsody on a Windy Night," *Poems*, p. 16, ll. 23–29.

11. MC, *Plays*, pp. 14–15, 28.

12. For this interpretation I am indebted to David Perkins, *Wordsworth and the Poetry of Sincerity* (Cambridge: Harvard University Press, Belknap Press, 1964).

13. "Choruses from 'The Rock,'" *Poems*, p. 168, ll. 22–28.

14. Ibid., p. 167, l. 20; p. 168, l. 21.

15. *Poems*, p. 6, l. 80; p. 26, l. 3, ll. 23–24; p. 69, l. 417; p. 79, l. 11; p. 163, l. 29, ll. 33–35; p. 128, l. 37; p. 178, ll. 88–90; p. 189, ll. 194–95; pp. 198–99, ll. 210–12; p. 195, l. 106; p. 194, l. 92; *Plays*, CP, p. 170.

16. *Poems*, p. 176, l. 33; p. 180, ll. 142–43; p. 181, l. 162; p. 185, l. 84; p. 185, ll. 86–88; p. 208, ll. 236–37.

17. *The Compact Edition of the Oxford English Dictionary*, Vol. I, A-O, (Oxford: Clarendon Press, 1971), p. 27.

18. SW, p. 11.

19. SE, p. 115.

20. "Philosophy, precisely as 'Being speaking within us,' expression of the mute experience by itself, is creation. A creation that is at the same time a reintegration of Being: for it is not a creation in the sense of one of the commonplace *Gebilde* that history fabricates: it knows itself to be a *Gebilde* and wishes to surpass itself as *pure Gebilde*, to find again its origin. It is hence a creation in a radical sense: a creation that is at the same time an adequation, the only way to obtain an adequation." Maurice Merleau-Ponty, *The Visible and the Invisible*, ed. Claude Lefort, trans. Alphonso Lingis (Evanston: Northwestern University Press, 1968), p. 197, quoted in Remy C. Kwant, *Phenomenology of Expression* (Pittsburgh: Duquesne University Press, 1969), pp. 32-33, 46.

21. "Choruses from 'The Rock,'" *Poems*, p. 167, 11. 16-18.

22. "The Metaphysical Poets," *Times Literary Supplement*, London, 1031 (20 October 1921), pp. [669]-670, reprinted in SE, p. 247. [Gallup entry C128.]

23. *Milton* (London: Geoffrey Cumberlege, 1947), included as "Milton II" in OPP, p. 173. [Gallup entry A49.]

24. "East Coker," *Four Quartets*, in *Poems*, p. 189, 11. 181-84.

25. "Coriolan," *Poems*, p. 125, 1. 12.

26. "Below the surface-stream . . . , " *The Poems of Matthew Arnold*, ed. Kenneth Allott (New York: Barnes & Noble, 1965), p. 543.

27. TCC, p. 134.

28. OPP, p. 110.

29. Ibid., p. 106.

30. Ibid., p. 107. (Italics added.)

31. SE, p. 29.

32. OPP, p. 93.

33. Browne, [CP/1], p. 192.

34. SE, p. 29.

35. OPP, p. 93.

36. UPUC, p. 155.

37. "Beyle and Balzac," *Athenaeum*, 4648 (30 May 1919), p. 93. [Gallup entry C80.]

38. OPP, p. 23.

39. Ibid., p. 9.

40. Ibid., p. 7.

41. FR, in *Plays*, p. 96.

42. OPP, p. 7.

43. Ibid., p. 264.

44. "A Note on War Poetry," *Poems*, p. 215, ll. 12–14.

Chapter 2

1. TCC, p. 18.

2. Letter to Paul Elmer More (20 June 1934, Princeton University Library), quoted in Margolis, p. xv note.

3. Walter Jackson Bate, *The Burden of the Past and the English Poet* (Cambridge: Harvard University Press, Belknap Press, 1970), pp. 6–7.

4. SE, p. 385. (Italics added.)

5. Ibid., p. 387.

6. Ibid., p. 385.

7. Ibid., p. 388.

8. Ibid.

9. Ibid., p. 384.

10. For a historical account see Margolis, Ch. 4, pp. 103–35.

11. SE, p. 420.

12. Ibid.

13. Ibid., p. 401.

14. Ibid., p. 424.

15. Ibid., p. 422.

16. Ibid., p. 189.

17. Ibid., p. 423.

18. Ibid., p. 379.

19. Ibid., p. 375.

20. Ibid., p. 373.

21. Ibid., pp. 374–75.

22. Ibid., p. 364.

23. Ibid., pp. 360–61.

24. Ibid., p. 361.

25. Ibid., p. 359. (Italics added.)

26. Ibid., p. 329.

27. "An Emotional Unity," *Dial*, 84 (February 1928), p. 112. [Gallup entry C246]

28. "Religion Without Humanism," in *Humanism and America*, ed. Norman Foerster (New York: Farrar and Rinehart, 1930), p. 110. [Gallup entry B12]

29. Letter to Bonamy Dobrée (12 November 1927), quoted in Bonamy Dobrée, "T. S. Eliot: A Personal Reminiscence," in *T. S. Eliot: The Man and His Work*, ed. Allen Tate (New York: Delacorte Press, 1966), p. 75.

30. TCC, p. 169; p. 170; p. 171; p. 185.

31. SE, pp. 282, 283.

32. Ibid., p. 285.

33. KE, pp. 134, 132.

34. Ibid., p. 44.

35. Ibid., p. 132.

36. SE, p. 273.

37. Ibid., p. 284.

38. Ibid., p. 285.

39. Ibid., pp. 282–83.

40. Ibid., p. 284.

41. Ibid., p. 285.

42. Ibid., p. 185.

43. Ibid., pp. 53–54.

44. Ibid., p. 48.

45. Ibid., pp. 93–94.

46. Ibid., p. 406.

47. Ibid., pp. 415–16.

48. Ibid., p. 290.

49. Ibid.

50. Ibid., p. 166.

51. Ibid., pp. 394–95. (Italics added.)

52. Ibid., pp. 308–9.

53. Ibid., pp. 302–3.

54. Ibid., p. 305.

55. Ibid., pp. 125, 124.

56. Ibid., p. 124. (Italics added.)

57. Ibid., p. 125.

58. *Titus Andronicus*, II. iv. 36–37.

59. SE, p. 125.

60. "East Coker," *Four Quartets*, in *Poems*, p. 189, ll. 188–89.

61. SE, pp. 122–23.

62. Reuben Brower, *Hero & Saint* (New York: Oxford University Press, 1971), p. 314.

63. SE, p. 123.

64. Brower, p. 310.

65. Kenneth Burke, "Semantic and Poetic Meaning," in *The Philosophy of Literary Form* (New York: Vintage Books, 1957), pp. 125, 144.

66. SE, p. 126.

67. Ibid., p. 137.

68. Ibid., p. 135.

69. Ibid., p. 130.

70. Ibid., p. 229.

71. Ibid., p. 201.

72. Ibid., p. 204.

73. Ibid., p. 208.

74. Ibid., p. 233.

75. Ibid., p. 204.

76. Ibid.

77. Ibid., p. 206.

78. Ibid., p. 205.

79. Ibid., p. 218.

80. Ibid., p. 205.

81. TCC, p. 16.

82. SE, p. 248.

83. Ibid.

84. Ibid., p. 254.

85. Ibid., p. 242.

86. Ibid., p. 245.

87. Ibid., p. 446.

88. Ibid.

89. Ibid.

90. Ibid., p. 247.

91. Ibid., p. 243.

92. William Wordsworth, *The Poetical Works of William Wordsworth*, 2nd ed., ed. E. de Selincourt, Vol. II (Oxford: Clarendon Press, 1965), pp. 438, 441.

93. SE, pp. 256–57.

94. Ibid., p. 261.

95. Ibid., p. 252.

96. Ibid., p. 250.

97. Ibid., p. 256. For comprehensive histories of this dispute see especially Walter Jackson Bate, *From Classic to Romantic* (New York: Harper, 1946) and Stuart M. Tave, *The Amiable Humorist* (Chicago: University of Chicago Press, 1960).

98. Ibid., p. 255.

99. Ibid, p. 185.

100. SE, p. 252.

101. Ibid., pp. 260, 262.

102. Ibid., p. 258.

Chapter 3

1. Bernard Bergonzi, *T. S. Eliot*, Masters of World Literature Series, ed. Louis Kronenberger (New York: Collier Books, 1972), p. 61.

2. UPUC, p. 155.

3. Browne, [FR/H MS], p. 132.

4. OPP, pp. 235, 225, 226.

5. SE, p. 277. (Italics added.)

6. WLMS, p. 43.

7. William Hazlitt, "On Modern Comedy," in *Prose of the Romantic Period*, ed. Carl R. Woodring (Boston: Houghton Mifflin, Riverside Editions, 1961), pp. 334, 333.

8. OPP, p. 235.

9. Matthew Arnold, "The Buried Life," *The Poems of Matthew Arnold*, p. 272, ll. 16–22; p. 274, ll. 60–63; ll. 72–75; p. 275, ll. 84–85.

10. CP, *Plays*, pp. 134–35. (Italics added.)

11. Ibid., p. 135. (Italics added.)

12. Browne, [CP/1], p. 191.

13. Ibid., [CP/1], p. 211. (Italics added.)

14. W. B. Yeats, *Essays and Introductions* (New York: Macmillan, 1961), p. 226. (Italics added.)

15. Ortega y Gasset, *Man and People*, trans. Willard R. Trask (New York: W. W. Norton, 1957), pp. 156–57. (Italics added.)

16. "The Love Song of J. Alfred Prufrock," *Poems*, p. 5, l. 56; p. 4, ll. 42–43, l. 51.

17. SE, p. 27. (Italics added.)

18. Ibid., p. 29.

19. Ibid., p. 28.

20. Ibid., p. 110.

21. Ibid., p. 111.

22. Ibid., p. 9.

23. Ortega y Gasset, *History As A System*, pp. 199–200; pp. 203, 205, 214, 217. (Italics added.)

24. Herbert Howarth, *Notes on Some Figures Behind T. S. Eliot* (Boston: Houghton Mifflin, 1964), p. 209.

25. Josiah Royce, *The Problem of Christianity*, Vol. II, Lecture IX, *The Community and the Time-Process* (Chicago: Henry Regnery, Gateway Edition, 1968), pp. 40–41. (Italics added.)

26. SE, p. 142.

27. Browne, [CP/1], p. 196.

28. SE, p. 4.

29. Ibid., p. 9.

30. "Burnt Norton," *Four Quartets*, in *Poems*, p. 175, 11. 1–2.

31. "East Coker," *Four Quartets*, in *Poems*, p. 182 1. 1; p. 190, 1. 211.

32. "Little Gidding," *Four Quartets*, in *Poems*, p. 208, 1. 239.

33. Matthew Arnold, "Growing Old," *Poems*, p. 539, 11. 23–24.

34. "Gerontion," *Poems*, p. 30, 1. 31.

35. "The Waste Land," *Poems*, p. 64, 11. 301–2.

36. CP, *Plays*, p. 211.

37. Calvin O. Schrag, *Experience and Being: Prolegomena to a Future Ontology* (Evanston: Northwestern University Press, 1969), Chapter 2 passim.

38. Ibid.

39. Ibid.

40. "The Dry Salvages," *Four Quartets*, in *Poems*, p. 192, 11. 40–47.

Chapter 4

1. "The Love Song of J. Alfred Prufrock," *Poems*, p. 4, 11. 32–33; 1. 48; p. 6, 1. 80; 11. 88–89; p. 7, 1. 120.

2. "Eyes That Last I Saw in Tears," *Poems*, p. 133, 1. 9; 1. 15; 1. 2; 1. 9; 1. 3; 1. 11.

3. MC, *Plays*, pp. 26–27.

4. Ibid., p. 46.

5. "The Love Song of J. Alfred Prufrock," *Poems*, p. 7, 1.113.

6. FR, *Plays*, p. 77.

7. Ibid., pp. 111, 109.

8. CP, *Plays*, pp. 156–57.

9. Ibid., p. 169.

10. Ibid.

11. Ibid., p. 170.

12. Ibid., p. 176.

13. Ibid., p. 189.

14. Ibid., p. 184.

15. Ibid., p. 192.

16. Ibid., p. 193.

17. Ibid., p. 210.

18. CC, *Plays*, p. 235.

19. William Wordsworth, "My Heart Leaps Up," *The Poetical Works of William Wordsworth*, vol. I, p. 226, ll. 8–9; ll. 3–5.

20. "Ash-Wednesday V," *Poems*, p. 93, l. 181.

21. "The Waste Land," *Poems*, p. 62, l. 242; l. 255.

22. "Ash-Wednesday," *Poems*, p. 85, l. 10.

23. "The Hollow Men III," *Poems*, pp. 80–81, ll. 48–51.

24. "La Figlia che Piange," *Poems*, p. 26, l. 20; ll. 23–24.

25. "The Waste Land," *Poems*, p. 53, ll. 17–18.

26. Ibid., pp. 68–69, ll. 402–410.

27. MC, *Plays*, p. 46. (Italics added.)

28. "Portrait of a Lady," *Poems*, pp. 10, ll. 61–68. (Italics added.)

29. CP, *Plays*, p. 189. (Italics added.)

30. "The Love Song of J. Alfred Prufrock," *Poems*, p. 4, ll. 45–46.

31. "The Hollow Men," *Poems*, p. 79, l. 19.

32. "Burnt Norton II," *Four Quartets*, in *Poems*, p. 177, ll. 54–55.

33. "Animula," *Poems*, pp. 103–4, ll. 26–30. (Italics added.)

34. "The Love Song of J. Alfred Prufrock," *Poems*, p. 5, l. 72.

35. "Gerontion," *Poems*, p. 30, l. 51.

36. ES, *Plays*, p. 342.

37. SE, p. 9. (Italics added.)

38. Stephen Spender, "Remembering Eliot," in *T . S. Eliot: The Man and His Work*, ed. Allen Tate, pp. 55–56. Quoted in Frank Kermode, Introduction to *Selected Prose of T. S. Eliot*, ed. Frank Kermode (New York: Harcourt Brace Jovanovich; Farrar, Straus and Giroux, 1975).

39. SE, p. 212.

40. "Reflections on Contemporary Poetry," *The Egoist*, July 1919, p. 39. [Gallup entry C84.] (Italics added.)

41. SE, p. 4.

42. Ibid.

43. UPUC, p. 33. (Italics added.)

44. Ibid.

45. SE, pp. 348–49. (Italics added.)

46. UPUC, p. 35. (Italics added.)

47. Ibid., p. 141. (Italics added.)

48. TCC, p. 21.

49. SE, pp. 7–8.

50. UPUC, pp. 78–79.

51. Ibid., p. 148. (Italics added.)

52. SE, pp. 18–19. (Italics added.)

53. SW, p. 5.

54. Ibid.

55. Ibid., p. 11.

56. SE, p. 96. (Italics added.)

57. OPP, p. 203.

58. Ibid., p. 299.

59. Ibid.

60. SE, pp. 10–11.

61. OPP, pp. 109–10.

62. UPUC, p. 115.

63. Ibid., p. 138. (Italics added.)

64. OPP, p. 301.

65. Ibid., p. 276. (Italics added.)

66. Ibid., p. 306.

67. TCC, pp. 177–78. (Italics added.)

68. "The Hawthorne Aspect," *Little Review*, August 1918, p. 52. [Gallup entry C67.]

69. OPP, pp. 301, 297, 301.

70. Ibid., p. 47. (Italics added.)

71. Ibid., p. 43.

72. Ibid., p. 272.

73. UPUC, p. 44.

74. SE, p. 153.

75. Ibid., p. 141.

76. Ibid., p. 170. (Italics added.)

77. Ibid., p. 179. (Italics added.)

78. OPP, p. 48.

79. Keats's letter to Benjamin Bailey, November 22, 1817 (Hampstead) quoted in UPUC, p. 101.

II: The Historical Paradigm

Chapter 5

1. TCC, p. 57.

2. OPP, p. 21.

3. Ibid., p. 191.

4. Ibid., p. 27.

5. Ibid., p. 31.

6. Ibid., p. 191.

7. TCC, p. 57.

8. OPP, p. 21.

9. Ibid., p. 28.

10. "A Commentary," *The Criterion* XII.46 (October 1932): 78–79. [Gallup entry C337]. Hence a full and self-informed recognition of the "notion of . . . language as perpetually in change," insofar as it indicates acquiescence to process, signals for Eliot, if not the birth, nevertheless a moment of vital importance in the development of modern self-consciousness. Needless to say, this attitude "is not one which had impressed itself upon the age of Johnson. He looked back some two centuries and marked in language, as in manners, a continuous improvement." And even "Wordsworth himself," continues Eliot, fails to "evince any more consciousness of the constancy with which language must change than does Johnson: what he thought he had established was return to a diction of popular simplicity and rural purity. In his perception that the language of literature must not lose its connexion with the language of speech, Wordsworth was right; but his standard of the right poetic diction was no more relative than Johnson's." OPP, p. 213.

11. Ibid., p. 76.

12. TCC, p. 184.

13. OPP, pp. 28–31.

14. TCC, p. 49. (Italics added.)

15. OPP, p. 29.

16. TCC, p. 147.

17. SE, p. 5.

18. Ortega, *The Dehumanization of Art*, p. 42. Quoted by Walter Jackson Bate, *Criticism: The Major Texts*, Enlarged ed. (New York: Harcourt Brace Jovanovich, 1970), p. 662.

19. OPP, p. 55.

20. Thomas S. Kuhn, *The Structure of Scientific Revolutions*, 2nd ed. (Chicago: The University of Chicago Press, 1970), pp. 2, 7, 112.

21. Ibid., p. 113.

22. Ortega, *The Dehumanization of Art*, p. 42. Quoted by Bate, *Criticism*, p. 662.

23. Kuhn, p. 7. A theoretical discussion of "The Historicity of Genres" may be found in E. D. Hirsch, Jr., *Validity in Interpretation* (New Haven: Yale University Press, 1967). Although Hirsch invokes the formidable figure of E. H. Gombrich in support of his point that a "new type of meaning"—be it a genre or individual work—while always involving a "leap of imagination," would be impossible unless one "were capable of perceiving analogies and making novel subsumptions under previously known types" (pp. 104–5), he fails to pursue the full implications of what he terms "the process of metaphor." The principal reason is, of course, Hirsch's strong conviction that "validity," if not "certainty" of meaning, is possible. Both Gombrich's *Art and Illusion* (Princeton: Princeton University Press, 1969) and Thomas Kuhn's *The Structure of Scientific Revolutions* (Chicago: University of Chicago Press, 1970) stand as contemporary monuments to the attempt to integrate the insights of "Gestalt" psychology into an epistemology of scientific or artistic creation, without which any attempt to erect an aesthetics or poetics of process becomes virtually impossible. Much of their success rests on a powerful unwillingness to allow their speculative hypotheses to harden into intellectual dogma, or to allow their essentially *heuristic* speculation about the "active mind" and its "effort after meaning" (Gombrich, p. 395), combined with the rise and fall of canons of artistic, linguistic, or scientific convention to degenerate into a narrow philosophy of historicism, periodicity, or the archaic remnants of nineteenth-century dialectical metaphysics. No age escapes the temptation to resurrect historical determinism or the myth of a *Zeitgeist*: much of the popularity of contemporary structuralism is little more than nineteenth-century philosophy writ large—but often lacking its original depth of insight and intellectual excitement. And it is a perilously short distance from the questing heuristic which underlies Kuhn's notion of "paradigms" to the jungle of structuralist platitudes and deterministic premises in *Les mots et les choses* which form the essence of Michel Foucault's *epistemes*. But although "Foucault's *epistemes* are strikingly reminiscent of . . . Kuhn's 'paradigms,'" even so partisan a critic as Jean Piaget is compelled to recognize the shortcomings of the former: "[Foucault] has no canon for the selection of an *episteme's* characteristics; important ones are omitted, and the choice between alternative ones is

arbitrary" (pp. 132–33). Piaget is forced to the unenviable conclusion that "Foucault has it in for man; the human sciences he views as a merely momentary outcome of 'mutations,' 'historical a priorities,' 'epistemes'; these follow one another in time, but their sequence has no rationale" (p. 129). "What we would want of Foucault is, accordingly, that he prepare the way for a second Kant to reawaken us, along with himself, from dogmatic slumber" (p. 129). Instead, he abandons exploration entirely, miring us beyond rescue in a static—and often indecipherable—dogmatics. Jean Piaget, *Structuralism* (New York: Basic Books, 1970).

24. "I," in *Revelation*, p. 31.

25. Bate, *Criticism*, p. 659.

26. SE, p. 34.

27. "A Commentary," *The Criterion* XII.46 (October 1932): 76–77.

28. SE, pp. 15, 19, 22. I have been guided by W. J. Bate's excellent observation that "'The Function of Criticism' . . . should be read as a supplement to 'Tradition and the Individual Talent.'" Bate, *Criticism*, p. 521.

29. SE, p. 5.

30. Introduction to *Savonarola: A Dramatic Poem*, by Charlotte Eliot (London: R. Cobden-Sanderson, 1926), p. vii. [Gallup entry B4.]

31. TCC, p. 152.

32. Introduction to *The Art of Poetry*, by Paul Valéry (New York: Random House, Vintage Books, 1958), p. xxiii. [Gallup entry B79.]

33. Introduction to *Savonarola*, p. vii.

34. OPP, p. 114.

35. SE, p. 6.

36. Peter L. Berger and Thomas Luckmann, *The Social Construction of Reality: A Treatise In The Sociology of Knowledge* (New York: Doubleday & Co., Anchor Books, 1966), p. 3.

37. UPUC, p. 108.

38. SE, p. 5.

39. UPUC, pp. 18–19.

Chapter 6

1. OPP, p. 57.

2. SE, pp. 178–79.

3. OPP, p. 187.

4. Ibid., p. 192.

5. Ibid., p. 188.

6. Ibid., p. 187.

7. See *Notes*, p. 103.

8. OPP, p. 212.

9. Bate, *Burden of the Past*, p. 19.

10. OPP, p. 61.

11. Ibid., p. 62.

12. SE, p. 237.

13. UPUC, p. 122.

14. OPP, p. 108

15. UPUC, p. 13.

16. Ibid., p. 14.

17. Ibid., p. 135.

18. Ibid., p. 136.

19. Ibid., p. 140.

20. TCC, p. 39.

21. Ibid., p. 41.

22. Ibid., pp. 39–40.

23. Ibid., p. 40.

24. Ibid., p. 41.

25. Ibid., p. 40.

26. "I," in *Revelation*, p. 8.

27. TCC, p. 39.

28. Ibid., p. 40.

29. T. S. Eliot, Introduction to *The Art of Poetry*, by Paul Valéry (New York: Random House, 1958; Vintage Books, 1961), p. xvi. [Gallup entry B79n.]

30. OPP, p. 10.

31. Ibid., p. 15.

32. Ibid., p. 16.

33. Ibid., p. 12.

34. Ibid., p. 8.

35. Ibid., pp. 9–10.

36. Ibid., p. 3.

37. Ibid., p. 9.

38. See the essential monograph by Justus Buchler, *The Concept of Method* (New York: Columbia University Press, 1961).

39. OPP, p. 121.

40. Ortega, *History As A System*, p. 171.

41. OPP, p. 122.

42. Ibid., p. 124.

43. Ibid., p. 122.

44. Ibid., p. 119.

45. MS entry to CP [CP/1] in Browne, p. 208. (Italics added.)

46. SE, p. 356. (Italics added.)

47. OPP, p. 44.

48. Ibid., p. 42.

49. SE, p. 21.

50. Ibid., p. 181.

51. T. S. Eliot, "I," in *Revelation*, ed. John Baillie and Hugh Martin (London: Faber and Faber, 1937), p. 29. [Gallup entry B32.]

52. George Kubler, *The Shape of Time: Remarks on the History of Things* (New Haven: Yale University Press, 1962), p. 72.

53. Paul Valéry, *History and Politics*, trans. Denise Folliot and Jackson Mathews (New York: Pantheon Books, Bollingen Series, 1962), pp. 58, 62, 64.

Chapter 7

1. SE, p. 36.

2. Ibid., pp. 36–37.

3. Ibid., p. 118.

4. Ibid., p. 138.

5. A number of pioneering studies explore the complex and shifting relations among realism, comedy, and satire. "At the bottom of much so-called realism," declares Irving Babbitt, "is a special type of satire, a satire that is the product of violent emotional disillusion." *Rousseau and Romanticism* (Cleveland: World Publishing Co., Meridian Books, 1947). Harry Levin has explored the problem both in "The Example of Cervantes," in his *Contexts of Criticism* (Cambridge: Harvard University Press, 1957) and *The Gates of Horn: A Study of Five French Realists* (New York: Oxford University Press, 1963). A more recent discussion focusing on the intersection of critical theory and novelistic practice occurs in Chapter 1 "Realism, Pure and Romantic" in Donald Fanger, *Dostoevsky and Romantic Realism* (Cambridge: Harvard University Press, 1965). It should not go unobserved that both in idiom and idea the germ of Eliot's remark owes much to Henri Bergson's *Le Rire* [1900], whose conception of the comic as "something mechanical encrusted on the living" is reflected not only in Eliot's scattered critical *aperçus* but even more so in his own aesthetic strategy.

6. SE, p. 36.

7. TCC, pp. 38–39.

8. SE, pp. 35–36.

9. Ibid., p. 36.

10. Wallace Stevens, "The Motive For Metaphor," in *The Collected Poems of Wallace Stevens* (New York: Alfred A. Knopf, 1964), p. 288. (Italics added.)

11. KE, p. 132. Cf. S. T. Coleridge's assertion that the imagination "gives birth to a system of symbols, harmonious in themselves and consubstantial with the truths of which they are the conductors." *Statesman's Manual*, App. B, *Works*, ed. H. N. Coleridge (1839), p. 229.

12. Preface to *Transit of Venus*, pp. viii–ix.

13. SE, p. 231.

14. Ibid., p. 118.

15. Herbert Spiegelberg, *Phenomenology in Psychology and Psychiatry: A Historical Introduction* (Evanston: Northwestern University Press, 1972), p. xxxii.

16. Ibid., p. xxix.

17. SE, p. 118.

18. Ibid., p. 233.

19. Ibid., pp. 93–94.

20. Jean-Paul Sartre, *The Words*, trans. Bernard Frechtman (Greenwich, Conn.: Fawcett Publications, 1964), pp. 78–79.

21. Jean-Paul Sartre, *Nausea*, pp. 33–34, 58, 234–35.

22. "The Family Reunion," in *Plays*, p. 79.

23. "The Dry Salvages," *Four Quartets*, in *Poems*, p. 199.

24. OPP, pp. 93–94.

25. Ibid.

26. Michael Polanyi, *The Study of Man* (Chicago: University of Chicago Press, 1959), p. 18.

27. Michael Polanyi, *The Tacit Dimension* (Garden City, NY: Doubleday & Co., 1966; Anchor Books, 1967), p. 83.

28. Michael Polanyi, "Experience and the Perception of Pattern," in *The Modeling of Mind: Computers and Intelligence*, ed. Kenneth M. Sayre and Frederick J. Crosson (New York: Simon and Schuster, Clarion Book, 1963), p. 220.

29. "East Coker," *Four Quartets*, in *Poems*, pp. 118–89.

30. Polanyi, *The Study of Man*, p. 25.

31. OPP, p. 93.

32. For a slightly different translation see Friedrich Schlegel, *Dialogue on Poetry and Literary Aphorisms*, trans. Ernst Behler and Roman Struc (University Park, PA: Pennsylvania State University Press, 1968), p. 136.

33. TCC, p. 172.

34. OPP, p. 183.

35. KE, p. 136.

36. "Burnt Norton," *Four Quartets*, in *Poems*, p. 178.

III: The Search for Form

Chapter 8

1. TCC, p. 156.

2. OPP, p. 251.

3. Ibid., p. 299.

4. Ibid., p. 17.

5. Ibid., p. 93.

6. Ibid., p. 107.

7. *Poems*, pp. 99–100.

8. *Plays*, p. 102. For a brilliant discussion of the origins of the drama of radical temporality and the dilemma of the missing present in Romantic thought and literature, see M.H. Abrams's "Structure and Style in the Greater Romantic Lyric" in *From Sensibility to Romanticism: Essays Presented to Frederick A. Pottle*, edited by Frederick W. Hilles and Harold Bloom (New York: Oxford University Press, 1965). Using as an example Coleridge's "Frost at Midnight," Abrams portrays the literature of radical temporality as a temporal drama in which " . . . the meditative mind disengages itself from the physical locale, moves back in time to the speaker's childhood, still farther back, to his own infancy, then forward to express, in the intonation of a blessing, the hope that his son shall have the life in nature that his father lacked; until, in anticipating the future, it incorporates both the present scene and the results of the remembered past in the enchanting close. . . . Plainly, Coleridge worked out the lyric device of the return-upon-itself—which he used in "Reflections on Having Left a Place of Retirement" and "Fears in Solitude," as well as in "The Eolian Harp" and "Frost at Midnight"—in a deliberate endeavor to transform a segment of experience broken out of time into a sufficient aesthetic whole." But the principal focus of Abrams's article is a special case—a subset, really—of this generic temporal paradigm, just as Euclidean geometry constitutes a special case of non-Euclidean geometry. As a special case of the literature of radical temporality, the "Greater Romantic Lyric," as Abrams calls it, displays a " . . . repeated out-in-out process, in which mind confronts nature and their interplay constitutes the poem. . . . " More specifically, the " . . . speaker begins with a description of the landscape; an aspect or change of aspect in the landscape evokes a varied but integral process of memory, thought, anticipation, and feeling which remains closely intervolved with the outer scene. . . . Often the poem rounds upon itself to end where it began, at the outer scene, but with an altered mood and deepened understanding which is the result of the intervening meditation." Needless to say, however, the poem's temporal structure can round back upon itself *without* recourse to the assumption that spiritual sustenance is to be found *only* in nature.

    In terms of my argument, superimposing the "repeated out-in-out process" upon the temporal pattern of "return-upon-itself" is rooted in the Romantic assumption that the poem's speaker could indeed find adequate meaning for the sudden accession of feeling that signaled unity between subject and object, speaker and nature. But failure to achieve this sudden accession of feeling, or inability to sustain it or to embody it in an adequate intellectual or theological framework resulted in what the Romantics themselves termed *dejection* or *despair*. If the speaker were successful, he would succeed in defeating linear temporality by binding his "days . . . each to each"—as Wordsworth puts it—in a continuity of felt joy. But if the strategy failed, the speaker would achieve not a moment of simultaneity from which sprang the illusion of a completed or authentic self but rather an overwhelming sense of alienation, disconnection, and despair.

This is what Paul de Man seems to suggest when he speaks of the " . . . temptation . . . for the self to borrow, so to speak, the temporal stability that it lacks from nature, and to devise strategies by means of which nature is brought down to a human level while still escaping from 'the unimaginable touch of time.' " Continues de Man in his essay "The Rhetoric of Temporality" in *Interpretation: Theory and Practice*, edited by Charles S. Singleton (Baltimore: The Johns Hopkins Press, 1969): "Whereas the symbol postulates the possibility of an identity or identification, allegory designates primarily a distance in relation to its own origin, and, renouncing the nostalgia and the desire to coincide, it establishes its language in the void of this temporal difference. In so doing, it prevents the self from an illusory identification with the non-self, which is now fully, though painfully, recognized as a non-self. It is this painful knowledge that we perceive at the moments when early romantic literature finds it true voice. . . . The dialectical relationship between subject and object is no longer the central statement of romantic thought, but this dialectic is now located entirely in the temporal relationships that exist within a system of allegorical signs. It becomes a conflict between a conception of the self seen in its authentically temporal predicament and a defensive strategy that tries to hide from this negative self-knowledge." When M. H. Abrams asserts that " . . . the descriptive-meditative-descriptive poem was precisely the one described and exemplified in T. S. Eliot's 'East Coker,' which begins: 'In my beginning is my end,' and ends: 'In my end is my beginning,' " *his analysis fails to take account of Eliot's endless struggle to shape a lyric whose form would avoid the inauthenticity of the completed self while coming to grips with temporal distance and nostalgia.* On the other hand, Paul de Man is open to the charge that his philosophic standpoint precludes a sympathetic understanding of symbol, synecdoche, or sacrament; at best he speaks of them in terms of "defensive strategy." An alternative to de Man's point of view is the Rev. Joseph Appleyard's "How Does a Sacrament 'Cause by Signifying'?" in *Science et Esprit*, 22, No. 2 (1970), 167–200.

9. *Poems*, p. 29. (Italics added.)

10. Ibid., p. 66. (Italics added.)

11. Ibid., p. 80. (Italics added.)

12. *Plays*, p. 44.

13. *Poems*, pp. 178–79. (Italics added.)

14. Ibid., p. 209. (Italics added.)

15. KE, p. 158.

16. Ibid., pp. 147–48.

17. Ibid., p. 132.

18. Ibid., p. 104.

19. Ibid., p. 61.

20. Richard M. Zaner's Introduction to Alfred Schutz, *Reflections on the Problem of Relevance* (New Haven: Yale University Press, 1970), pp. xv–xvi.

21. Alfred Schutz, "Multiple Realities," *Collected Papers I* (The Hague: Martinus Nijhoff, 1962), p. 207 and *Reflections on the Problem of Relevance*, p. 7.

22. Ibid., p. 12.

23. OPP, p. 77.

24. *Plays*, p. 96. (Italics added.)

25. OPP, p. 32.

26. Ibid., p. 25.

27. James Olney, *Metaphors of Self* (Princeton: Princeton University Press, 1972), p. 262.

28. "The Love Song of J. Alfred Prufrock," in *Poems*, p. 3.

29. Characteristically, Eliot here invokes as a central term in his criticism a phrase whose true significance is apparent only as it points directly to his own aesthetic strategy. Although he touches upon "the incantatory element in poetry" in "From Poe to Valéry," a more revealing definition occurs in "Johnson as Critic and Poet," OPP, p. 193: "Besides the poetry of sound—and, from one point of view, occupying an intermediate position between the poetry of sound and the poetry of sense—there is poetry which represents an attempt to extend the confines of the human consciousness and to report of things unknown, to express the inexpressible".

30. David Perkins, *The Quest for Permanence: The Symbolism of Wordsworth, Shelley, and Keats* (Cambridge: Harvard University Press, 1959), p. 103.

31. See *Waste Land* MS, especially p.22ff.

32. Cf. Harry's speech the first time he catches sight of the Eumenides in "The Family Reunion," *Plays*, p. 64:

> No, no, not there. Look there!
> Can't you see them? *You* don't see them, but I see them,
> And they see me. This is the first time that I have seen them.
> In the Java Straits, in the Sunda Sea,
> In the sweet sickly tropical night, I knew they were coming.
> In Italy, from behind the nightingale's thicket,
> The eyes stared at me, and corrupted that song.
> Behind the palm trees in the Grand Hotel
> They were always there. But I did not *see* them.
> Why should they wait until I came back to Wishwood?
> They were a thousand places where I might have met them!
> Why here? why here?

33. James Olney, *Metaphors of Self*, p. 314.

34. *Poems*, p. 26. (Italics added.)

35. For this observation I am indebted to Professor Anne Ferry of Boston College.

36. *Poems*, p. 34.

37. *Waste Land* MS, p. 5.

38. Virginia Woolf, *A Writer's Diary*, ed. Leonard Woolf (London 1954), pp. 50–51.

39. For a brilliant discussion see Hugh Kenner's "The Urban Apocalypse," in *Eliot in His Time: Essays on the Occasion of the Fiftieth Anniversary of The Waste Land*, Ed. A. Walton Litz (Princeton: Princeton University Press, 1973).

40. *Poems*, pp. 125–29.

41. Monica's words about her father in "The Elder Statesman," *Plays*, p. 300.

42. *Plays*, p. 80.

43. Ibid., p. 19.

44. *Poems*, p. 200.

45. Ibid., p. 89.

46. TCC, p. 32.

47. *Poems*, p. 138. An analysis by rhyme group of the rhyme scheme in "New Hampshire" clearly shows how sound retards the pursuit of sense:

Group a:	Between the		and the
	Between the		and the
Group b:	Golden head	head	
	Golden head		
Group c:	wing	wing	
		spring	
		wing	
	Cling,	swing	
	Spring,	sing,	
	Swing		
Group d:		hover over	
			over
	Cover over		
Group e:	grieves	grieves	
		leaves	

48. *Plays*, pp. 106–7.

49. Ibid., p. 11.

50. Ibid., pp. 29–30.

51. *Poems*, p. 139. A diagrammatic look at the rhyme scheme in "Virginia" again demonstrates the strong incantatory effect, and how it is achieved:

Group a: Red river,   red river
                              river,
             Red river,   river, river

Group b: Slow flow

Group b¹: heat
               heat

Group c: will   still
               Still.   Will
               Still   hills

Group d: move
               Never moving. Ever moving

Group e: Wait. Gates wait.
                     wait, wait,

Group f: Delay, decay.

Group g: Living, living,

52. *Poems*, pp. 175–76.

53. Ibid., p. 85.

54. Browne, Martin. *The Making of T. S. Eliot's Plays* (Cambridge: The University Press, 1969). Hereafter referred to as Browne.

55. SE, p. 39. Quoted in Michael Goldman's "Fear in the Way: The Design of Eliot's Drama," in *Eliot in his Time: Essays on the Occasion of the Fiftieth Anniversary of The Waste Land* , p. 155.

56. Stephen Spender, "Remembering Eliot," in *T. S. Eliot: The Man and His Work*, ed. Allen Tate, pp. 55–56. Quoted in Frank Kermode, Introduction to *Selected Prose of T. S. Eliot*, ed. Frank Kermode (New York: Harcourt Brace Jovanovich; Farrar, Straus and Giroux, 1975).

57. OPP, p. 86.

58. Browne, p. 41.

59. *Plays*, p. 18.

60. Ibid., pp. 27–28. (Italics added.)

61. OPP, p. 86.

62. *Plays*, p. 51.

63. SE, p. 118.

64. Browne, p. 91.

65. Browne, p. 92.

66. Ibid.

67. Ibid., p. 93.

68. Ibid., p. 100.

69. OPP, p. 90.

70. Ibid., p. 88. About the conclusion to *The Family Reunion* Eliot remarked in "Poetry and Drama" that " . . . we are left in a divided frame of mind, not knowing whether to consider the play the tragedy of the mother or the salvation of the son. The two situations are not reconciled. I find a confirmation of this in the fact that my sympathies now have come to be all with the mother, who seems to me, except perhaps for the chauffeur, the only complete human being in the play; and my hero now strikes me as an insufferable prig." See OPP, pp. 90-91. But in a letter dated 1938 Eliot had described Amy as " . . . a person of tremendous personality *on one plane*. What happen to Arthur and John are not meant to be 'disasters', but minor accidents typical of each: she *is* affected by these. But I admit that her behaviour on Harry's departure needs clearing up. But Harry's departure is not a disaster for *him*, but a triumph. The tragedy is the tragedy of Amy, of a person living on Will alone." See Browne, p. 107.

71. *Plays*, pp. 82, 108-9. "What have we been saying?" asks Harry at the conclusion to the first of the lyrical duets, signaling his return to a different plane of consciousness. In the second of the lyrical duets, Agatha, as the stage directions indicate, "goes to the window, in a somnambular fashion, and opens the curtains, disclosing the empty embrasure. She steps into the place which the EUMENIDES had occupied." At the conclusion of her duet "She moves back into the room" and echoes Harry's words: "What have I been saying? I think I was saying/ That you have a long journey."

72. OPP, p. 88.

73. *Plays*, p. 19.

74. Ibid., pp. 106-7.

75. *Poems*, pp. 175-76. (Italics added.)

76. *Plays*, p. 108.

77. Ibid., p. 105. (Italics added.)

78. *Poems*, pp. 111-24.

79. Browne, p. 91.

80. OPP, p. 91.

81. *Plays*, p. 235. (Italics added.)

82. *Writers at Work: The Paris Review Interviews*, Second Series, (New York, 1965), pp. 104-5.

83. Browne, p. 329.

84. Russell Kirk, *The Conservative Mind: From Burke to Eliot* (South Bend: Gateway Editions, 1978). See also Russell Kirk, *Eliot and His Age* (New York: Random House, 1971).

85. Ibid., p. 7.

86. ASG, p. 28.

87. Ibid., p. 13.

88. Ibid., p. 42.

89. Ibid., pp. 35–38.

90. Ibid., p. 54.

91. Ibid., pp. 29–30.

92. Ibid., p. 13.

93. See Karl Popper, *The Open Society and Its Enemies* (Princeton: Princeton University Press, 1971). See also the important discussion by F. A. Hayek, *The Confusion of Language in Political Thought*, 1968, The Institute of Economic Affairs, Occasional Paper 20.

94. Charles E. Lindblom, *Politics and Markets: The World's Political-Economic Systems*, (New York: Basic Books, Inc., 1977), pp. 249–52.

95. *Idea*, pp. 50–51.

96. Ibid., p. 6.

97. Ibid., p. 27.

98. Ibid.

99. Ibid., p. 30.

100. Ibid., p. 26.

101. Ibid., pp. 48–49.

102. Ibid., p. 32.

103. *Notes*, p. 86.

104. Kenneth Burke, *A Grammar of Motives* (Berkeley and Los Angeles: University of California Press, 1945), pp. 507–8.

105. *Notes*, p. 104.

106. Ibid., p. 121.

107. Ibid., pp. 87–88.

108. "Five-finger Exercises. V. Lines For Cuscuscaraway and Mirza Murad Ali Beg," in *Poems*, p. 137.

109. OPP, pp. 25–26.

110. *Notes*, p. 79.

111. Ibid., pp. 132–33.

112. Ibid., p. 136.

113. Ibid., pp. 142–43.

114. Ibid.

115. Ibid., p. 170.

116. Ibid., p. 114.

117. ASG, p. 28.

118. From "Two or Three Ideas," *Opus Posthumous*, ed. Samuel French Morse, New York, 1957, pp. 206-9, reprinted in *The Modern Tradition*, edited by Richard Ellmann and Charles Feidelson, Jr., (New York: Oxford University Press, 1965), pp. 217-18.

119. See the brilliant discussion in Peter L. Berger and Thomas Luckmann, *The Social Construction of Reality: A Treatise In The Sociology of Knowledge* (New York: Doubleday & Co., Anchor Books, 1966), especially Chapter III, "Society as Subjective Reality."

T. S. Eliot: Works Cited

For a complete bibliography of works by T. S. Eliot see Donald Gallup, *T. S. Eliot: A Bibliography*, revised ed. (New York: Harcourt, Brace & World, 1969). The following list is arranged according to Gallup's classification of Eliot's works into Books and Pamphlets by T. S. Eliot; Books and Pamphlets Edited, or with Contributions, by T. S. Eliot; and Contributions by T. S. Eliot to Periodicals. Under each group the works are listed in chronological order according to their first appearance in Gallup.

The Sacred Wood: Essays on Poetry and Criticism. 7th ed. London: Methuen & Co., 1950; University Paperback, 1960. [Gallup A5]

For Lancelot Andrewes: Essays on Style and Order. London: Faber & Gwyer, 1928. [Gallup A12]

Selected Essays. New ed. New York: Harcourt, Brace & World, 1964. [Gallup A21]

The Use of Poetry and the Use of Criticism: Studies in the Relation of Criticism to Poetry in England. London: Faber & Faber, 1964. [A24]

After Strange Gods: A Primer of Modern Heresy. London: Faber and Faber, 1934. [Gallup A25]

The Rock: A Pageant Play. New York: Harcourt, Brace & Co., 1934. [Gallup A26]

The Film of Murder in the Cathedral. New York: Harcourt, Brace & Co., 1952. [Gallup A29j]

Old Possum's Book of Practical Cats. New York: Harcourt, Brace & World, Harbrace Paperbound Library, 1967. [Gallup A34]

"The Idea of a Christian Society." *Christianity and Culture.* New York: Harcourt, Brace & World, 1949. [Gallup A35]

"Notes Towards the Definition of Culture." *Christianity and Culture.* New York: Harcourt, Brace & World, 1949. [Gallup A51]

Poems Written in Early Youth. New York: Farrar, Straus & Giroux, 1967. [Gallup A56]

On Poetry and Poets. New York: Farrar, Straus & Giroux, Noonday Press, 1957. [Gallup A69]

The Complete Plays of T. S. Eliot. New York: Harcourt, Brace & World, 1967. [Gallup A72]

Collected Poems 1909-1962. New York: Harcourt, Brace & World, 1963. [Gallup A74]

Knowledge and Experience in the Philosophy of F. H. Bradley. New York: Farrar, Straus & Co., 1964. [Gallup A75]

To Criticize the Critic and Other Writings. New York: Farrar, Straus & Giroux, 1965. [Gallup A76]

The Waste Land: A Facsimile and Transcript of the Original Drafts Including the Annotations of Ezra Pound. Edited by Valerie Eliot. New York: Harcourt Brace Jovanovich, 1971.

"A Brief Introduction to the Method of Paul Valéry." Introduction to *Le Serpent Par Paul Valéry*, pp. 7-15. Translated by Mark Wardle. London: R. Cobden-Sanderson, 1924. [Gallup B3]

Introduction to *Savonarola: A Dramatic Poem*, by Charlotte Eliot. London: R. Cobden-Sanderson, 1926. [Gallup B4]

"Religion without Humanism." In *Humanism and America: Essays on the Outlook of Modern Civilisation*, pp. 105–12. Edited by Norman Foerster. New York: Farrar and Rinehart, 1930. [Gallup B12]

Preface to *Transit of Venus: Poems*, by Harry Crosby. Paris: Black Sun Press, 1931. [Gallup B18]

"Donne in Our Time." In *A Garland for John Donne*, pp. 1–19. Edited by Theodore Spencer. Cambridge: Harvard University Press, 1931. [Gallup B19]

Introduction to *Nightwood*, by Djuna Barnes. 2nd ed. New York: Harcourt, Brace & Co., 1937; New Directions, 1946; New Directions Paperbook, 1961. [Gallup B31]

"I." In *Revelation*, pp. 1–39. Edited by John Baillie and Hugh Martin. London: Faber and Faber, 1937. [Gallup B32]

Foreword to *Contemporary French Poetry*, by Joseph Chiari. Manchester: Manchester University Press, 1952. [Gallup B67]

Introduction to *The Art of Poetry*, by Paul Valéry. Translated by Denise Folliot. New York: Random House, 1958; Vintage Books, 1961. [Gallup B79]

"The Hawthorne Aspect." *Little Review*, V. 4 (August 1918), pp. 47–53. [Gallup C67]

"Beyle and Balzac." Athenaeum, 4648 (30 May 1919), pp. 392–93. [Gallup C80]

"Reflections on Contemporary Poetry." *Egoist*, VI.3 (July 1919, pp. 39–40. [Gallup C84]

"The Metaphysical Poets." *Times Literary Supplement*, 1031 (20 October 1921), pp. 669–70. [Gallup C128]

"An Emotional Unity." *Dial*, 84.2 (February 1928), pp. 109–12. [Gallup C246]

"A Commentary." *Criterion* XII.46 (October 1932), pp. 73–79. [Gallup C337]

Index

Abrams, M.H., 170-71
Adequation. *See* Adequation, Dynamic; Adequation, Static (Failed)
Adequation, Dynamic: its relation to historical sense—cycles of art, 75-81 *passim,* 91-93 *passim;* its relation to multiple realities, 109-12; as noun of action, 7-9; as poet's obligation to language and sensibility, 10-13; in social criticism as "ideal" over "bewildering minute," 141-51 *passim;* as three-stage method of interpretation, xiv-xvi, 60-66 *passim,* 134-35, 138. *See also* Adequation, Static (Failed)
Adequation, Static (Failed): as "baffled emotion" in art, 20-29; as compensatory myth in design of *Selected Essays,* xiv-xv, 15-35 *passim,* 75; as defence of Eliot's own poetry, 31-32; as inadequacy of doctrinal thought, 17-20; its relation to allegory in prelapsarian cosmos, 29-31; metaphors of, in design of *Selected Essays,* 16; as metaphysical catastrophe of "dissociation of sensibility," 9-10; as opposite of "wit," 34-35; as theological compensatory myth, 142-49 *passim; See also* Adequation, Dynamic
Aeschylus, 78
Andrewes, Lancelot, 25-26
Appleyard, J.A., 170-71
Arnold, Matthew, 10-11, 17-18, 38, 47, 85, 107, 122
Art: as double perspective—point of view between realism/liturgy, 91; spectator/participant, 93; style/story, 93; sound/sense, 126; emotional character of, 87, 92; as *harmonia/mimesis* conflict, 78; and imposition upon/perception of order in reality, xv, 96; polymorphous, in function, 92; relation to belief, theory of, 94, 133; relation to religion, according to law of inverse proportions, 91-92; use of conventions, 95

Babbitt, Irving, 18, 168
Bate, Walter Jackson, xiii, 16, 160, 166, 167
Baudelaire, Charles, 18-19
Bell, Daniel, xvii
Benn, Gottfried, 11
Berger, Peter L., xix, 166, 177
Bergonzi, Bernard, 160
Bergson, Henri, 168
Bradley, F.H., 4, 24-25, 102
Brower, Reuben, 27-28
Browne, E. Martin, 130, 156, 160-61, 168, 174, 175
Brzezinski, Zbigniew, xvi
Buchler, Justus, 167
Burke, Kenneth, 159, 176

Carlyle, Thomas, 17
Chesterton, G.K., 17
Christ, xiii, 105
Coleridge, S.T., xiii, xv, 34, 93-94, 101, 107, 109, 119, 145, 170-71
Criterion, The, 17, 118

Dante Alighieri, xv, 10, 16, 29-31, 33, 61
de Man, Paul, 171
Derrida, Jacques, xiii
De Saussure, Ferdinand, xiii
Dial, The, 118
Dickens, Charles, 23
Dobrée, Bonamy, 158
Donne, John, 25, 28
Drucker, Peter, xvii

Eliot, T.S., works cited: *After Strange Gods: A Primer of Modern Heresy,* xvii, 142-45, 147, 149
  "American Literature and the American Language," TCC, 75
  "Andrew Marvell," SE, 31-34
  Animula, 59-60
  "Arnold and Pater," SE, 17-18
  Ash-Wednesday, 58, 114, 126, 129, 140